DETECTIVES
Don't Wear
SEAT BELTS

DETECTIVES
Don't Wear
SEAT BELTS

True Adventures of a Female P.I.

CICI McNAIR

CENTER
STREET®

New York Boston Nashville

Center Street
Hachette Book Group
237 Park Avenue
New York, NY 10017

Visit our website at www.centerstreet.com.

Center Street is a division of Hachette Book Group, Inc.
The Center Street name and logo are trademarks of Hachette Book Group, Inc.

Printed in the United States of America

First edition: September 2009
10 9 8 7 6 5 4 3 2 1

Library of Congress Cataloging-in-Publication Data
McNair, Cici.
   Detectives don't wear seat belts : true adventures of a female P.I. / Cici McNair.
      p. cm.
   ISBN 978-1-59995-187-4
  1. McNair, Cici.   2. Private investigators—Biography.   I. Title.
   HV8083.M35A3 2009
   363.28'9092—dc22
   [B]
                                                            2009006918

This book is dedicated to all the men I've spent the night with in a parked car, to every partner on a stakeout, to all the private investigators who let me watch them, who taught me...
with boundless gratitude to Kevin F. Dougherty and Anthony G. Spiesman.

I also dedicate this book to my mother,
Clarissa Walton McNair, and to my patron saint,
Giacomo Casanova. Their blithe spirits inspire me to be curious and optimistic, resourceful, relentless, and brave.

Contents

Acknowledgments

Thank you to Vinny Parco for having the imagination to hire me when no one else would give me a chance. I'll never forget that. You changed my life.

Thank you to Glenn Hales for being my ally and for all I learned from you.

Thank you to Mary Ellen Young, who is always in my heart. Beautiful, strong, and true. My moral compass from the age of eleven and a last surviving witness to the craziness on the Old Canton Road.

Thank you to Dorothea Halliday, who is a production editor without equal. Her big, beautiful, brilliant brain and her love of the English language delighted me. She truly understands nuance.

For common sense, for shelter, for professional expertise and for cheering me on: Arthur G. Altschul, David M. Anderson, Pete Beveridge, Lawrence Block, James C. Esposito, Elizabeth Gainsborough, Frank Gray, Heather Hanley, Caro Heller, Vivienne Heston-Demirel, Charley Hill, Charles Intriago, Herbert Irvine, Perri Klass, Julie Lombard, Diana Marley-Clarke, Renwick Matthews, Judith Natalucci, Hayko Oltaci, Sesto Quercetti, Stanley Rosenfeld, Avery Russell, Robert Spiel, Litsa Tsitsera, Arish Turle, Baroness von Goetze-Claren, Baroness von Karger, Sian Willson, Larry Wolff, and Hervé Zany.

Preface

When my agent said my manuscript was being sold as a memoir, I thought it was wildly pretentious to label my capers that lovely French word. Almost as lovely as *surveillance*.

Detectives Don't Wear Seat Belts is exactly as I saw and heard the events, as true a surveillance as I can present. I did change most of the names and some of the identifying details, but there is no conscious embellishment. How could anyone possibly embellish Vinny or Mickey or my mother?

I'm named after my mother. I'm the fifth Clarissa in her family; the first Clarissa was born before the Civil War, a Quaker in Pennsylvania. In my detective life and on my business cards, I am Cici McNair, P.I., so this book is written by that persona.

I hope you will be inspired by my adventures and driven to do what makes you feel most alive. Sail into the eye of the storm.

As Ben Kingsley said in *Sexy Beast*, "It's not the money, is it? It's the charge, the buzz, the bolt. The sheer fuck-off of it all."

That's it. That's exactly what it is. Detectives don't wear seat belts.

Clarissa McNair aka Cici McNair, P.I.

DETECTIVES
Don't Wear
SEAT BELTS

PART I
Starting with Poison

April Fools' Day, 1994.

"Relax! Lemme do the work. Go limp." Errol grasped my thumb, pressed it in the ink, and then rolled it on the paper. Hard. "Relax," he commanded again.

Barbie Doll was on the phone saying, "No, no, no. Mr. Parco is unavailable," as Vinny was telling us that he wanted to play "hide the salami" with the new client who had the missing husband.

"You're done," announced Errol with cheeseburger on his breath. The prints would be sent to Albany and registered.

I wiped my hands on paper towels, which just smeared the black ink over a wider range of skin. Smudges like bruises covered both forearms. "Here," yelled Rodriguez as the sponge he tossed hit me in the face. "I wet it for you!"

Errol guffawed and Rodriguez grinned. "What a dirty mind! I just spit on it."

Get tough, I told myself. I threw the sponge back and left for the ladies' room.

I looked at myself in the mirror over the sink as I scrubbed my hands with gray suds. It was official. I'd been hired as a private detective.

Later that first day, I was told it was because Vinny liked

me and because Nick, his partner, was out with the flu and couldn't object. I laughed when I heard this, and Vinny chortled, "Bodda-bing, bodda-boom!" and did a series of bumps and grinds in his brown double-breasted suit. He was built like a fireplug; his shaved head gleamed under the fluorescent lights of the windowless office.

I had just sat down at my desk, was still drying my hands, hadn't even opened my new notebook, when Vinny bounded over to me. "Hey, got this guy arriving from Milwaukee into LaGuardia at ten-thirty, checking into a hotel on Park Avenue. His wife wants pikchuhs of the broad he's screwing. Get 'em gettin' outta the cab. Get over there, get the photos, get back."

"Okay." I nodded and pulled on my jacket. Photos. Hotel. Adultery. Like in the movies.

"A swanky hotel means a doorman. Watch yourself," said Vinny. He looked at his watch and then at me. "Here's the address. Get outta here. Hurry."

"Okay," I said as I grabbed the paper and then the camera Errol held out like the baton at a relay race. *How will I do this?* I shrieked silently. *If there's a doorman, I can't stand on the sidewalk and just wait for the taxi to pull up. Park Avenue. Maybe I'll have to lie on my stomach in the daffodils on the island in front of the hotel.*

"Guy's six foot four. Got bright red hair. Can't miss him," shouted Vinny from the doorway as I started down the hall.

I turned around to wave at him, to let him know I'd heard. Errol and Rodriguez had both popped their heads out the door. Three heads in a vertical row, like cartoon characters, all watching me. Vinny's shiny bald head was on the bottom since he was shortest. The send-off. The kiss-off. Maybe my new career would be over before lunch. Later I'd hear that they took bets on whether I'd come back.

I jammed the camera into my pocketbook as the elevator

doors opened. Rats flashed through my mind as I descended. I'd heard there were rats on those Park Avenue islands. There had to be another way to get the pictures. "I can do this," I said aloud as I stepped into the lobby. Out on the sidewalk in the sun I started toward Third Avenue, reminded myself to stand up straight, and whispered, "I've been fingerprinted and I'm a private detective and I can do this."

Circumstantial Evidence

The idea to be a detective had occurred to me about a month before, on a snowy February afternoon, as I thumbed through the Manhattan phone book. Some people turn to the Bible for inspiration, but for me it's the Yellow Pages. I'd never met a detective, but suddenly I wanted to be one. It seemed obvious that all I had ever accomplished or endured had led to this.

I was divorced and broke and camping out in a borrowed apartment with an open suitcase under a dining room table. I look back and wonder why this wasn't cause for despair, but at the time, I saw it as just part of the ride, another chapter, the ending of something or the beginning of something else. I was back in New York after a long time in Europe via a stint in Beverly Hills. After college I traveled all over the world, living in cheap hotels or ones with five stars, cottages, consulates, cabins, flats, penthouses, houseboats, villas, chalets, châteaux, or palaces, depending upon my ever changing circumstances. I'd been a cat sitter, a mail getter, a plant tender, someone who drove a boy to his piano lessons from Switzerland to France on Thursdays, a houseguest, a writer in residence, a lover, a fiancée. Just nothing on paper—no leases, no licenses. Married to a Canadian for a few minutes, which was quite long enough.

My best address for about a decade was a post office box on Lexington Avenue. I'd call Avi the Israeli and tell him that I'd be in Cyprus for the next three months or in Sicily for the spring if things worked out, and he'd laugh and write down a new place for the forwarding.

Rome had been home base the longest. I'd worked for Vatican Radio and been on the air at least twelve times a week with the international news, interviews, my documentaries. On Sunday evening, I was the weekend news anchor for a local TV station. I'd go tearing up the Spanish Steps at six and race through Piazza Barberini, worried about the sweat stains under the arms of my silk blouse, which cost (to the lira) exactly as much to clean as I was paid. I'd write my copy, powder my nose, flirt with the *tecnicos*, and then perch on a stack of Italian telephone books in front of the one camera. I had published two novels, with three more gathering dust on a high shelf in my mother's garage. One novel I'd written in a bikini on my terrace in Rome overlooking Castel Sant'Angelo across the Tiber, another in an elegant hotel room gazing out from my balcony at Lake Geneva and Mont Blanc.

A decent journalist can organize facts, decide what's relevant, and move ahead, so becoming a detective made sense. But once I was one, it tapped something in me that I thought I'd lost. I liked finding the feeling again. Kid stuff, tomboy talents. Long-ago games on summer evenings with lightning bugs.

All the stories overlap other stories. Circles of past and present and memory. When it's going well and it's very physical, I feel about nine. A little girl wearing sneakers, having adventures in the woods, far away from the house, harboring the wish that no one would ever call her home for dinner.

I look back to that first spring of my new life and realize that I knew nearly nothing about being a detective. Yet on some level, I was prepared to embrace everything it entailed.

The chance of an income also figured in this wave of desire—oh! what naïveté!—for I was slowly and fashionably starving to death in Murray Hill right on Madison Avenue. A friend of a friend, Robert the Englishman, had gone to Eastern Europe and left me his apartment for a small rent, which loomed larger every time I thought of it. He was supposedly becoming a millionaire selling tractors to Romanians while I fought with a novel that was going nowhere.

When I first had the idea to become a detective, I suddenly remembered Caro and called her up. I'd met her in Haiti years before, and we'd always liked each other. Once, for a month in 1974, Caro worked for a detective agency and found a missing person that not even the FBI could find. Caro was euphoric, but family obligations interfered and she hasn't been a sleuth since.

She shares an enormous loft with her sculpture and a man her husband calls Silent Pete. I'd go to foreign movies and drink champagne at Café des Artistes with her husband, John. They were quite sophisticated about it.

Caro had a broken leg in Brooklyn Heights, so at noon the next day I was tromping through the snow under a giant bridge, bearing turkey sandwiches. When I arrived, she limped across the room and told me she lived for the day when it would be necessary to change wigs in a phone booth. We sat down in front of the bookcase holding twenty years' worth of magazine articles and books on private eyes; her list of the best was topped by Bo Dietl. I borrowed his autobiography called *One Tough Cop*, went home, and read it.

The following morning, I called Bo Dietl's office and he agreed to meet me at the Doral Inn at 49th and Lexington at five-thirty. I was told to "ask the bartender for Dietl."

Then I hung up and leapt around in a state of high spirits, wondering what to wear. I changed my blouse three times during *Donahue* and yanked off one pair of earrings after another. I opted for subdued good taste and wondered if he'd show up undercover. Then I wondered if you could do that.

A detective in the flesh, my first. I grinned triumphantly in the bathroom mirror. Columbo has that ratty raincoat. Matlock is southern small-town seersucker. I took off my earrings and replaced them with gold hoops. Don't want to overpower him, I decided. I felt like a teenager with first-date jitters. I thought of interviewing a cardinal in Rome. Royalty of another realm. Bo Dietl! I kept wanting to say Bo Diddley, and this worried me.

At ten past five, I reskimmed the last ten pages of *One Tough Cop*, standing up to remain unwrinkled; then, after deciding perfume might be unprofessional for this profession, I sprinted out the door toward Lexington. Caro had made me promise to call her afterward "even if Nancy Kerrigan is skating. Even if you're in bed with him."

The bar was as black as a nightclub. I obediently asked, "Where is Bo Dietl?" and the bartender answered me with a little head tilt. Bo was over by the window in a dapper double-breasted suit and cowboy boots; his silk tie looked expensive and just barely in good taste. Without the police cap he'd worn in the jacket photo, I could see his bald spot. We shook hands, but he didn't look happy to see me. He didn't make eye contact and immediately turned away to introduce me to his "attorney." Stubby had just arrived from Miami aglow with sunburn in his nearly white double-breasted suit. The pouf of handkerchief in his pocket was the color of strawberry ice cream. He had perfect, Chiclet-capped teeth and a tie that made me imagine flowers from a jungle on Coney Island, even though I've never been to

Coney Island. Stubby was easy to talk to, which was lucky for me since Bo was constantly greeted by other men who were invited to sit down and have a drink. "One tough cop" blatantly ignored me, so I talked to "the attorney." Bo drank Diet Coke and ordered one for me; I had pictured him throwing back jiggers of Scotch and wiping his mouth on the back of his hand.

The suits were stunning. I felt like a drab female bird as the males flaunted their plumage. I'd never been with men who would wear such suits. I guess I've been a Brooks Brothers baby my whole life, if you leave out Rome and London and Geneva. Now I sat across from a banquette lined with men from Brooklyn and the Bronx and Queens. Foreign boroughs. A convention of bodyguards. It was dark outside, and the Waldorf=Astoria glowed behind them across the street.

I noticed texture, pinstripes, lapels of proud notched triangles. Door-frame-brushing shoulders. Silk ties with big knots printed in colors I associated with Pucci. Cuff links glittered on French cuffs. I saw diamond rings and remembered someone from my childhood warning me to stay away from any man who would wear one. I drank in the sartorial splendor of another kingdom. I think I may have entered *Guys and Dolls* territory. And I knew I wanted to stay.

There was Stubby and Teddy and Lennie and Bobby. Little-boy diminutives for massive men wearing boots made from reptiles I'd never dreamed crawled on this earth. I would later guess that these men had all worked with Bo Dietl during his NYPD days. They stuck together, year after year. They had the same backgrounds, often the same neighborhood in common, the same habits, and the same perspective on life. They'd seen combat together, gotten drunk together, been in each other's weddings.

Suddenly Bo Dietl slumped forward on the banquette with

his head between his knees and pointed back for Stubby to read his collar label. "Do you like it, do you like it?"

Stubby squinted at the label with pursed lips. "It's pretty good. I like it."

Bo straightened up and tilted his head toward Stubby. "This guy monitors my wardrobe."

Conversation swung toward Teddy, who had just returned from Indiana trying to get a check from a man who owned a billion-dollar communications empire. "So this guy drives me out ta da woods ta this giant effing warehouse and says he's got da check inside. I start ta get outta da car. 'No, you can't come in,' he says ta me. 'Because you'll spread bacteria among the machines.'"

We sophisticated New Yorkers sitting in the darkness of the Doral Inn decide he's worried about a virus in the computers and laugh. Teddy doesn't get it and continues, "I tell him I took a shower this morning. I don't have any bacteria!" He is deeply offended. "But he tells me ta wait and he goes in and locks da door after him. I stand in da snow until I think about a back door and I run as fast as I can around da warehouse and sure enough da door pops open and I call his name and he says, 'Oh, Teddy! Hi! Come on over here!' He leaves da door open and I rush over when he goes ta get da check and I see da inside of the effing warehouse. Two phones on da floor! That's it!"

Stubby's face went red under his tan. His mouth opened and closed with no sound coming out. He looked like a fish drowning in air. Mopping his face with the pink handkerchief, he searches for words. "I gave that guy sixty-five thousand bucks last summer! Whaddya mean there were just two phones on the floor?"

"I'm tellin' ya. Looked just like a bookmaker's."

Raised voices. Another round. More Diet Cokes arrive.

The men are ranting about lost money, about cheats. "Whaddya expect?" bellows Lennie. "Whaddya expect?"

In later months, I would be privy to countless conversations like this one.

Meanwhile, Bo Dietl was not even looking at me. He is a man's man. His shirt was so white, it looked blue white; I think I have never seen French cuffs so deep. A gold cuff link twinkled as he put down the Diet Coke. All the men fell silent. Bo appeared small beside his linebacker "attorney," but Bo was definitely the top dog. They all sat shoulder to shoulder and stared at me. At last Bo spoke. "So ya wanna be a private dick."

I hope I didn't gasp. All I could think of was *public penis.*

I managed to nod. Silence. I took a deep breath and said that I'd done lots of different things, but the pattern was that I loved interviewing and research. I thought about working for the Madison Avenue art gallery and the charming, womanizing French owner who'd ended up in handcuffs, arrested for possession of stolen paintings. *No, don't talk about that. Maybe Bo arrested him.* Citibank. No. National Audubon Society. That was temporary. I was a bad typist and would give letters to my boss with tiny holes from my erasures. It appeared that moths had gotten to his thoughts. Time Inc. had lasted four days; I'd hated it. Air France. Club Med. The travel agency. The advertising firm in the PanAm Building. Me as dessert chef. Me as interior decorator. No. No. No. I took a deep breath and talked about doing research for CBC television. The documentary on organized crime. I said that I'd coauthored a documentary on contemporary celibacy in the Catholic Church and that for a year I had interviewed nuns and priests about their sex lives. None of the men blinked. I wondered if they were still breathing. I soldiered on.

Then he told me that he only hired people with law enforcement experience or from other detective agencies and that he couldn't hire me. I would not surrender. I suppose in hindsight I should have waved a cocktail napkin like a little white flag and run from the room through the hotel lobby and out the revolving door to lose myself in the evening crowds.

But no, that's not my style. I blundered on. "Why can't I be a detective?" I insisted. "I can learn." Silence from the men. There was the whirr of a blender from the bar behind me. Something being crushed, pulverized. "What about finding a missing person, since I hear that's a lot of work on the phone? I could start there."

Finally Bo said, "Maybe I could pair you with an experienced person."

"Super," I breathed.

Then he said, "Would you do surveillance?"

"Oh, yes, of course." What a lovely word. So French. "Would it be a hotel lobby?" I ventured.

"I don't know."

"Would it be out on the street watching a doorway?" I hid my nervousness at the thought of being sent to Harlem in midwinter to stand in the snow under a streetlight and pretend I belonged.

"I don't know."

"Doesn't matter," I said. "I'll do it." Pause. "If you tell me how, I'll do it. If you would just give me a few tips." Silence. "I could start out in the office, if you wanted me to."

"Yes, you'd learn a lot listening to the jargon."

I agreed enthusiastically. *Jargon? That's the problem—I simply don't know the jargon.*

Bo Dietl was poker-faced and hard-eyed before me in that very expensive suit. I felt writhingly stupid. Like a Girl Scout offering a cookie to a man who's just announced he's a cannibal.

Suddenly he repeated, "Maybe surveillance." My heart

soared. That lovely word again. Oh, the romance of it! He continued, "Because I noticed when you came in there was not a ruffle of interest. No one gave you a second glance."

Death, I thought. But I smiled gamely. "Oh, so you mean I shouldn't rush out and buy a blond wig?"

"No." Bo played with the swizzle stick. "Some girls, uh, women... want to work for me and they walk in the room and they are these baudacious blond broads and everyone stops and stares..."

"Oh," I say brightly. "Then the trick is to have mud brown eyes and brown hair like me and to be a chameleon." I'm five foot nine, with shoulder-length hair, usually weigh 133 pounds, and always feel... never gorgeous, but adequate.

"You know the city?" Bo is looking down into his Diet Coke as if the mysterious dark liquid contains the answer.

"Manhattan very well, but Queens or Brooklyn? I'll get a map and figure them out." I'd lived on the Upper East Side before marriage and then on the West Side for a year afterward, which was before decamping for Rome. I knew "the city" to Bo Dietl meant a lot more than a few square blocks between the two rivers north of Grand Central Station and south of Harlem. I made a mental note to be able to say, the next time, that I knew the city.

Why wasn't I getting through to him? I told him more about my work on the Canadian television documentary on organized crime. I told him that I used to sit in bars in Toronto for hours with a hidden camera in a bag and that I'd plant myself next to Squeaker Franco, whose favorite thing in life was to drag people behind cars when they were late in paying the loan shark. Bo listened, then tilted his head in a gesture of dismissal. Stubby stood up. Teddy, Bobby, Lennie, all of them, scuffed to their feet in their pointy-toed boots. The audience with the Imperial Investigator had ended. He told me to call him on Wednesday and "remind me."

I ground my teeth. Bo Dietl told me to have a nice week-end, and we shook hands. He might as well have said, "I hear you're moving to the Yukon for sixty-three years."

THE NEXT DAY, I felt like a bag of dirty laundry. I realized it was the first time in my life I'd had an interview and not been offered the job. A part of me was on fire. Caro said not to give up; I said, "Are you kidding? This is just the beginning. I *will* be a detective."

I wrote a thank-you note on Monday and called Bo Dietl on Wednesday. He was polite, but I'm not an idiot.

So it was time to attack Caro's and my second choice. Irwin Blye's book explained everything you have to know about surveillance. No bright colors, please. Forget the red convertible. I decided not to drink anything for days in advance of a stakeout. I would be superlative at surveillance until I was carried away, bravely half-dead from dehydration and only barely strong enough to report to the client. Preferable to peeing in wide-necked plastic bottles. Irwin Blye, Private Eye. A knight in shining armor in a parked car.

Mr. Blye refused to even see me. Two down, but approximately 6,098 New York detectives to go. At this rate, I could be ignored and/or deselected twice a day for the next ten years.

March would be forever remembered as the month of rejection. Every morning I would get up and run a mile, shower, dress, put on lipstick, and prepare myself for a potential interview. Then I would sit down at Robert's desk, open the Yellow Pages to yesterday's place under "Investigators, Private," and start dialing, crossing out names one by one with ballpoint pen. I would introduce myself to anyone who answered the phone, and I'd tell him I wanted to be a detective. When the snickering stopped, I would ask for an appointment—resisting the urge to grovel, always thinking that if they could just see me, just talk to me face-to-face, they could be convinced of my potential merit. But they never wanted to see me, they were never hiring, they always wanted experience—preferably "a law enforcement background," which, along with electrical engineering, was about the only thing not on my résumé. They didn't want to hear that I'd been a journalist or spoke Italian or had written novels. I kept putting my foot in it. "Oh, yeah?" barked one. "You'll just work here for two weeks and then turn around and write a book about me!" Keep dreaming! I cursed him when I heard the dial tone.

I'd phoned and crossed out all the ads from Aardvark to Cheetah, and still no one would see me. Worse, they laughed; they actually snorted with contempt. By "D," I was getting used to it. "I can learn," I told one man after another. "Give me a chance." Making it a game, I got better and better at keeping them from hanging up. I'd ask if they knew any firm that was hiring, how many people worked in the office. I'd ask what kinds of cases they handled. Anything to delay hearing the dial tone. And no matter how rude they were, I pleaded for advice.

"Stay away from Vinny Parco," they would growl.

"Why?" I asked again and again.

"He's poison. Gives investigators a bad name," they'd say in voices laden with loathing. "Parco is poison." They'd hang up, and I'd wonder, *Who is Vinny Parco?*

"E" did not look promising, so I changed tactics and began calling the companies with the biggest ads. When the address was midtown and reasonable, when we'd done the dance of not hiring, I would thank them sweetly and rush out of the apartment. Arriving at the appointed skyscraper, out of breath and primed for confrontation, I would scan the big wall directory in the lobby, then ask the porter where the Never-Go-

Wrong Agency was located. Astonishingly, he would deny it was even in the building. "Do you have an appointment? Slither Investigations would have given you the suite number if you had an appointment." I would stare at banks of elevators labeled 1–20 and 21–40 and 41–60 and walk home.

Not being able to get an interview was one thing, but not being able to assault these men at their desks because I couldn't even *find* their offices was quite another when I was trying to tell myself how good a detective I would be if only someone would give me a chance.

Then I'd write a postcard in bright green ink saying how much I had enjoyed speaking with them and remind them that I was available if they decided to hire anyone in the next decade. I'd put a stamp on it and pace around the little apartment, then I'd pull on my coat and rush out again and hand-deliver it to a stone-faced doorman. I dashed in and out of countless lobbies in the month of March.

I began to twig on to a few things. A 212 number in the phone book often rang in Queens, where a retired cop had an answering machine in his basement. No wonder my offer to come over immediately for a job interview would evoke great guffaws. I realized I was asking one retired cop after another for a job, each of whom had twenty years of experience and a permit to carry a gun. They didn't want me, and I didn't blame them, but that didn't stop me from being furious that they wouldn't give me a chance. I imagined desks and ringing phones and people running between them discussing new cases.

One morning, I realized I'd skipped a "B" and punched in the number for Patrick Bombino Investigations. When his office put me on hold, the twanging chords of "Secret Agent Man" blasted forth: "They've given you a number and taken 'way your name..." I longed for that to happen to me. Mr. Bombino actually came on the line and we talked, but after that he seemed to be perpetually "out in the field." The field? Magnetic? Cotton? Was it just another way of saying his trench coat was at the cleaners?

His office was between two wholesale bead shops on West 38th Street, and the porter there told me that he hadn't seen Mr. Bombino for months and months. I thought, *Ha! You just think you haven't seen Patrick Bombino for a long time, but he is probably a master of disguise and is constantly coming and going.* The porter took the postcard from me with great reluctance, but I felt good about it. It is much more satisfying to hand a note to a real person than to slip it under a frosted glass door with a padlock. The following day, Patrick Bombino agreed to meet me at four o'clock, but an hour before my appointment a woman called and told me not to come, that that very afternoon his office had caught fire and that Mr. Bombino was moving to Brooklyn. Torched? Was Bombino the target of a whack?

In a brave attempt not to be devastated, I bought a Hershey's bar and took the afternoon off—slamming closed the Yellow Pages, eating chocolate, and watching talk shows.

I soldiered on.

Intercontinental Investigations sounded sophisticated, grand, and important and had a big ad. I dialed the number and talked to somebody named Nick. Tired of rejection, I simply said I wanted to find someone, and before I could finish, he said, "Come on over to the office." I nearly wept with delight.

"Now?" I breathed. "Really?" In ten minutes, I was in an elevator ascending to the third floor, then making my way down a hall with signs saying, "Intercontinental." Another sign and another. At last I found myself walking through the waiting room, then through the examining room of an ophthalmologist with eye charts covering the walls, then down another corridor, turning left at a framed print of Van

Gogh's *Sunflowers*. Significant? That Dutchman had terrible problems with his vision. An eye doctor renting space to a private eye? Ideal. Eye deal.

The door had no name, but it was open. I walked past a coatrack and an umbrella stand into a large, windowless room where I was assailed by the smell of barbecue. Nick was a large man in his sixties with white curly hair and a Sicilian last name. His desk chair squeaked when he leaned forward to shake my hand. "So you want to find a missing person?" he said, picking up a pen and preparing to take notes. He waved me to a chair.

"I want to find a person who will help me find missing persons," I said carefully. I realized that there was someone at a desk behind Nick. He looked very young and very skinny, dressed in black, with Elvis Presley pomaded hair. A beefy character in a white T-shirt was eating potato chips at a nearby desk. He looked mean and bored. Nick, the teenager in black, and the thug all stared at me.

"So. Go on. I'm listening." Nick was ready for me.

"I mean I want to find the best person there is to find missing persons." *A real detective agency*, I thought as I glanced around the gray, fluorescent-lit room.

Nick grinned. "You found him! He's right here!" he crowed. "I'm it!"

"Great. I want you to teach me how to do it. I want to work for you." I smiled radiantly.

Nick didn't smile back. The chair on rollers squeaked as he folded his arms across a large belly, regarding me. I sensed he felt tricked, which was not good, but I threw myself into my how-much-I-want-to-be-a-detective oratory. It had never before been delivered in its entirety or to a person I could see. I finished my spiel; there was silence in the room except for the crunching of potato chips. Three pairs of eyes drilled through me.

"How much do you think you're worth?" asked Nick.

I said I didn't know.

Suddenly the thug waved the potato chip bag and jeered, "Yeah, how much? How much you gonna charge?"

I shrugged, and then the skinny one in black called, "How much per hour?"

They all three began yelling at me, "How much how much how much how much!"

I shouted over the din, "The going rate! Of course, I'll charge the going rate!" and that stopped the noise and there was silence again. There was the crunch of potato chips, then the crinkling of the cellophane bag. The thug had a sheen of grease around his mouth and on his cheeks. "Maybe I'd even accept a little less than the going rate since I'm just starting out."

Then they were all insisting again, shouting, "How much how much how much!"

They wouldn't stop, so I finally said, "Oh, all right! Forty dollars an hour."

They started screaming and pounding the armrests of their chairs as they whirled around on the rollers. Loud, snorting laughter. I felt hot and sat up straighter and crossed my legs, attempting to appear poised. "Where do ya wanna be a private dick?" one shouted. "Monte Carlo?"

I blinked. *That would be nice*, I thought. *I like Monte Carlo*. Nick told me, as he wiped tears from his eyes, that "investigators on the island only get twenty-five dollars an hour, and they own their own agencies." *Which island?* I wondered. *Puerto Rico? Capri?*

Nick explained, "You'll only get seven dollars an hour."

"I'll take it," I said.

I talked to him for a while, but he wouldn't hire me because business was slow and I had no experience. I kept pushing, and he said he'd talk to his freelance friends, who were all ex-cops the way he was. I didn't feel very optimis-

tic about it because he looked at my résumé and started laughing. "If I got this in the mail, ya know what I'd do with it?"

I said, no, I didn't know, and he said, "I'd toss it right in
the wastebasket."

"Well, since you didn't get it in the mail and I'm right
here, maybe it would be nice if you waited until I leave so
you don't hurt my feelings." His face looked quite blank for
a moment. Maybe he was ashamed of himself. Nick sighed.

"The way you look. You...uh...you're not right for this.
You don't look...I dunno."

I stared down at my black trousers and black patent-
leather flats and shrugged my shoulders in the black-and-
white houndstooth blazer. I resisted the urge to pinch off my
gold earrings. "What's the matter with the way I look?" I
tried to sound offhand, as if it didn't matter.

"You're too classy. Too much class." Nick scowled.

"Oh," I said hollowly. "Thanks...I guess."

He was shaking his head, frowning, as if I were hopeless
to not realize this. Later he admitted, "It took guts to pull
that missing person bullshit," and by the time I said good-
bye, I had the feeling he almost liked me. But before I was
even in the hall, I heard them all shouting, "Forty dollars
an hour!" and hooting like wild animals. I walked home
thinking that at least I had now seen the inside of a detective
agency. A small victory.

March seemed cheerless and eternal. When I met friends
for dinner, I'd pretend to be hard at work on my abandoned
novel. I imagined myself some future evening quite casually
announcing over dessert that I was now, quite suddenly, a
detective. Not an investigator, because I thought it sounded
clinical; a detective sounded far more romantic. Meanwhile,
I spent my days deep in the Yellow Pages.

There was no one to teach me how to be a detective, no

school for it. I hadn't even read a detective novel since my
James Cain glut a decade and a half before. As a kid, I'd read
Nancy Drew but preferred the Hardy Boys. Didn't any girl
you ever liked? I'd read all of Sherlock Holmes. He was mar-
velous, but in 1990s New York he wasn't helping me. The
Mafia, past and present, was seductive. Sometimes I worried that I daydreamed too much to be a detective and that
it showed. Or maybe it was something else. Perhaps these
investigators were such savvy judges of human nature that
they *knew* and would have nothing to do with me because
they sensed qualities in me I never imagined. Were detectives
born, not made? Were they possessed of instincts and a certain brand of intelligence I could never even aspire to have?
I thought of Bo Dietl. Nick. Maybe not. But one thing was
clear: I didn't even know what I didn't know.

One evening, I joined two hundred people in the ballroom
of a cheap hotel to hear a lecture called "How to Have a Mega-
Memory." The next evening, I took a two-hour course called
"How to Get Anything on Anybody." Caro and Pete went
with me. The class was taught by Vincent Parco, who'd been
described as "poison" by every investigator I'd spoken with
on the phone. This only made me more curious. He charmed
the class; I liked him. He was funny and self-deprecating,
and he was quick on his feet. There were forty-seven people
in the room who wanted to be investigators, but somehow in
the swarm of groupies afterward, Vincent Parco scrawled his
number on the corner of my notebook and told me to call. The
next morning, we talked at nine; he gave me his address, and I
fairly ran toward First Avenue in a spring thunderstorm.

Oh no, oh no, I thought as the elevator rose to the third
floor. *Oh no, oh no* ... I walked through the ophthalmologist's office and past *Sunflowers. Can't be. Oh no.* I stood
in the open door and saw Vincent Parco, shiningly bald
with a big dark mustache. He grinned and waved at me to

come in. I froze, hoping he'd come out into the hallway. I leaned weakly into the coatrack festooned with dripping raincoats and wet, half-open umbrellas. "Come on in here!" he boomed. "I want ya ta meet Nick, my partner!"

I was introduced to Nick and instructed to sit in the same chair as eight days before. Parco bobbed around, snapping his fingers and saying, "We need good people," as Nick repeated mournfully, "We don't have any money." I pulled a strand of hair over one eye à la Veronica Lake but decided that putting on sunglasses on a rainy day in a windowless office was a bit too affected. I'd just have to wait it out. Nick was staring at me, and I was thinking, *Oh no, oh no, oh no. When he recognizes me, he'll start whirling around in that damn chair again, shouting, "Forty dollars an hour!"*

Parco asked me why I wanted to be a private eye. Nick stared at me. The two characters in the back of the room talked on the phone. I tried to have a strong southern accent as I delivered my transformed monologue. I pulled my hair over my face and finally put my elbow on the desktop and fanned my fingers out over the one eye closest to Nick as he scrutinized me from the vast distance of three feet. Parco paced around Nick's desk and asked me questions; he raised his arms, shrugged, tilted his head, waved his hands. Totally Italian. The double-breasted brown suit rose and fell over his round belly.

Suddenly Nick said, "Uh, didn't I see you before? Didn't you come in here with some wild ideas about making lots of money?"

"I...yes, I did! I'm so happy you remember me!" I smiled brightly as I flipped my hair back. "You and I had a wonderful conversation. I was very glad we had the time to talk."

Nick smiled. Parco was perched on the edge of Nick's desk, swinging one stocky leg back and forth. His silk sock was olive green. Suddenly he popped off his perch like a squirrel and said, "Let me walk you to the elevator."

I said good-bye to Nick and followed Parco out into the hall. "Come on, this way." He tilted his head. "Follow me."

He led me past closed doors through an empty suite of offices and out to a balcony. "We can talk here. I need some air." He told me he really wanted to hire me, but he couldn't without Nick's say-so because he needed Nick, who held the license for the agency.

"Ya got a videocamera?"

"No."

"Ya got a car?"

"No."

"How ya gonna do surveillance in Jersey without a car?" he demanded.

"I can take the train," I said.

"Yeah, yeah. Ya gonna lean out the window of a speeding train and take pictures with your Brownie as the train goes by."

"I have an Instamatic," I stated with dignity.

Parco looked at me and shook his head. He sighed. "Oh, that's good." He seemed defeated, and then he rallied. "But I dunno. I gotta feelin' about you. I wanna use ya. I just don't have anything going on around here right now."

"I don't believe it." I smiled. "No evil in all of Manhattan?"

"Well, I got this guy who lives in Jersey. I'm watchin' him for his wife. He comes inta the city to go to a club, where they sorta ... well, they dress up ... it's a bunch of transvestite types. Could you go to the club and keep an eye on him?"

"Sure. I could do that," I said in a strong voice. *Be positive. Sound capable. But what will I wear?*

Parco reached up and clapped me on the back. "So, look, I'll call you if I can. I really wanna use ya, but it's like I said. I got this partner thing. He's got the license for my company and he has the checkbook."

I walked out of the building and straight to the library on

42nd Street, waved at the lions, and dug into the microfiche. It was all there. I'd been in Europe at the time. Vincent Parco, New York City private investigator, being grilled on the stand during a murder trial a few years back. He had given not only a gun to a client, but also a silencer—which is totally illegal for anyone to even *have*—and she'd turned around and killed her lover's wife. Parco was the link to the murder weapon, and all hell broke loose. So he lost his business and his reputation was in shreds and he surrendered his P.I. license to avoid having it taken away. Now I knew why, when I asked for advice on the phone from the detectives who wouldn't even see me, they would all say the same thing: "Stay away from Vinny Parco." I met with him and Nick on Wednesday, and Vincent Parco called on Thursday night and said he could "use" me. *I knew it, I knew it!* cried a little voice inside. The worst had happened. Just my luck. I knew what I had to tell him. Then I heard myself say, "Tomorrow? Eight o'clock? Sure. And thanks."

Caro was elated with the news. We shrieked on the phone like teenagers, and I imagined this was what it would have been like to tell my best friend in tenth grade that I'd just gotten picked to be cheerleader. But I had never wanted to be a cheerleader, so this was off-the-charts better. We decided that I could always quit if I were asked to do strange or illegal things. If I lasted till lunch, that would be three hours of experience as a private detective, which I had zero of at the moment. She agreed that I could be a good person and still work for someone who was poison.

I thought about being a detective until dawn. I couldn't sleep because I couldn't stop smiling. That night had the feel of Christmas Eve.

April Fools' Day

At half past seven the next morning, I had tiny ID photos taken at a one-man shop on Second Avenue. Friday, April the first, was a blindingly beautiful spring day. The photographer warned me not to expect much. He said the police department used the same camera for mug shots. Appropriate, I decided as the flash went off. I looked like a happy kid in the picture—over-the-moon ecstatic. I paid the photographer, took the envelope, and half ran, half skipped, toward the office.

Today the office smelled like pepperoni pizza.

"I'm Barbara." I was dazzled by the statuesque platinum blonde wearing spike heels and a skirt short enough to be described as a belt. I would learn that the men all called her Barbie Doll and that she didn't mind. Gesturing with a slender arm that jingled with bracelets, she told me to wait in the next room, then disappeared into a closet-size cubicle with a desk and a computer and file cabinets. "Nobody's here yet," she called over her shoulder. Then the phone rang, and she answered and said, "Yes, okay, yes, she's here, no, okay, yes, oh, for Pete's sake! I will, okay," and hung up.

"He's going to be late. That was Vinny," she shouted, then she appeared in the doorway with legs that started at her throat and that movie-star hair. "He's about to step into the shower and he only lives a block away but he hasn't even shaved yet and he doesn't have any clean underwear so he'll be..." She threw up her hands and with loud jangles of irritation said, "Oh, that man takes forever to get dressed! If I were his boss, I would fire him." Exit Barbie Doll to answer the ringing phone.

I pictured Mr. Vincent Parco, short, husky, naked, standing on a polar bear rug in a palatial penthouse, worried about his underwear. Here was a man with a strongly developed sense of the dramatic—in silk ties and lapel size. It was this yearning for flair that determined which women he chased and the cases he took, and it was this yearning for flair that made his life so complex.

Barbie was answering the constantly ringing phone. In between calls, she played back the overnight messages—an equal mix of call me's, hang-ups, and threats of physical violence. I couldn't help but listen and for the first time in my life thought maybe I shouldn't be ashamed, maybe wanting to listen would prove to be an asset in my new profession. Then I walked around the room and read the framed newspaper accounts of my new boss's past exploits. He'd gone to the D.A. and told all when one of his investigators had been hired as a hit man. A White Plains business executive had been saved from death by him. Parco's grin dominated photo after photo. The walls were covered with praise by the press—the *Post*, the *Daily News*. Vincent Parco was the stuff of tabloids.

On the wall above a desk in the back was a nearly naked calendar girl smiling over the month of March. I wondered what bimbette April would bring when the page was turned. There was the strong smell of hot dogs at that end of the room.

The phone rang, rang, and rang. Barbie Doll fielded calls,

and I waited. My hero finally chugged in, barrel-chested, out of breath, complaining about how long it took to shave his head. There was a tiny bloodstained pinch of toilet paper stuck on the back of his pink scalp. "Used ta be losin' my hair and then I decided ta shave it all off, and ever since— you never know about broads! Women come up ta me on the street and ask if they can touch me! And so they pat my head, they rub my head! And wow! On a bus, they rub their breasts—you know it's just the right height—and I—well, it drives me crazy! But the broads! They love it! Shaving my head in the morning is a bitch, but my sex life—never been better!" I didn't know what to say. I hadn't counted on hearing about his sex life so soon. Or so early in the day.

He suddenly asked me if I liked his new suit. It looked like it might have cost a lot of money. I called him Mr. Parco and he laughed, then I called him Vincent and he cackled. "Call me Vinny," he said with a roguish grin, a shrug of his shoulders, and a tilt of his shining pate. "It makes me feel young."

Vinny opened his jacket, displaying celadon green paisley lining. "Hadda get all new suits this year. See this? All my suits wear out right here on the inside under the left arm 'cause that's where I used ta carry my gun." He closed the double-breasted jacket and buttoned it. I wondered about the gun. "What a bitch. All my suits wore out the same day." His perfect little white teeth gleamed under the walrus mustache. Suddenly, gracefully, on tiptoe, Vinny pirouetted. "So do you—" Suddenly he stopped and shouted, "Barbie Doll, get in here! Whaddaya think of the new suit?"

One of the "how much" screamers arrived, and I was introduced to my first skip tracer. I would later learn that a skip tracer was, originally, a person who pursued anyone who skipped town or skipped out on a debt. Now it has come to define someone who gleans information over the phone from anybody who knows anything.

Errol was a twenty-two-year-old, five-foot-ten drink of water with paper white skin and slicked-back black hair. He was eternally clad in his favorite color—black, right down to his combat boots with jingling chrome chains— and reminded me of a vampire who should not be seen in daylight. Errol hung around clubs till three or four every morning, then drifted into the office from Queens as if in a trance. The first thing he did was pick up the phone to call the corner deli for an emergency order of clam chowder and ginger ale. An hour later, he was consuming his weight all over again. Sometimes it was bacon and grits and French fries and a peanut-butter sandwich with "Ya got any a that banana cream pie from yesterday?" on the side. A skip tracer who convinced and connived and wheedled and cooed over the phone with grace and quick wits. Scary to meet, but telephonically like silk. People who worked for a bank, a hospital, the phone company, an insurance company—secretaries, accountants—they told him everything. Then he'd hang up, dial the deli, and order a liverwurst sandwich and hot chocolate with whipped cream and a double order of onion rings. When he wanted to crack me up, he would stand by the fax machine and mimic tough-guy Sergeant Joe Friday: "The fax, ma'am, just the fax."

A Class Act

I reinvented myself on the crosstown bus. My first case in person. I'd been telling stories on the phone for two days, but now I was to do it in front of someone. I was to lie to their face, to look in their eyes and lie.

Being a detective had given me permission to lie. It astounded me. It delighted me. It was bad to lie—the smallest child was warned against it. That must be why it felt so *good* to do it now.

On the phone you could crinkle cellophane and say, "Oh, what terrible static! I'll call you back." There were a hundred ways to escape gracefully if you took a deep breath and refused to get rattled, and of course, no one could see you. I looked down and sighed. The skirt, the shoes, the blazer—all wrong! But Vinny said it had to be taken care of today. "The client's getting antsy." *Yes*, I thought, *but to send me out like this?* I didn't think I could pull it off dressed like this. I thought of Bo Dietl's "baudacious blondes" and wished I were one.

I felt like a six-year-old and that Vinny had just pushed me off the high diving board at the country club. I love to swim, so I wasn't worried about drowning, but I wondered if there was any water in the pool. My assignment was to find out if one Tony Persico ran an escort service to supplement his income as a real estate agent. Our client was his boss, the owner of the real estate firm.

As the bus wound through Central Park, I tried to decide on my story. I would make sure that Tony Persico believed me. He *had* to. I would make it really believable. Vinny said, "I don't care how you do it. Use your imagination." And what if Tony Persico didn't believe me? Would he grab me and shake me like a rag doll and demand to know what was going on? Would he shout at me? Call the police? Would he hit me? I decided I would deny everything if my bluff was called, and then...then I would just run. I opened my compact, checked my lipstick, reapplied blush, and told myself I felt better.

Truth was, I felt rotten as I opened the glass door that said, "Cortina Realty." There were several rooms with desks and I could hear a man on the phone, but I couldn't see anyone. A girl in jeans materialized and asked if she could help me. I told her I was there to see Tony Persico about an apartment. She went into the room with the closed door, and I heard him stop talking on the phone and hang up. The door opened.

"I'm Tony. Boy, that was fast. I didn't think you'd be here for another hour." He was in his late thirties with a big smile, dark hair, a striped shirt, a tie, and khaki trousers. He shook my hand and motioned me to a chair on the other side of his desk. "Sit down. Now you said something not too expensive—ha! That's what everybody says—but let's see." He started to flip through an open box of index cards. "Oh, better fill this out first so we can get it out of the way." I winced when he handed me an application form because Vinny had told me to use my own name "because they might check the Social Security number and it hasta add up." I had resisted, but he had insisted. I'd only been a detective since last Friday, so who was I to argue?

Tony looked okay, but you can never tell. He was reading over the application form when the girl called from the hall-way, "I'm going to lunch. The service'll pick up the phones." She slammed the door, and we heard the elevator doors open and then close out in the hall. I was alone with him. I took a deep breath and thought, *I have to start this. Somehow.* Over his shoulder, I could see the buildings across the street and hear the traffic outside. His office was messy with maps and photographs of buildings stuck on the walls as if the entire room were one big bulletin board.

"So on the phone you said you didn't really care about the location as long as it wasn't expensive."

I nodded. "You see, I'm living with someone in the Village and it's just not working out. I need my own place. It's hard to get phone calls, no privacy—it's impossible."

He looked up from what he was writing and gave me a big smile. "What should I call you? Cici?"

"Yes." I cringed mentally. I was summoning courage, but I hated having him know my name.

"You new in the city?"

"Yes. Been here a month. It's tough. A tough town."

"Where you from? I can hear a southern accent. You from the South?"

"Georgia. Little town about a hundred miles from Atlanta."

"What's it called? I might know it."

Panic. "Oh, I don't think so." The calendar that said, "Marcus Insurance," caught my eye.

"Try me." He smiled.

"Marcus. Marcus, Georgia."

"Marcus, Georgia!" he sang in an exaggerated southern drawl. "You are far from home! But you'll love New York once you're settled. Everybody needs a place of their own." He flipped aside a few cards in a little metal box, then pulled one out. "Let's see... I've got a studio a few blocks away. Very sunny. High ceiling. Good closets. For nine hundred." He wrote down the address on the pad. "There's a studio for eight fifty in a walk-up, but I haven't seen it yet. I think it's the third floor facing the back. It may be dark. What about taking a look?"

Suddenly I said, "I have to tell you something. This isn't easy. I feel that I should apologize for wasting your time."

Tony stopped writing and looked up.

My voice had cracked and my eyes suddenly filled with tears. "What I mean to say is—oh, this is hard—oh, I'm sorry..."

"Here. Here you go..." He was yanking Kleenex out of his desk drawer.

"I think... oh, I'm sorry. It's just been such a day, and on the way over here... on the bus... I..." I swallowed noisily. "What I'm trying to say is—I can't afford any of these apartments. I wasted your time, and I'm sorry. I have a job and it pays three hundred a week and I thought that would be fine. I thought that when I called you last week. But today I got my first paycheck and they took so much out of it that I don't even see how I can live... how I can buy groceries..." I blew my nose. Tears kept welling in my eyes. Was I crying because I really couldn't afford an apartment on Vinny's salary? I stumbled on. "I don't really believe this is happening. I mean I came back here—to the U.S.—after a long time away, a time of having anything I wanted—a huge apartment, jewelry, trips, fur coats, champagne, a Ferrari..."

Tony was leaning forward. I tried not to let him know I was looking at him over the wad of Kleenex I held to my nose. "What happened? Did you come here from Georgia?"

I shook my head. "Oh, no. I left Georgia right after high school and went to California." California. I can wing California. I'd endured a year in Beverly Hills. "You know, the glitter of Hollywood and—"

"Were you an actress?" Tony was getting interested. "Have I seen you in anything?"

"Oh, no! I wasn't very good. I did a few walk-ons, and time went by and...well, I had a very nice life." I sighed and didn't know what to say.

Tony was a big help. "But...the Ferrari?"

Men were always so nuts about cars. He would pick up on that. "The Ferrari? It was a present. That came later." Later, when I figured out how and where and how much later. Oh, God. "The Ferrari was in Rome, but that's...much later. I...well, I can't believe that all this would happen and that I'd be in this position now!"

"What did you do in California? When you weren't acting?" Tony seemed genuinely concerned.

"I didn't have an easy time at first. Not when I first left Georgia. I lived in a little dumpy West Hollywood apartment and tried to get work and...then I met this woman who said I could do much better and she asked me if I wanted to go out to dinner with someone nice and I thought it was a blind date and I said yes." I sighed and dabbed at my nose again. "Monique was very polished, very beautiful, but older. She was in her mid-fifties, I guess, but was always going shopping or on her way to get a manicure, and her apartment was incredible. She was very generous and she had a lot of younger women as friends, but she treated them like daughters. Anyway, I borrowed a dress and went on this date, and the man took me to Morton's and we drank champagne. He was some businessman from out of town and he didn't know anybody except Monique." I shrugged. My southern accent got stronger. "She changed my life. She bought me clothes and took me to get my hair cut and...I don't know how to describe this, but..." I sounded uncertain about how to proceed because I was. "I know what it must sound like, but I never...did anything with them. I just...well, kept them company, and my life was fine." I couldn't believe it, but tears were running down my face.

Tony handed me another Kleenex. "What happened?"

"Well, I met this Italian named Pietro and he kept taking me to dinner and kept coming into town and he always stayed at the Beverly Hills Hotel and I... I fell in love with him and he gave me this four-carat diamond ring and asked me to marry him, and all the girls and Monique gave a big going-away party for me." *Oh, for Pete's sake*, I thought. *All the girls! Can I be serious, can I possibly pull this off?* "It was the happiest time of my life." I dabbed at my nose and looked off into the distance out the window. "I went home to..." I glanced at the calendar. "To Marcus and told everybody in town how wonderful he was and how I'd send Mama a ticket when we picked the wedding date, and then I flew up here to New York and Pietro and I stayed at the... the Pierre Hotel and then we went off to Rome because that's where he wanted the wedding. He had this incredible apartment overlooking... Piazza Navona." I could see it. My old apartment at Piazza della Rovere: high ceilings, dark beams, a fireplace, two terraces, a penthouse without equal.

I could see Pietro, too. How many Pietros had I had dinner with? "I trusted him. Even though he was Italian. Oh, I'm sorry! But, you're an American, really. Italian men— Roman men—they are entirely different animals! Pietro told me we would be married and he bought me clothes and fur coats and he gave me the Ferrari." *There. Keep going. Don't get tripped up. Make everything dovetail. What happened next?* "And we spent every weekend on Capri and we drank gallons of champagne, and Italy is so beautiful..." Yes, those delicious weekends on Capri with somebody incredibly attractive and truly wonderful who really did want to marry me. *Don't start thinking about it now! Don't get sidetracked.*

"Do you speak Italian?" Tony leaned forward.

"*Sì.*"

"It sounds perfect. What went wrong? What happened?" insisted the Realtor.

"It was perfect for a while. But I realized I wasn't meeting his mother and he wasn't setting a date and sometimes he had 'business' on the weekends and..." My eyes filled again. "I found out he had a wife already! And three children! And he just wanted to keep me as his mistress!"

Tony was the soul of sympathy. He handed me more Kleenex. I got myself under control, and I continued with the story. "So I left him and I came here and I'll have some money when I sell the ring, but...but look at me! I bought these ridiculous clothes so I could look businesslike! Plain skirt, flat shoes! I have so many black dresses I can't count them and more evening bags than the law allows, and look at me! I'm dressed like this to make a decent living, to start over, to get an apartment, and I...I won't make it!" I blew my nose. "I realized today on the bus...coming over here...if they take all that out of my check, then I can't make it. I can't get an apartment, I can't even live in New York!"

"You've had a rough time." Tony stood up, handed me another Kleenex. "You left Rome, Pietro, everything behind to come here and start over?"

I nodded. "Stupid, I guess."

"No, you're not stupid. You're just having bad luck, but...listen...let me take you to lunch."

"No, I'd better go. I've wasted enough of your time. I'm sorry to go on and on about it." I stood up clutching a Kleenex and wondered if I had two black stripes of mascara running down my cheeks like some African tribesman. "You've been so sweet to even listen to all this." *And I'm so sweet, I might be coming down with tooth decay.*

"I want to take you to lunch." He looked at his watch.

"But I have to make some calls first. Can you meet me at the Irish bar a few doors down in half an hour?" When I didn't answer right away, he said, "Come on. Everything's better when you have food in your stomach."

THREE MINUTES LATER, I punched in the number and waited while Barbie Doll put me through. "Vinny, it's me. I'm on Seventy-second Street at a pay phone. He's asked me to have lunch with him." I listened. "Yes, yes, yes, but he hasn't said anything about the escort service yet." I listened. "Well, I think he will. I think he's leading up to it. I've certainly been leading up to it." At this point, he thought I was a major hooker with a bad case of denial. "Listen. How much should I charge?" I tried not to remember the morning of my humiliation with Nick and Errol and Rodriguez. "How much per hour?"

Vinny told me seventy-five dollars, then he said, "You've got class. Make it a hundred."

I sighed. Gee whiz. This class thing. And Vinny was paying me, with all my class, eight dollars an hour to be a detective. Nothing made sense. "Okay. Yes, I'll call you right afterward. I'll be in this bar called Donahue's." I listened, curiously touched. "Yes, I'll be careful. Promise. Bye."

The bar was dark, but I saw Tony wave at me from a bar stool. He was smiling as he ordered two beers. I asked him where he lived and then about the pictures of the sailboat I'd seen above his desk and we talked about sailing and he told me about finally making enough money to leave the city and to have a house near Sheepshead Bay. I liked the way he talked about loving New York and all it had to offer. He was a decent person. Wasn't he? The club sandwiches came. I started to think, *No, don't say it to me. Don't mention it. Don't offer me a job.* I was sending him brain waves and crossed my ankles, thinking, *Don't do this, Tony. Don't do this.*

"Do you like the real estate business?" I asked.

"Love it! Can't imagine ever doing anything else." He grinned. "Meet a lot of interesting people, like you."

Oh, no. You'll rue the day you met me if you say the wrong thing. You'll lose your job. They are watching, I thought. *I'm watching. I'm one of* them, *even though I like you.*

He ordered two more beers and said, "Now, I think we should decide what to do about you." I stared at his open, likable face as he went on. "Can you go home to Marcus?"

I felt confused. Suddenly realizing I'd let down my guard. *Marcus who? Marcus Welby?* "Oh! I can't go back home. Not after telling everyone I was getting married. Oh, no, I couldn't! Not yet!"

"I understand. But what about Monique? She of all people would understand how awful this has been for you!"

Good idea, I thought. *I'll go back to Monique. No! Can't do that because I have to get a job* here. I sighed. "No. I can't do that either."

"Why not?" Tony began to encourage me to go back. I'd had a good life in Hollywood, hadn't I?

"Monique . . . Monique was killed when I was in Rome."

Tony gasped. "Killed?"

"Car accident. On the way to Malibu." My eyes filled with tears, and I took a swipe at them with my paper napkin. I was becoming a veritable Niagara Falls.

"Oh, God." Tony stared down into his beer mug.

"My life is a mess. A real mess." Yes, it certainly was. I couldn't go back to Marcus, Georgia, wherever the hell that was. I had killed the Hollywood madam. My dirty rat fiancé was in Italy and had probably already installed a new mistress in *our* beautiful apartment . . . what a scum. Life was rotten.

"What about the Ferrari?"

"What?"

"Where is it?" he insisted. "You could sell it."

Damn. Where had I left that damn car? Hollywood or Rome? "I...I didn't want to take it. I never felt it belonged to me." At least that part was true.

"Your fur coats? You could sell those."

"I left them behind. And all the jewelry except my engagement ring." I took a deep breath. Well, that takes care of all my possessions. Easy. Much easier than paying storage every month, which is what I did in real life. The closet in Harlem. Plus the warehouse outside Rome. Seven years and I was still planning to go back and live in Italy.

He took a swallow of beer. "You need money and...well, I get the idea you don't want to go back to what you were doing, but...what if you...what if you did it once in a while?"

"Did what once in a while?"

"What you did for Monique. What if you went out to dinner, out to parties, with a man once in a while?"

I sighed and looked up at him. "It's so sad for me to go back to that. I thought I'd left it all behind. I was getting married." I smiled what I thought might be a bitter half-smile. "I guess I could do it again," I said slowly. "But only until I can save something and move into my own apartment." Tony nodded. "But I wouldn't want to work for someone I didn't know."

"Oh, don't worry about that." He was flipping through a small address book.

"Would I be working for you?" There. It was out in the open. Cards on the table. Would he bite? *Oh, please, please, Tony, say no.*

"No. I don't have anything to do with this, but I have a friend named Luke who has two girls working for him. Really nice. Really okay."

I felt like shouting with relief. "So what do these girls do, exactly?"

"They used to work at a club and Luke and I were always around and I was in charge of security, which is a way to say I was a bouncer...anyway, Crystal and Tiffany were exotic dancers and they wanted extra money and Luke helped 'em out. They give massages."

He looked at my face and elaborated. "You know with the AIDS problem a lot of yuppies don't want sex, but they want...they want relief, and it's just a massage with baby oil. I mean, if you didn't want to, you wouldn't have to, but that's what Tiffany and Crystal do. Luke sends them out. They give him something every week and he gives them business." He paused. "I can call him for you. Once he meets you, he'll give you work. I'm sure of it. You've got class."

"Thanks," I said weakly. Class. It was a curse when I wanted to be a detective, and it was a blessing when I wanted to work for an escort service. What does this say about being a detective?

We finished lunch. I was very happy that Tony was not what the owner of Cortina Realty suspected he was and couldn't wait to tell Vinny. There was no distasteful little sideline to supplement his real estate commissions. Tony and I talked about all kinds of things until the check came, and then he invited me to come to his house that evening. "You're thin. I want to cook a great big steak for you tonight. And we'll call Luke together."

I told him I was overwhelmed at how nice he was, which was utterly and totally true. "But tonight I have to move my things from one apartment to another. I'm taking care of somebody's cats for a few days and it means I can stay there, but I have to go downtown and move before six."

Out on the sidewalk in the bright sunlight, I gave him my phone number. My real phone number in Robert's apartment in Murray Hill, because I didn't know any better. He told me to call him when I wanted to speak to Luke, and meanwhile he would get in touch with a few girls he knew who might want a roommate. "You're nice. You're really okay. I don't want you to have a bad time in New York. Call me tomorrow and I'll have some news. Think about calling Luke. And call me anyway if you have a problem. We could have dinner. I'd really like that." He kissed me on the cheek and gave my hand a squeeze. "Keep your chin up. You're going to be fine."

I walked to the phone booth on 72nd Street and Columbus, happy that Persico was not running an escort service and that I hadn't failed Vinny, but there was this bad feeling under my breastbone that I had lied to someone inherently decent. For hours. As I ate the lunch he'd paid for. I winced. Does the end justify the means? I dialed Intercontinental. "Hey, Vinny, it's me. I've got terrific news…"

AT JUST AFTER MIDNIGHT, I called Cortina Realty and left a message on Tony Persico's voice mail: "Tony, I want to thank you for being so kind to a stranger. You'll never know what was going on in my mind when you were offering to help me. So thank you for lunch and for listening to all my problems. I called my mother tonight and I've decided to go home to Marcus."

LITTLE DID I KNOW I would be going home to my mother soon. Not to some mythical town called Marcus—to Turtle Creek. But that's another story.

From the Vatican to Vinny

The last time I'd had a job, my desk had been in the pristine, hushed atmosphere of La Radio Vaticana on Vatican territory in the center of Rome. I'd been the only Protestant.

Working for Vinny Parco was not working for the Pope. I guess the only thing the two men had in common was me and being Catholic. It stopped right there. Vinny was fond of declaring, with a bump and a grind and a leer, "I ain't no choirboy."

The office situation alone was quite a contrast. The large open space meant everyone heard everything, and there was constant calling back and forth, nonstop wisecracks. Only Vinny and Barbie had partitions giving them offices of a sort; but the partitions did not reach the ceiling, so everything could be heard. There was serious eating going on at Errol's desk; in between mouthfuls, he made scam calls. Barbie Doll was on the phone—one call after another, with someone on hold. Rodriguez was usually telling positively disgusting jokes and trying to get a rise out of me as I feigned deafness. Nick was grousing about the sad state of the finances and insisting that if a time sheet showed a person worked from ten a.m. to four p.m., that was five hours, and how did anybody think they could get away with charging for six? Nobody wanted to answer him. Vinny was bobbing between us all, kibitzing, cajoling, telling stories, talking about going on another new diet, asking where reports were, and giving orders.

At least twice a day, a man wearing a wrinkled, mysteriously stained lab coat would wander in, looking as if he hadn't combed his hair in years, head down over a crossword puzzle. He might mutter, "Hat with a pom-pom. Three letters." Vinny, quick and alert, would shout, "Tam!" and the doctor would slowly write it in, never raising his head, and wander out like a somnambulist.

"He has no patients," Barbie told me. "Not one patient." And then she would raise her arms with a jangling of bracelets and exclaim, "Well, look at him! Just look at him! I mean, maybe if he cleaned himself up! Did you see the dirt under his nails?" She took a breath. "Well, don't even look. It'll make you sick." She sighed dramatically and with a last jangle stalked back to her office to answer the ringing phone.

Barbie was dynamite. Worked hard. Bright. Capable. She was in a constant state of outrage over the money going out and the money not coming in. I would sometimes be dispatched with two or three thousand dollars in cash to "run, don't walk—go ahead and take a taxi" to pay the overdue phone bill.

"Vinny says don't bill him, he's a friend. Don't bill her, she's special. Yeah, well, where are these friends when we owe the rent, and who is that 'special' whoever anyway, and by the way, so special that I've never even heard of her and I've been with Vinny for ten years! Do you know that last week he arranged to accept a boat—a boat in Maryland—in exchange for that missing persons case? Some kind of boat! Honestly! A special situation, Vinny says! Because the guy is a friend! Where are these friends when he's in trouble? They're such good friends they don't know his name when he needs them! And so he says, 'Barbie, don't bill this one and that one,' and honestly this is no way to run a business! We could be out on the street tomorrow!"

But we weren't. We were in the gray, windowless room under fluorescent lights, and the cases were coming in. All kinds of cases. I was introduced to plots via excited explanations from Vinny, over the phone, and overheard. Characters paraded past my desk. Big Paulie Castellano's locksmith, Joey, developed a crush on me. Big Paulie had been the Capo di Tutti Capi until John Gotti had had him gunned down in front of Sparks Steak House a few years ago. Big Paulie had been the most powerful mobster in the United States. I looked at Joey the locksmith and wondered what secrets he knew. I looked at Vinny with new eyes, too.

The dumb, the desperate, the devious...all of them wandered through the eye doctor's office, past Van Gogh's *Sunflowers,* looking for Vinny Parco to take care of their problems.

One morning, Barbie Doll told Vinny that Precious O'Keefe had arrived, and in teetered this rather large, elderly woman in five-inch white patent spike heels, black fishnet stockings, and a Dolly Parton–style red wig. Her breasts seemed to be tumbling, like twin waterfalls, out of a tight black satin sheath. This gave new meaning to Bo Dietl baudacious. Barbie stood behind her and gave me a look like "Do you believe this?" I tried not to let my eyes pop out. Strictly Times Square. Vinny was like a nervous child bobbing up and down on his toes beside her great height. He did manage to shake her hand in the elbow-length black glove and ask her to come into his office. She took tiny steps, teetering through the open area as we gawked in stupefied silence. Errol said later he forgot how to swallow, had some French toast lodged right in there, and thought he might have to ask Rodriguez to Heimlich him. Vinny closed the door as Nick swiveled around in his chair and told us in a stage whisper that she was a very famous madam.

My first madam. In the flesh. And so much of it. I was delighted. Precious O'Keefe left when I was down at the courthouse and was never mentioned again.

I don't know if it was the office atmosphere, or Vinny, or just becoming a detective that imbued everything with a difference. It was exhilarating, it was secrets, it was sometimes so ticklishly exciting that I couldn't sleep. Yet I embraced the newness quickly. Vinny lived under an assumed name in his apartment building. This had gone on for years. I was told to leave any packages, messages, or reports at that address for Mr. Forrestal. I blinked and then accepted it. It was just Vinny's way. All the doormen knew he was a famous private investigator, and I imagine they were pleased to be in on this delightful duplicity. Once a doorman was asked, "Hey, isn't that Vinny Parco?" and the doorman answered, "Yeah, that's his stage name. His real name is Thurston Forrestal." The name on the lease *was* Forrestal, for there was a real Forrestal. Robert Forrestal. By necessity, even though he was only about thirty years old, this man became Vinny's father.

Down the hall from our office was a portly mysterious figure who always wore black, double-breasted, pin-striped suits and reminded me of a very large penguin. He was doing something on the telephone with banks, but I never knew what; Barbie said darkly, "Don't ask." A link to Switzerland? Who knew? He looked serious, spoke quietly when he talked to Vinny, and kept to himself. The Penguin wore those suits with pinstripes so wide that when I blinked, I thought they veered into the arena of convict.

Errol and Rodriguez were often told to "break the bank," and they would disappear for a half hour or more to use a phone, I assumed, in an empty room. They would tell me nothing about the technique. "If I tell you, then you can do it. And if you fuck it up, then it's fucked up for me and I can't do it anymore. It's ruined. Everybody has ta develop their own way. So I won't tell you."

These two would discuss, within earshot of me, the most sordid, wincing details of their sex lives, but I could never get them to divulge the tiniest clue about "breaking the bank."

The office was comedy, tension, food smells, and ringing phones. New cases came in constantly; from that first day, I realized there would never be the luxury of focusing on just one. Research was done, clients were called back, cases were closed. In the middle of it all, darting between our desks, was the ringleader of the circus—a character in a double-breasted suit with a gleaming bald head and a walrus mustache—sometimes raising his arms over his head and gleefully exhorting, "C'mon, you guys! Let's rock 'n roll!"

Bahama Triangle

The day after I finished the escort service case, the phone rang and Barbie called, "Hey, Vinny, it's a Mr. Smith in Nassau. Says he's a private investigator." He picked up and I could hear over the partition that separated Vinny's office and the common area that he was saying, "What?...What?...What?... No. Must be the connection...Yeah...Say, lemme call ya back. Gimme your number." I heard him slam down the phone, and he barreled out of his office and right at me. "Listen, C, there's this guy in the Bahamas and I can't understand a word he's saying. Ya speak pretty good. See if you can unnerstand him. Here's the number. Find out what he wants."

Ten minutes later, Vinny was leaning over my desk asking for a translation. "Well, Alistair Smith says he needs some work done here in New York. He got your name out of the WAD book." The World Association of Detectives membership book. "He has this client named Frederick Chapin who is old-money English, very wealthy family, good name. His daughter has fallen in love with an American multimillionaire who keeps his yacht there—but it's not really his even though he says it is. Little things don't add up, and Chapin is concerned that his daughter may have made a bad choice for a husband." I circled Alistair's phone number in green ink, feeling suddenly panicked, wondering if there were things I should have asked, obvious things I'd missed. I took a deep breath.

"They married yet?"

"No. But she's evidently in love with him and they are definitely engaged. Smith is sending all the details this afternoon with an international bonded courier."

Vinny made a whistling noise.

"There's a photograph of the fiancé—the only one available—and the daughter's in the picture, too. No one outside of this office is supposed to see it because Chapin doesn't want his daughter dragged into this."

"No shit, Sherlock. And the old man doesn't want his daughter to ever know he's checking on her sweetheart. Well, we can do that. You can do that. That stuff'll come tomorrow and you take care of it. Have any questions, ask me."

I flinched and then thought, *I can do this. Somehow.*

"Nick!" called Barbie. "It's a collect call from Riker's. Will you accept? It's Chuck the Chopper."

Errol explained to me, "Ya know Nick used ta be a cop. Used ta put 'em in thuh slammer, and now he gets 'em out." He lowered his voice. "Everybody calls him the Chopper because he used ta make hamburger outta his victims."

BARBIE HANDED ME THE package at eleven the next morning. "Vinny says this is for you."

In twenty minutes, I had read everything and had made a list of what I thought should be done to check out the subject, Wilton Baskerville. I almost giggled out loud. "It *has* to be his real name," I told Errol as he stood over me, eating French fries.

Errol repeated it with his mouth full. "He could have a million dollars and a big boat and be named that. But I think he made it up. That's just my gut talking." I looked up at the long, skinny lizard body in black T-shirt, black pants, and black combat boots with silver chains. His gut talking. Barbie had told me a lot of skip tracers were drug addicts who had to leave the room and do lines or shoot up before they made their calls. Rodriguez had told me that skip tracers were antisocial misfits, misanthropic. I was surprised he knew the word. He said the best one he ever knew was a pathological liar, the second best one just died of AIDS. I took another quick glance at Errol with his whiter-than-death pallor and the slicked-back Elvis hair and turned to the photograph.

"Lemme see the picture." He inspected it, then handed it back with a speck of ketchup near Baskerville's left ear. Wilton was a well-built, olive-skinned, handsome man grinning into the camera with a sail and blue sky behind him. His muscular, tanned arm was around a slender blonde in a two-piece bathing suit with a large X over her face.

"I'd know her anywhere," said Rodriguez, leaning over me. "Just by those fuckin' breasts. Looka this, Errol. Didja see this little piece, Errol?"

I tried to tune out. Rodriguez was telling Errol he'd decided on the girl of his dreams. "A bitch with tits like this I kin knock around a little who'll sleep in the wet spot."

Nick spun in his chair to take a look. I handed him the photograph and heard him begin a story. "Now, things are gettin' so bad that guys are afraid ta make a good, legitimate pass. I used ta run a strip joint—" He cleared his throat for my benefit, but I didn't look up from my file. "I mean a ... singles joint. Out on the island. And I never had time ta learn the waitresses' names. They were all ... I had 'em all dressed as bunnies, ya know. I used ta call 'em 'sweetheart' and 'honey.' Ya couldn't do that today."

I reached for the phone and called Manhattan directory assistance for Baskerville's company phone number. The Baskerville Corporation. No listing. I checked the Cole crisscross directory for all the companies in the building at 666 Fifth Avenue. No Baskerville Corporation. Odd. He gave that as his company address. Should be suite 327, but that was something called Ackerman Investments. A front for Baskerville? Why would old Wilton want to hide his hugely profitable business? I called Manhattan directory assistance for his residence. Nothing. Then I tried Queens, Staten Island, Brooklyn, the Bronx, Long Island, and Westchester County.

Vinny was shouting in his office, "I don't have excess to that! No! Nobody's got excess to that!" He slammed down the phone, then came back to lean on my desk and ask how it was going with Baskerville. "Maybe he's so rich he doesn't list himself, that's all. Doesn't want ta be bothered. Maybe. But maybe not." His hand went up to smooth the mustache. "Go on down to Sixty Centre Street and check the articles of incorporation. See what you can find."

I grabbed a notebook and left the office for the subway downtown, hoping someone at 60 Centre would have mercy on me and tell me what to do. Somebody did. I realized they always would if I were polite and stood in line. The books were heavy and handwritten. Nothing from 1900 to 1990, so I checked 1991, 1992, and 1993, but the Baskerville Corporation was not listed.

I walked back to the subway, went down the steps into the station, pushed my way through the turnstile, stood lost in thought on the platform, and waited for the roar of the train. I imagined Alistair waiting for my report in his office. Maybe it overlooked clear blue water. Nassau. I rode the train in a daze. The subway doors slid open at 33rd Street and I leapt out and made my way through the turnstile and up the steps.

When I got back to the office, Nick was reading *Prison Life* magazine and Errol was telling Rodriguez why he liked Queens. "Queens is thuh best a both worlds. Ya got trees, ya kin have a backyard, but it's not like you're in the country. It's not slow. It's still peppy."

I sat down at my desk and heard Vinny on the phone. "I'll get you a real motherfucker of a lawyer . . . Yeah, yeah. He's a cock crusher, a hungry bastard. He'll take calls at ten o'clock at night." Pause. "No, no, no. He's a classy guy."

Ten minutes later, I tell Vinny that there are no articles of incorporation. "I think I should just go to the address and see if the offices are there. What do you think?"

"Yeah, do that. Go up ta the floor, look around, maybe go in—yeah, go in and ask the receptionist for a brochure. Ya know what to do."

Vinny leaned over toward Errol's desk, grabbed the extra plastic spoon, and dipped into the ice cream as Errol pleaded, "Aww! Don't do that ta me! Come on! They're makin' the banana splits smaller than they used to!" Vinny ignored him, took the bite.

"Six Six Six Fifth is a big building. Good address." He took another bite.

Errol put his head down on his desk and moaned in despair.

Barbie called, "Vinny! It's Schlomo calling from Israel! Can you pick up on two?" Vinny, still holding the red plastic spoon, chugged toward his office. He was singing "My Way" in a pretty fair imitation of Sinatra.

As I pulled on my raincoat, Errol and Rodriguez started chanting, "C is going to the Devil's building, the Devil's building, the Devil's building!" I was laughing as I walked through the ophthalmologist's office and out to the elevator.

Buckets of rain were coming down. It was midafternoon, but the sky was black when I crossed Fifth in my sodden, paper-thin leather flats. Dozens of us clutched umbrellas with gritted teeth, squinting against the blowing rain. The second I looked up at the number 666, my umbrella flipped inside

out with a *gwok* noise; I was soaked as I fought to right it in
the near darkness. Maybe Errol and Rodriguez were right.

The revolving door spat wet people out into the big marble
lobby. They seemed to nearly stumble, then lean on dripping
umbrellas for balance before deciding which elevator to take.
Two epauletted doormen manned a large desk in front of a
giant wall directory, which I scanned quickly. No Baskerville
anything. No Wilton anything. No company with the initials
WB. I went up to the third floor anyway and walked down the
hall to glass double doors that read, "327, Ackerman Investments." The receptionist said they'd been there for five years,
had never heard of Wilton Baskerville or any company with
a similar name. I thanked her and left, then checked the floor
directory and walked up and down the long hallways, seeing
for myself. I went down in the elevator, wondering if it could
be suite 3270 on the thirty-second floor. Just a little typo.

One of the doormen approached me. No, he'd never known
the company, but he would look in his book. He opened a battered black spiral log and traced down the columns under "B"
and "W" with one finger. Nothing even similar. I said I had
been told this was the address and confirmed it. We checked
suite 3270, which didn't exist since it was all one company on
the thirty-second floor. I went up anyway and talked to another
receptionist. Then I came down again. The other doorman
was interested, so I drew him into the conversation. Dead end.

I thanked them and left. Went out into the rain, holding
my umbrella with both hands like a flagstaff, wind blowing my hair into my eyes. It was cold for April. I might as
well have been barefoot; my shoes were destined for the
wastebasket. I crossed Fifth with a crowd at the corner,
then walked directly across the street and stared back. Huge
building. Up up up. Little windows lit. Offices. Hundreds of
them. They disappeared and reappeared between swirling
gray clouds and reminded me of the Gotham City scenes in

Batman. I stood there for a few minutes, wondering what to do, and then I crossed Fifth again and went back to the Devil's building.

This time, there was a third doorman there, a fresh one to attack. "Hey, you know what I'm thinking," he said. "I think there's one of them mailbox places next door. You can't see it from the street. You'd never know it was there."

I was electrified with joy. "That's it! Has to be. Do I go out the main door?"

I was directed out of the lobby using a side door, then down a steep flight of stairs. Below ground level was a very small Mail Boxes USA.

"Hi! What's the address here?" I asked the man behind the counter.

"It's Six Sixty-six Fifth Avenue. A good midtown address," he said. "You wanna rent a box?"

I wanted to tap-dance with delight. "No, I want to leave a message for somebody. I've got his box number. I hope this is right. The name is Baskerville, number 327." I was tearing a page out of my notebook and fumbling for a pen.

"Yeah, Wilton Baskerville. That's right."

I smiled as sweetly as I could. I was sure there were raindrops on my teeth. Leaning on the counter had left huge puddles, and I apologized as he swiped them up with paper towels. "When will he get my note? Does he come in once a week? This is Wednesday, does he come in on Fridays or maybe every Monday?"

"He comes in about twice a week, but I never know when. He came by yesterday."

"Oh, so he doesn't always come in on the same day?" Damn.

"No. He'll get this prob'ly by Monday, Tuesday at the latest. Ya want an envelope?"

I didn't know what to write, but I had to pretend to write something. I scrawled, "I missed you. Lots of love from Monique," folded it, and put it into the envelope. It seemed only right that Monique would return from the dead to haunt a flamboyant, handsome liar.

I couldn't wait to tell everyone at the office that Wilton Baskerville was running a multimillion-dollar corporation with hundreds of employees from a mailbox you could barely put your fist in. When I came dripping in with my news, Vinny was doing a little jig around the room, shouting euphorically, "I am the squire of sleaze, the lord of lust, the king of kink!"

When he saw me he stopped in midhop and demanded, "Hey, so whut happened?" and when I told him, he put his arms straight up in the air like an umpire and shouted, "I love you I love you I love you!"

It was not possible to stake out the mailbox. Too much manpower and wasted hours. I got on the phone, then on the computer. Errol helped me do the searches for a driver's license, car registration, Social Security number. Nothing. Wilton Baskerville was not on paper anywhere.

"Hey, Rodriguez, search for bank accounts!" ordered Vinny.

"I gotta tell this joke. Lemme tell this joke first," Rodriguez pleaded.

"Okay, but it better be good. Shoot." Vinny sat on the edge of my desk to listen.

"How can you tell when an Italian girl's not wearin' underpants?"

Nick leered. Errol was wiping butter off his chin. Vinny leaned forward in anticipation. "Cuz you can see the dandruff on her shoes!"

They all laughed, then Rodriguez searched for bank accounts and came up empty-handed. Vinny told me to call Alistair Smith and give him a full report, and I did. He and I talked over some things that he had not sent in the package, and pieces began to come together.

The biggest help was a telephone number that Chapin had found on an old phone bill. Baskerville had made the mistake of using a phone at Chapin's beach house, and one number showed up again and again. I had learned how to back out numbers the first day, and I did this and discovered it was at an address on the Henry Hudson Parkway in the Bronx. Apartment building. Phone listed in the name of Hester. Not a ritzy neighborhood.

Vinny had Greg, the freelancer, go out there that evening and check mailboxes. Then he did a stakeout and was asked to leave by the project's security force.

"I'll get Rodriguez ta go this afternoon," said Vinny the next day. "Meanwhile I got a new case," he addressed us all. "This is great. This real social guy called. He's the master of the hunt and they voted somebody out and now he wants to get back in. We gotta check him out."

Errol, Nick, and Rodriguez stared at him blankly. I didn't smile but just flipped open my notebook, ready to write. I wondered how Vinny would handle this.

"Ya know! Hey, you guys! It's a foxhunt! A very manly sport! All these grown men run aftuh those cute li'l foxes!" shouted Vinny.

The room erupted in boos. Rodriguez was loud, vehement. "That sucks! Ya should nevah fuckin' kill whut you ain't gonna fuckin' eat!"

"Yeah!" agreed Errol with a chicken drumstick extended over his head like a torch. "Go, Jeffrey Dahmer!"

That afternoon, Rodriguez did a stakeout, ID'ed the subject, and returned to the office. "His real name is Willem fuckin' Rosenblatt, and he is fuckin' married to some fuckin' broad named Trudy fuckin' Hester," he announced with a great sense of self-importance. Then he belched.

Hester, I discovered, was employed as a secretary in a small law firm, and it looked as if she supported Wilton, aka Willem. Willem was not using Rosenblatt, or Baskerville, but was living with his wife as Geoffrey Rudolph.

I was stunned. I never thought it would be this contrived. Yes, a nouveau riche fiancé might be after Chapin's money and social acceptance, but a fake name and a phantom corporation and a borrowed boat and a *total* impostor? Alistair Smith, in his English accent, was stupefied. Ever smooth on the phone, he still couldn't entirely hide his amazement from me. I took one last look at the photograph and, as requested, FedExed it back to him "for security reasons." The report was written and Barbie Doll did a bill and it all went out to Bay Street, Nassau, the Bahamas. Copies of everything were stuffed in a file in a metal cabinet under "C" for Chapin.

I closed the drawer and thought how sad it would be for Frederick Chapin to sit his daughter down and tell her about the phony Wilton Baskerville. I pictured them on a veranda with an aqua ocean view, and I saw the tanned, slender blonde, in tears, swearing that Wilton was the only man she'd ever love and that her father had made a mistake, that everyone had made a mistake. How she would suffer when told her fiancé was married to somebody else, had been married all along!

For me, the detective, this was to be one of those rare assignments that ended with the "aha!" factor. It was small and neat with a villain discovered, the lie uncovered, and the truth laid out like a winning hand of poker. I would learn that many times the client gets tired or feels it's too expensive to go on, and the investigator never experiences the satisfaction of putting the last puzzle piece into place. I would be introduced to the characters, pulled into their lives, told their secrets, be privy to their rage, worry, fear, and suspicions, and then...it would be over. Like leaving a movie in the last fifteen minutes.

I sat at my desk and stared at my open spiral notebook. A neat, tied-up-with-a-ribbon ending. Chapin's daughter didn't realize it then, but she was lucky.

Errol was talking on the phone, Barbie was telling Vinny that she had to pay Con Ed, and Vinny was telling Nick he had to write the check. I thought of Trudy Hester supporting her husband as he frolicked with someone else. How did he explain the long absences and his return to their crummy little apartment with a tan? How did he pay for his luxurious life on Lyford Cay? The boat was borrowed, but he had to have clothes, the appearance of wealth. It took a lot of money. Was Trudy in on it? She must have been unless Geoffrey/Wilton lied to both women. The novelist in me saw plots within plots, action mysteriously linked to past events I would adore to imagine, and endless, kaleidoscopic repercussions. Were they planning to kill the young blond heiress after the wedding and take her money and leave the Bronx forever? And who would they be when they did? Mr. and Mrs. Geoffrey Rudolph or Mr. and Mrs. Wilton Baskerville?

Vinny had said, "Hey, it's just your first week! You'll get used ta this stuff!"

I wasn't sure I would.

The phone rang and Barbie Doll called out, "C, pick up on line one! It's Mr. Riccardo." I grabbed the Riccardo file and took a deep breath. Vinny was standing in front of my desk. He wanted to talk.

"You know I'm gonna be in *Penthouse*. A big interview. They're taking the photographs tomorrow." He sighed. "I gotta get my head shaved professionally." I glanced up at Vinny. I'd never seen him look so worried.

"Vinny, I better take this." I picked up the phone. "Hello. Mr. Riccardo? . . . Yes. I'm fine, thanks. I think I finally talked to the right person. Now I know exactly what's what." I listened. "I have a statement from the director about Maria and can fax it over the minute we hang up." Vinny grinned and gave me a thumbs-up sign. I smiled back at him, then looked down and flipped to my notes. "The number you gave me is old, no longer in service. Here's the new one. It's unlisted. Do you have a pencil, Mr. Riccardo?"

One First After Another

had never so entirely embraced a job before. The days' events were being absorbed, I imagined, into my very skin, and the thought of the following day's possibilities kept me from sleep. I worked very hard for Vinny, and he worked me very hard. The reports were easy, but I was starting to learn about the computer databases—I'd never even used a fax machine before—and there was always work on the phone and trips for research at one courthouse or another. The subway—sometimes three round trips in a day—was exhausting in itself. Rodriguez was rarely sent out on anything if there was any talking to do because he had a bad temper and a rough manner and, like Errol, created a certain impression. Errol hated to go anywhere because he would invariably be told to go to a back door to make the delivery, and this both hurt his feelings and enraged him. So I was sent out all the time.

My life was filled with firsts. The first time I had to go to the Bronx criminal courthouse, I casually asked if anyone knew which subway line. This excited them all because it was apparent I'd never been to the Bronx before. The men were mocking and out of control with this tidbit.

My nickname was sometimes Mary Tyler Moore, which I

hated being called, so Errol and Rodriguez shouted, "Mary Tyler Moore is goin' ta da Bronx!" over and over again. Vinny told me what train and advised me to "be careful" as the office erupted into catcalls. "Goin' ta da Bronx! Goin' ta da Bronx!" I slung my bag over my shoulder as Errol marveled, "Nevuh been ta da Bronx before!" for the third time.

I turned in the doorway and smiled. "No, but I've been to Patagonia."

If I was foreign to them, they were foreign to me. Their language was entirely new. The vulgarity was there, of course, and "fuck" was an adjective, a verb, a noun, a curse, or an exclamation. I'd never thought of it before but decided that their plural of "you" made perfect sense. There was a plural in Spanish, Italian, French, probably in hundreds of languages. Southerners had "y'all," and these New Yorkers had "youse."

They all complimented my work, and I was afloat with joy. Vinny seemed to know how to do everything, and the other two often amazed me with their skill on the phone, but I would surprise them, too. They were disbelieving when I said I was going directly to the Korean consulate the next morning and would be late coming into the office. I wanted to find out if a Korean with the highly unusual name of Lee might be registered anywhere. He wasn't, but I did meet with the consul. Something else occurred to me, and in three days of phone calls, mostly in California and Texas, I found this man with the Korean equivalent name of John Jones, who had been missing for seventeen years. I was ecstatic. My first missing person. But that night, lying in bed, I wondered if he had wanted to be found. He certainly hadn't imagined himself as missing...he'd been with himself all that time. Did I do the right thing to "find" him?

You Don't Exist

I guess it was my third week in the office that I sensed a change when I came into the room. A quiet. Rodriguez and Errol seemed to have a secret, and I caught Nick staring at me in an odd way.

"You leavin'?" Vinny asked at the end of the day. "I'll walk wich ya."

He chattered a bit for a block or two and then seemed embarrassed. "I don' know how to say this, but there's a problem."

"What problem? What do you mean?"

He spread his hands out in a gesture of helplessness. "Listen, I gotta tell ya, you are the best person I've ever had in all these years. Maybe one other person caught on as quick as you. Maybe one." His voice died. I waited. "Ya know when I hired ya we really needed someone fast. There was alluva sudden a lotta work and we didn't check your references, and now—"

People were passing us on the sidewalk. "I don't understand. What's wrong with my references?"

"Well, first thing we did was check and there is no one in the country with your name except a woman in Mississippi's gotta be seventy, eighty years old."

"That's my mother!" I laughed with relief.

"There's more," Vinny said with a sigh. "We called that company, that film company in Hollywood, and they never heard a ya."

"Did you talk to Steve Friedman?" I asked.

"No. We never ask ta speak to the person on the résumé. We ask in general." Vinny looked very sad about this. It was as if I had lied to him, let him down. As if everything were ruined.

"Steve Friedman is the president, and I worked for him. Only for him. I didn't have an office there but worked at home and with Steve on the weekends. He'd be the only one to talk to about me."

"There's more."

"What else could there be?" I looked at Vinny in profile, framed by the New York skyline. It was dusk in April; a peculiar shade of yellow was in the very air. He was talking over my shoulder, refusing to look me in the face.

"Well, you don't exist. Not anywhere. There's no record of you. No credit rating. We've searched all the databases. Nothing." His voice was ice cold. "You don't exist."

I felt weak. "What? How can I not—" Then suddenly it came to me. "Vinny! That's because of all those years in Europe. I only have one credit card, and it's from London— Barclays Bank in London. It probably doesn't show up here."

"Why don't you have a credit rating?" he demanded, but at least he was looking at me again.

"Because I guess I've never borrowed money. I've never owned a car or a house—"

He was still angry. "Once I asked you if you had a driver's license and you said yes."

I nodded. "I do."

"According to our research, you don't. Not in any state."

"That's because it's in my married name and Mississippi won't change it until I present my divorce papers and they're in a warehouse outside Rome..."

Vinny, whose moods were as changeable as a child's, gave a little delighted bark of a laugh. "Hey, ya got a passport?"

I took it out of my pocketbook and handed it to him. He turned the pages, studied it, then grinned and gave it back. "Ya bin a lotta places," he purred. "That's great."

We walked a few more blocks together. "Vinny, if you have any more questions, just ask me."

"Bring the passport in tomorrow and I'll make a copy and put it in your file." He sighed. "Ya gotta admit. It looked bad. No trace of you." He shrugged apologetically. "Ya know the others, everyone in the office has been very upset about this. Because you were so good. And they were startin' ta think you were too good."

"I'm older, that's all. I was a journalist. It helps."

He didn't agree or disagree but stared at me and then said seriously, "You're really good."

I left him on Lexington Avenue and walked over to Madison in the spring twilight. It had been odd. I had felt like water when he'd told me that I didn't exist. Standing on a sidewalk as people surged past us. *You don't exist.*

What a chance, I thought that night as I was falling asleep. A chance to start over, to begin again with no background, no memories, no bad dreams.

THE NEXT MORNING, I walked into a silent room. Rodriguez scowled at me, Nick had his head down, and Errol didn't say, "Good morning." Then Vinny bounded in and asked for my passport and held it up and made a little speech about the coincidences. "So we can all relax now."

Rodriguez said, "I wuz plannin' a Bensonhurst bat party." When I asked, he explained that a group of friends got together with baseball bats in an alley at night and beat the person to death. Nick said he was worried that I might be planning to write an article on sexual harassment.

"Come on, Nick!" I said. "Why would I still be here? I could have gotten enough material in the first half hour." They all laughed.

That night, Barbie called me at home. "Every time you'd leave the office they'd run to the computer and try to trace you. And then they'd warn each other and run back to their desks when you'd come down the hall." They couldn't understand why I didn't have a real apartment, why I joked about a sleeping bag, why I'd used a New York post office box as my address for the last eight years. Barbie said they weren't telling me what they'd really thought. "It drove them crazy that you were so good. They went on and on about it all the time." Greg, the freelancer from New Jersey, had been in on it, too. There was a lot of talk about my being in the CIA. Nick thought I was a plant. Rodriguez thought I was infiltrating them and reporting back to someone else. Vinny just moped around, felt bad, and went along with the CIA theory.

Barbie and I talked again the first chance we were alone the next day. She said there had been a lot of talk about the gaps in my résumé. "That's several years," she said. "There was the idea that you'd been in prison. For murder." I burst out laughing and then stopped when I saw the look on her face. "Barbie! You don't—? Come on!"

"No, I don't. But watch out. The others—"

"Well, it's over, isn't it?" I smiled. She was a good friend.

PRISON AND MURDER I thought hilarious. The Company stuff didn't amuse me. It had happened before.

The gaps in the résumé made me smile. The gaps were my best times. Adventures that didn't count unless you were there, really sucking in the oxygen of that place and time with your eyes wide open to the palette of colors. There were gaps when no one who knew me knew where I was. When every alliance was a few minutes or a few days old. When the depth of my involvement with any other person might be just a conversation one taxi ride long. Lighter-than-air freedom.

At one point, in my twenties, I thought I could live nowhere forever. It didn't work—poste restante was a place. An envelope with my name on it, handed out through the wicket when I came for my mail, meant I had a past, was connected to another venue, another time. No matter how long ago it had been written, no matter how long it had waited for me in a hot, dusty, foreign city.

I would take a deep breath each time the plane landed in a new country where I knew no one—often I couldn't spell the name of the capital. Sometimes it was a country that no longer had an American embassy; I'd roll my eyes when told that the United States had broken off relations the week before. I knew I would alight in this new place, have my bags searched, change my money, bargain with taxi drivers, fight off lepers, beggars, pickpockets, and con men, and find a place to eat and to sleep. It took enormous energy...living on so little money, perpetually launching myself into the unknown.

I was the only woman on a train through Sicily while brown-shirted men stared and clicked the safeties of their rifles off and on, hour after hour, as we clattered through the parched countryside. I once swam with a school of barracuda in the bay of Port-au-Prince and later shivered in fear on the deck of the boat as Christophe threw me a towel and told me my silver jewelry was attracting them. I can still feel the exhilaration of being kissed as I crossed the equator over Africa in a tiny plane—the noise, the touch, my arms around khaki-clad shoulders, the kick of it!

I lived in a Belgian's big white Colonial house in Kinshasa.

The African guard posted in front, armed with a machete, sang beside his fire all night in a valiant effort to stay awake. His only job was to kill thieves and the snakes that fell from the trees in the land of the black mamba, the green mamba. Death in minutes. How I hated walking up the long gravel driveway under the overhanging branches in the dark.

One evening, I unexpectedly found myself at a wife-swapping party in an elegant house with zebraskin rugs on the shining wooden floors. Most of the guests were sex-crazed, expatriate Belgians. Maybe it was the contraband meat from South Africa that made them that way, maybe it was the malaria pills. Maybe it was the French movies. I remember my confusion, my hurried departure. They wife-swapped when they had wives to swap. The Congo was littered with unhappy Belgian businessmen whose unhappy mates had fled to Brussels. Lonely, the men made pots of money and waited for their return. How many silver-backed hairbrushes gathered dust on dressing tables in Kinshasa?

In Mombasa, I lived for a while in a very pretty hotel with a big lobby, ceiling fans, and potted palms. The only draw-back was being wakened at one every morning by police in white pith helmets running up and down the wide staircase, blowing whistles and shouting as beautiful African women, some absolutely naked, ran back and forth on the galleries, squealing. I was rescued from the Palm Court after a gin and tonic with the German consul. It was settled before we even ordered dinner. I had not felt the least bit in need of rescuing and was astonished to be told I was living in a whorehouse. He was firm about it. I would live with him in the German consulate, looking out at the Indian Ocean.

He was a thirtyish bachelor from Bavaria, English edu-cated, sophisticated, adorable, and we were to have hilarious, wonderful times together. There were two things I should know, he told me in his English accent that first evening.

First, it was imperative that I learn Swahili in order to deal with the servants. I said, "Oh, absolutely and immediately." Second, I must promise never to give the manservants my underwear to wash because they were convinced they would lose their virility. So, a few hours later, as I got into his chauffeured Mercedes with my knapsack and my straw hat from Togo that was one meter in diameter, I thought, *It's just two things: Swahili and underwear. Yes and no. Okay.*

The German consulate was a tremendous white-columned house on the edge of the Indian Ocean. I was given a wing. The consul and I talked incessantly, flirted nonstop, and were basically inseparable as servants brought us tea, vodka, whatever. There were long conversations on a veranda gazing out at blue water. I swam every morning after our breakfast, and he'd go into town to his shipping firm and then come back for lunch with me. Servants made my bed, drew my bath, constantly checked on my well-being. Swahili was as easy as breathing.

It was quite a happy day-to-day existence. A gap of such sweetness. Once in a while, we'd give a rather successful dinner party with African ministers and diplomats and a smattering of British expatriates. The revelry invariably lasted until dawn.

I had lovely days and nights with the German consul. I left him for Ethiopia.

My gap that was Ethiopia. I would get up at three in the morning, go to the airfield, and get on an old plane called a Dakota. We'd watch the sky lighten, wait for dawn, then I'd climb up a rickety ladder and someone would help me close the door. Nobody told me to wear a seat belt or to sit down. A couple of times, it was just me and the pilot. The propellers would start with an inspiring *clackety-clack* as children in rags cheered and shepherds cleared the animals away. We'd start to move over the grass, trying to pick up speed, but it never felt fast. The earth was like a sponge in the rainy season and water would spray up in arcs from the wheels and pelt the windows. Then there was that hold-your-breath moment of realizing we had left ground not because we had ascended, but because we had simply driven off the side of the mountain, right off the cliff into midair. Green peaks loomed in front of us and below. Would the nose rise in time? Great noise, great tension, a moment never to forget. Something would catch, we made it, we defied gravity every glorious morning. I would crow with relief and know that no one could hear me over the joyful racket of the metal beast.

I was curious about Massawa, an Ethiopian port devastated by the loss of revenue from the closing of the Suez Canal. The whores cost eighteen cents. I went by plane from Asmara—though I'd wanted to take the train—because this cute Italian promised to take me sailing on the Red Sea, but only if I flew with him that day. The next morning we heard the news: My train had been stopped in the desert by Eritrean rebels riding on camels and all the passengers had been ordered off. The rebels had then pushed the train over the hillside and destroyed the tracks. I was plunged into despair to have missed it. Still am. The Italian was mystified but did his best to make it up to me.

Years later, in Rome, I'd hurry over the cobblestones through Piazza San Pietro before dawn with a full moon above me, hearing the splash of the fountains and seeing the light in the Pope's bedroom window. I would be on my way to sort out hundreds of feet of the overnight telex, to write the international news, and then to say the words that would be heard all over the world. I would tell myself to never forget what it felt like, no matter what happened to me.

I remember fighting the undertow that curious white afternoon in Togo and the crystal-clear possibility that I might be sucked to the ocean floor. Afterward, exhausted, too weak to stand, I crawled on hands and knees in the shallows, then lay on my back in the sand, staring up at an empty sky, and thought, *That was almost it.*

There was a python shot and pulled from the Nile that I measured with my size eight feet—twenty-four of my sneakers long—as the robed women screamed at me to stay away.

I remember my plane landing in Tripoli; the only other passenger to disembark was bleeding from a head wound. That searing heat, that man and his blood-soaked bandages and me—the start of a complicated few days in Libya.

A Chinese gangster in Hong Kong once gave me a very expensive jade ring at dinner—I didn't want to take it—and then tried to kidnap me for what he called a weekend in Singapore. The sense that I was in danger had come as we were led to a table, but Mother and good manners kept me talking and smiling as I noted that everyone in the restaurant knew him, was obsequious, in his thrall, even frightened of him. After dessert, his bodyguards tried to force me into the chauffeur-driven black car. It was happening in front of the brightly lit shops, the crowded sidewalks, and no one would help me. After running to my hotel through back alleys, I took the elevator to the wrong floor and then hid on the stairs as his men waited outside my room.

I remember the Catholic priest in Côte d'Ivoire, far away from the capital, in a place of lagoons and crocodiles, who led me to a storehouse filled with coffins. It was past midnight. He held the kerosene lantern over his head so I could see and told me in French to pick one and to close the lid before I fell asleep—"because of the wild beasts."

Can't decide if the coffin was better or worse than my nights in the whorehouse run by the Lebanese in Abidjan. I thought it was a cheap hotel like the Palm Court in Mombasa.

One summer I was engaged to a Portuguese count and wore that heavy gold ring with his family crest on my fattest finger. João kept deserting from the Portuguese army in Angola and flying back to Lisbon to meet my train as I arrived on the all-night local from Madrid. We'd speed in his little red Mini Cooper to the Algarve, where we sunbathed and drank sangria between swims in the icy Atlantic.

Gaps. Rattling through India all night on the crowded train with the snake charmer's basket at my feet—full of angry, hissing cobras. Being led into the desert by the Egyptian peasant to see the mummies he'd hidden in the caves. At dusk in Montevideo, wearing amethysts and drinking wine in a plaza beside a splashing fountain, I thought: *I could stay here forever.*

The adventures are part of me—whatever animal I have become. The sights and sounds, the scent of jasmine, the colors and the music never show up on a résumé. Writing novels, sailing on the South China Sea, nearly getting sold to a tribal chieftain in Afghanistan for an exquisite lapis lazuli box, nearly getting married to a king in Ghana, eating caviar in Tehran with that witty gunrunner, admiring icebergs in Tierra del Fuego, eating banana-and-honey sandwiches at midnight in the casbah in Tangiers. Buying ivory from the terrified Chinese in Zanzibar in a hidden room lit by candles. The rats down by the wharves at night in Dar es Salaam. The huge husky dogs of Tuktoyaktuk who ate fish and rhubarb. Scenes of mystical beauty: the Mountains of the Moon, the fifteen minutes of night north of the Arctic Circle, the "lakes" of the Red Sea alive with sharks.

The gaps . . . I'd be nothing without my gaps.

I'll never forget Vinny Parco in the April twilight as the crowds swirled around us like water, telling me I didn't exist. My gaps were the reason the detectives had decided I wasn't who I said I was, but maybe it was during that time that I was more myself than ever. Those were the moments when I most keenly existed.

Transition

There have been several times over the years when my living situation in New York has become so complicated that I have simply left the country. But in the spring of 1994, I wanted to stay. I had the whole town on the lookout for a New York nest.

Nick thought maybe I could sleep in the office and use the shower of the health club on another floor. Vinny offered to let me stay with him. He had a tiny studio, neat, immaculate, dominated by a gleaming exercise bicycle. He was sweet, and I suspected nothing untoward about his offer because of that first Saturday in the office. We were alone, it was raining torrents outside, and I was happy to have his undivided attention. I felt special as he explained a tricky case and gave me the files. Out of the blue he told me that I was attractive, but, "You're not my type. I dunno why, but I go fer the sorta really cheap broads."

I feigned minor dismay—not too much dismay—followed by a quick moment of resignation. I was actually delighted. I've had testosterone ruin jobs for me before. The advertising agency, the dessert chef job, Air France. I was enduring sexual harassment before anybody put the two words together. But the fact of Vinny's not being attracted to me was not enough to make me want to live in one room with him. I kept asking around, kept throwing my nets out.

Meanwhile, even though I had presented proof of my existence, it seemed that my aptitude as a P.I. was feeding into the CIA rumors that had plagued me during my time in Italy, England, Cyprus, and Switzerland. Mistress of the Station Chief in Rome? Me selling arms to Qaddafi? It had actually been reported in Italian newsmagazines. The stories had made my life complicated, and I wasn't happy that they might resurface. And now, I was still—mysteriously—too "experienced." The drama of my true identity had not entirely dissipated. There was so much talk about how good I was that Vinny gave me a raise. "I talked ta Nick about it and he says okay." He hesitated. "Ya catch on so fast ta everything." He looked at me with squinted eyes. "Even Nick thinks you're really good."

"Wow," I breathed, delighted. I was standing beside his desk, facing a wall of framed glossy black-and-white photos. Vinny was shaking hands with prizefighters and show business personalities. No politician would risk a photo opportunity with Vinny Parco. "That's great, Vinny." Visions of affording an apartment danced in my head.

"So you'll be getting ten dollars an hour from now on."

Apartment idea sledgehammered. I blinked. But from eight to ten dollars *was* a 25 percent increase. I thanked him.

He sighed, rubbed his shining head, and said, "But don't come in tomorrow. Come in on Thursday. Nick says we gotta cut back or we can't make the payroll."

After work I took the subway to Brooklyn Heights, where I had been invited to have dinner with John, Caro's husband. It was a pale green sort of spring evening, and I walked along the water before going up to the Pierrepont Street apartment. Later we screamed with laughter at the big kitchen table as he poured me wine. "You're getting a raise—congratulations, you're great, the best—but, by the way, don't come back!"

PART II
Rural Detectivery

It is the luckiest thing in my life to have a mother who always greets me with open arms and no questions. I had no place to live, and my salary—with the enormous raise and the cutback in hours—could only be wryly described as a reversal of fortune. So I flew to New Orleans, had a gossip-laden lunch in the French Quarter with Susan Coates, who'd once helped me with a novel, and then she put me on the train. This is the cheapest way to get from New York to Turtle Creek. I sat with hands folded in my lap, counting off the Louisiana towns and then the Mississippi ones. Braced to endure exile.

I thought of Mother meeting me at the station in a few hours. Mother was not from the South, yet she'd adapted to it far better than I had. She was from Main Line Philadelphia, descended from Quakers who'd been among the first arrivals in Penn's Sylvania; one of her ancestors had signed the Declaration of Independence. Mother had grown up with governesses and tutors who taught her French. There were chambermaids, cooks, housekeepers and gardeners, a butler, and a chauffeur. There was a lake for skating in winter and a lake for boats in summer, the water lily pond, and a swimming lake. There were rowboats and canoes, a waterwheel, and a log cabin. There were tennis courts, a billiards room, a greenhouse, vegetable gardens and rose gardens, and great expanses of manicured emerald lawns in between. The houses on the two facing hills were impressive. One was my grandfather's in the English Tudor style, and the other was designed by my great-grandfather to look like a Spanish castle. It had sixty-five rooms. All the marble for the floors and fireplaces, all the fountains and the chandeliers, had come by ship from Europe, as had most of the furniture.

Mother was the oldest of eight, rather sheltered, with a serene brunette beauty in the manner of Gene Tierney. There was a quiet elegance to her even when she was wearing sneakers. She was sweet-tempered, not spoiled in any way, though she'd grown up going to private schools and taking adventurous trips with a father who never worked.

My father saw my grandfather's and my great-grandfather's houses on those two hills outside Philadelphia, and he courted my mother over tea in the Big House. Mother was fascinated by the tall, brown-eyed Mississippian who was going to become a doctor. She said that in those days you thought of a doctor not making money, but making sacrifices for the good of other people. On call twenty-four hours a day, long hours, being wakened in the middle of the night. She admired him, fell in love with him, accepted his proposal, stopped her classes at the Pennsylvania Academy of the Fine Arts, and they were married—for decades of acrimony. With conversation of any sort, disagreement was inevitable, Daddy's rage a sure thing.

I looked out the window of the train at the dark green leaves and thought of the ivy. Mother wanted ivy on our brick house, and the yardmen tended it year after year. When it had finally grown up to the second-story level, she was so pleased and it did look beautiful. It seemed only a week later, at dinner, that my father ordered Mother to "rip it off and have it burned." They argued, he shouted, he commanded.

I remember the stricken look on Mother's face as she supervised the men on ladders tearing down the vines and dark green leaves.

Arguments and criticism could materialize over the most bizarre. Sometimes at dinner Daddy would claim that one chandelier bulb was dimmer than the others. Mother and I would stare up as he shouted at her, "If you cain't run thuh house, jes' say so and Ah'll shell out money fer a housekeeper! You're too stupid to handle anything!"

I was stupid, too, and was told this several times a week. "You'll never amount to a hill a beans!" he would rant at me, and I would wonder what that meant. Lima or baked? With ketchup? I had "no ambition" and "no sense of competition," and I would never "better" myself.

"Jackson! Next stop Jackson!"

I snapped into the present, swiped a brush through my hair, zipped my pocketbook, and felt my stomach tighten. The black conductor was talking almost to himself as he threaded his way up the aisle. "Y'all don' fergit yore bu'longin's and mek sure y'all check round yore seats. Otherwise, everythin's goin' on up ta Memphis wid me." Then he shouted again as I felt the train slow. "Welcome to the capital of the great state of Mississippi!"

Mother was on the platform in a navy wraparound skirt, a white T-shirt, and her red sneakers without socks, smiling when she saw me. She'd always looked younger than her age, had been athletic and natural and un-made-up, in fresh contrast to the other mothers, who wore girdles and plenty of face powder and went to the "beauty parlor" twice a week. At age eighty-three, Mother's hair was still light brown.

The best thing about coming back was that I was immediately a private detective. No license needed so I didn't have to work for anybody. I stepped off the train—instantly and legitimately freelance.

Mother was not only delighted with my new profession—she even had a client for me. Darrell cut her hair at the Hair Depot for four dollars a whack way on the other side of town. I called him and we arranged to meet between haircuts the next morning.

I couldn't sleep the night before. I never slept well in Mississippi—not growing up and not now in the house Mother bought after the divorce. I worried about how much to charge Darrell. What if it were a very tough case taking many hours and I had to charge him a lot—say, one hundred dollars? That was twenty-five haircuts. Maybe this would only be a ten-haircut case. My mind raced. I had finally stopped having nightmares in Rome but Mississippi would always be the scene of the crime.

I was little again.

The Way It Was

I never thought I'd live to be twelve. For several reasons. I was constantly applying Band-Aids and Mercurochrome to scraped knees and forever explaining complicated events surrounding torn clothes. I remember dogs and turtles and catching lightning bugs and climbing high up in the butter bean tree. I'd mark how far up with my knife so no one could doubt it. Some of my happiest times were before the first grade—before I was yanked into the world of arithmetic and shoes.

I was a tomboy. All my friends were boys. The Robinson boys—Sidney and Craig—and the Grenfells—Raymond and Milton. A cut, a bruise, falling off the brick wall, crashing a makeshift sled into a mailbox going a hundred miles an hour (maybe not quite that fast, but we would swear it was at the time) down an icy street in Woodland Hills: "No, it didn't hurt. 'Course I'm not limping." Over 150 stitches to close the cuts after running through a plate glass door at a Halloween party. Scars? Who cared? I confess that I actually like my scars. My clothes were wet, muddy, ripped, and grass-stained, but I never broke a bone, was always just fine. And I'd rather have dropped in my tracks right there in the woods and been eaten by buzzards than ever confess to being tired.

I loved my dogs and once had twenty-seven turtles under my bed, but I also loved my dolls. I named them all. First names and then last names out of the Jackson phone book. I remember sitting on the top step of the staircase and hearing my father tell my mother to give away all my dolls because I was "too attached" to them. Then he said he was going to "git rid" of my dog because I was "too attached" to him, too.

My stomach used to ache with fear when I'd hear him talk about getting rid of my dog, but scarier still was when he'd stare me in the face and say he was going to get rid of *me*. He told me he hated me every time he caught me alone. This was far too often, even though I'd scamper away like a rabbit when I heard the Mercedes coming up the driveway. I study photographs now and see this skinny little girl with crooked teeth, bright, trusting eyes, and two ponytails. I did wonder why my father hated me. Maybe it was because everyone said I looked like my mother, and he hated her.

My father was over six feet tall and handsome, a back slapper with a southern accent who charmed both men and women. He was a well-respected eye surgeon known all over the state and even beyond the borders. When I was about four, we moved nearer to town from the farm to a big, two-story house with pine trees, live oaks, camellias, azaleas, gardenias, and magnolias on the property. There was a brick wall surrounding the back garden and a terrace and a fountain and fish pond. He held on to the farm for a while but sold it to developers years later.

He had oil leases, but I think there were a lot of dry holes, and land and cattle. Owning the first Mercedes in Mississippi and being admired behind the wheel of it gave him enormous pleasure. It was actually bought when he was in Stuttgart at one of his eye meetings and shipped over. He so enjoyed easing it into the country club parking lot and then being seen in the big dining room for Sunday lunch, smiling, with his wife and two daughters at his side. I used to pretend I was a prisoner of war. Mother and I, but not my sister, would drape the big damask napkins over our shoulders because the air-conditioning was always too strong. We were secretly gleeful that it enraged Daddy, who wouldn't dare explode in public.

My three older brothers were much older, away at military school or later in the army when I was growing up; my sister is a few years younger than me. The boys were seldom home.

Sometimes, in an eerily pleasant mood, my father would call Mother into his study where he watched Huntley and Brinkley before dinner. She would try to smile as he offered her a glass of sherry—already poured and on the table beside his chair. He would be drinking bourbon. She would perch on the edge of the couch across the pine-paneled room and pretend to be so interested in the latest newscast that she would forget to take the first sip. After a few minutes, she would stand up and say, "Oh, I must remind Mary not to put any salt on that fish," or "I must tell Mary about dessert," and leave the room. Mary would be spooning sweet potatoes into a serving dish or taking something out of the oven. Mother would hurry past her to the sink and carefully pour the dark liquid directly down the drain. Neither woman ever spoke of it until years later.

The dining room table was a battlefield. There were occasions, in my early teens, when I felt strong enough to stand up to him. I can hear my voice, trying to be brave, as Mother knocked over water goblets, first hers and then mine, then began on the iced tea glasses as Mary rushed in with cloths to stanch small rivers.

Our own little private war. Diversionary tactics, confrontations, targets, chinks in the armor, weapons, noise, and, in the end, survival. Getting the globs of food down a tear-choked throat. I never added salt to my food because the tears would course straight down my cheeks and drip directly onto my plate. I was very thin. If it wasn't rage at dinner, there was the silence. Other than the swish-swish of the swinging door as Mary came and went with serving dishes, there was only the occasional clink of silver against china, the noise of ice in a glass, our chewing, and Mother swallowing. Mother was a loud swallower. When Mary had announced dessert, I could finally say, "No, thank you. Mother, may I please be excused?" I can still hear my voice saying that. Thousands of times.

I used to wonder how he'd get rid of me. Maybe I would be taken out to the farm and weighted down with rocks and thrown off the dock. Or I'd be put to sleep with a lethal injection. He was a doctor, he could get rid of me. He'd never smother me with a pillow because I was awake all night.

I don't think I really slept until I was about fourteen and we got Tiny—the Chihuahua that was supposed to cure Daddy's asthma, which was brought on by me and by Mother. At least he always blamed us for it in a red-faced fury. An asthmatic dentist friend of Daddy's swore by his Chihuahua, so with much muttering about "Indian hocus-pocus," Daddy directed Mother and me to drive to a Chihuahua farm in south Mississippi "ta pick up the damn dog."

According to Dr. Colette, the dog was supposed to sleep with Daddy for maximum effect, but Tiny curled up on my bed that first night and then every night. The "hocus-pocus" worked anyway, for the little dog started to wheeze like Daddy, and Daddy stopped. It was eerie to hear a little cough and think he was in the next room. Tiny became my miniature bodyguard, pressed tightly against me, and I slept at last.

At least four times in my teenage years, Tiny woke me with a throaty growl, and reaching for her, I realized all her fur was standing on end. My bedroom door was closed, but the light from the walk-in linen closet across the hall was on. The first time, I'd turned on the bedside lamp and the door had opened instantly and Daddy had commanded me to "turn it off!"

"But what—but why..."

"Why are you awake? You shouldn't be awake! Turn off the light!"

Tiny showed all her little teeth, poised to leap at him in his pajama top. He closed the door, I turned off the lamp, and still he stood there. An hour passed, according to the alarm clock, with Tiny growling, me petting her, with all my muscles clenched and her fur on end. At last, I heard the *ka-shoo* of the cord being pulled, and the linen closet light went off. I heard his footsteps go down the hall. The other times were the same except I never turned on the lamp again. It would be two or three o'clock and he would stand there in the middle of the night, not moving, for an hour, as Tiny growled and I stared at the shadow of his feet and waited for him to turn the doorknob. It was as if he were deciding what to do.

NOW, SLEEPLESS IN THE summer of 1994, I told myself I was all grown up, that I lived in New York, that Daddy was dead. I knew he was dead because Mother made me go to his funeral. Stirling, my oldest brother, told me in between shaking hands with all the tearful fools, that he felt like tossing a few dollar bills into the open casket. Wish he had. Wish Daddy hadn't cut him out of his will. Wish Stirling hadn't killed himself.

I stared into the darkness for a long time and then fell into black dreams.

Clip Job

The next morning I was up early, in and out of the shower, wondering what to wear, thinking it was already one hundred degrees in the shade. A historic morning. My first client. Not Vinny's, but mine. I stared in the mirror, trying to look sympathetic, tough, and shrewd all at the same time; I felt sweaty. Mother hated air-conditioning and I wasn't crazy about it, either, but sometimes I'd say, "Mother, let's just close the windows and turn it on for an hour," and she would give in.

Mother told me it was complicated to get to the Hair Depot and that she would go with me. I was content with this but felt it might soften my reputation for being a hard-boiled detective if I rolled up in the little gray station wagon with my mother. There was also the issue of confidentiality.

"I understand completely," said Mother as she got out of the car at the Krystal.

I drove to the other side of the parking lot in front of the Hair Depot and waved at Darrell through the big plate glass window. He stopped between trimming sideburns (one was trimmed, one was not) and strode outside on his down-at-the-heels cowboy boots, which were worn in a very odd place because of the way he leaned during haircuts.

Darrell had a neatly trimmed black beard and bright eyes. He was tan and lean, with jeans hanging precariously from hipbones—very attractive, if you go for white trash. He was still holding the big shears in one hand.

After the initial greetings, and, "You down here visitin' yore momma?" he began.

"Yeah, well, I won' take up too much a yore time. Ya know the guy whut owns this place?" He tilted his head toward the Hair Depot, which is always packed with fat women wearing Easter egg–colored polyester shorts. The kind of fat women who haven't been able to cross their legs in ten years. "Well, he's got somethin' on me. I ain't supposed ta drink cuz I'm on medication, but I went in one night and busted up all his videocam'ras. Now he sez I cleaned out his safe, too. I'm payin' him back ev'ry week, but I want somethin' on him." He clacked the giant scissors open and closed. *Clack clack clack.*

"Thought we could git him pilled up and git him on video. I don' think adultery's enough. Git him with a girl and a guy on film." He kept clacking the scissors. *Clack clack clack.*

Pilled up? I wanted to shriek, but I told myself to be professional. "Is he married or gay or both?"

Darrell rocked back and forth on his boots. "Hell, he's married, but that don' make no diff'rence cuz I thank he'd go fer a guy given half a chance."

"Did it go to court? The problem with the safe?" This is me playing Friday on a Thursday. The facts, just the facts, man. No judgmental tone whatsoever. This is my client. I believe in my client.

"Hell, no. He jes' laks ta hang somethin' over me." Darrell is rocking back and forth on his heels, making clacking noises with the big shears. I imagine that the blades gleam evilly and tell myself to get real. The thumb of his free hand is hooked into a belt loop of his jeans.

"I can't help you with this," I tell him. "You'll have to find somebody else."

"Hell, that videocam'ra is easy ta git. And I know people who'd take care a this fer me. Used to. I quit that kinda life."

"Well, Darrell, I'll keep you in mind if I meet someone..." My voice trailed off. Pilled up? Some redneck honeypot scheme? I could see myself trying to buy drugs in Rankin County and then talking some honky-tonk angel in jeans cutoffs and a tank top into seducing the owner of the Hair Depot. *Oh, and yes, does your boyfriend want to make some money, too?* What would my mother say?

Clack clack clack. "Yeah, well, you must meet a lotta people, all kindsa people." We shook hands. "Tell 'em ta give me a call." He clacked the scissors one last time.

I wished him luck and got into the car. I looked up before starting the air-conditioning and saw the man with one trimmed sideburn, still in the chair, wearing a white cape, staring out the window at me.

I did a big circle around the parking lot and fished Mother out of the Krystal. She raved about how clean the place was and was excited by the white icing on her doughnut. I thought of her innocence. That thug cut her hair every six weeks.

She didn't ask a thing about the case. Nothing.

"I haven't been able to have him cut my hair the last two times because he's been away." She ate the last of the doughnut. I waited. "He goes away for months at a time." Her voice dropped. "I think he's in and out of Parchman."

I laughed. Parchman was the state prison farm. Maybe Mother wasn't so innocent after all. I told her that I could hardly believe the haircuts there only cost four dollars.

"And I always give him a dollar as a tip," she said vehemently.

I turn onto Highway 80. My first client. My first case.

It was over. I thought of the clacking of the big shears. An open-and-shut case. Or so I thought.

Darrell later exacted a vicious revenge for my not helping him. I was down visiting Mother the next year when he gave me the worst haircut of my life. I looked like a dog had gnawed on me. Once back in New York, the men in the office got a lot of mileage out of my anguish.

Return to the Yellow Pages

The next day, I dived into the Jackson Yellow Pages. I wanted assignments, didn't think I could get cases on my own. One call netted an investigator who said he'd like to meet me and what about lunch? We met at a Greek restaurant and ate salads under an umbrella on an elevated deck in 227-degree heat as I told him what I could do, had done. Then he told me he couldn't hire me because "I'd worry about you." I was silently livid. Then he said, "Your eyes sparkle so much, I think I'll call you Sparkle." It was all I could do not to push him over the railing, where I imagined him landing spread-eagle, cartoon style, on the hood of some truck parked below. I was polite right up to the last black olive, thanked him for lunch, and drove home. I was newly enraged when Mother said she thought it was "cute to be called Sparkle."

Next I called an investigator who listed an 800 number. I was thrilled at the sophistication. Johnny Bob Thompson told me he worked all over the country, and he had the idea that he was famous because he was once on a TV show called *Day One* for finding a kidnapped child. This man seemed to think he was doing me a favor by talking to me. On the phone, he was in turns flirtatious and belligerent. "I bin havin' a rough time. The last altercation I attended was last week. Up in Tunica. I turned mah back on the gal and she stabbed me with a steak knife. Nothin' real bad. Bled some."

I thought, *Well, I'm not the only woman unmoved by your charm.* Johnny Bob decided I could do a surveillance of a woman and child the next day at five-thirty in the afternoon. There was a bigamist involved. He would follow the bigamist. I wanted to follow the bigamist and felt like whining, "Please, please let me have the bigamist!" but I was businesslike and merely said, "Yes, that's fine. I can do a surveillance tomorrow."

"I'm not gonna tell ya how much I'm gonna pay ya until I meetcha."

"Good idea," I said quickly. "I want you to be convinced that you can trust me, that I don't have the IQ of a pineapple and can do the job."

Johnny Bob snarled suggestively, "Jes' as long as you don't have the figure of a pineapple."

Mother said it didn't mean anything. Johnny Bob was an oaf, but that didn't mean I wouldn't work for him. After all, I knew I could be hired by poison and come through unscathed. But I never heard from Johnny Bob again—not about the surveillance, not about anything. I called his office the following afternoon and a woman said that "something had come up."

This is the way those men handled it—they didn't handle it. They would tell me somebody from their office would call me back to arrange a meeting, but no one ever did. It was refreshing when one or two actually said, "We aren't hiring."

I called at least a dozen investigators. I can't prove it, but I think they balked because I was a woman. What did they think? That I'd show up for a stakeout wearing a hoopskirt, clutching a lace handkerchief and smelling salts? Maybe this was how it felt to be black in the sixties.

Turtle Creek Exile

I was restless. I opened the top bureau drawer every morning to stare at my plane ticket: New Orleans to LaGuardia. Still valid.

I blamed myself for having to be here. Since I'd left Beverly Hills a year or so ago, my life had become a saga of housing crises. I walked down to the dock and gazed out at water that looked brackish and hot at noon. *If I were married, I probably wouldn't be here; but if I were married, I probably wouldn't be a detective.* A sobering thought. I'd gotten married, but I hadn't liked it. I'd finally been allowed to cross the border with my silver, my typewriter, and Monty, my stuffed albino cobra. Six years later, at lunch, I'd opened an envelope with lots of colorful stamps and seen that he'd surrendered and signed the divorce papers. Meanwhile, I'd thrown the wedding ring in a river, moved to Rome, started a new chapter. I waved the documents in the air, waiters materialized with more wine, and my friends shouted, *"Bravissima!"* Not one of them had any idea I'd ever been married in the first place.

So—so far, I don't like to be married. I like to be engaged. Security, with its long chain of synonyms, seems a terrifying concept. Weren't we put on earth to have adventures? Isn't it our duty?

I tried not to think of Vinny Parco.

Another day went by. I swam. Sorted boxes of old books in the garage and tried not to wonder what Vinny Parco was doing in New York.

In the occasional morose moment, I labeled myself a failure. The other times I'd come to visit Mother had been triumphs, with book signings at Lemuria and even an article or two in *The Clarion Ledger*, and now I was not visiting but living with my mother, in a place I had always wanted to leave. Then I would think how lucky I was to know what it was like to be a detective, to find what made my spirits soar, to be driven mad by curiosity and high with the thrill of the chase. Granted, I didn't feel much like a detective at the moment and the days of Vinny Parco seemed like another lifetime.

The next morning, Mother called out name after name from my past as I wandered barefoot through the house, swigging Diet Coke. "No, Mother, I don't want to 'get in touch.' I don't want to 'arrange to get together.'"

Three old beaux were married and probably wouldn't take me to the movies. I'd once considered marrying a Jackson lawyer, once almost married someone whose family had a plantation up in the Delta. He used to call and break dates with the explanation "It's a real crucial time for the soybeans." And it *was*. I understood and I forgave. There were several beaux over my summers in between college years, but I think their strongest suit was proximity. We'd kissed to the point of having trouble breathing, gotten caught by the Reservoir Patrol skinny-dipping off the dock at Turtle Creek. We'd drunk beer and played pool in honky-tonk joints until it was time for breakfast, stayed up all night on boats, flown helicopters at dawn out to oil rigs in the Gulf. They asked me to marry them. Some asked more than once. Only thing worse than saying no is saying no again. And I never knew whether to say, "No, thank you."

Falling in love was dizzy and fizzy and fun, but even cali-brated at maximum intensity, it was tagged in a corner of my mind with an expiration date, like milk. I couldn't imagine that I would actually want to be with one person forever.

I sorted more boxes of old books in the garage. I tried watch-ing daytime talk shows. When Jerry Springer announced that his show would be all about circumcision and promised that the audience would "meet four men who will talk about how they want their foreskins back," I turned off the television, walked outside, and picked a pine tree from which to hang myself.

Then I started wondering what Vinny Parco was doing in New York. I returned to the kitchen stool and the Yellow Pages and began to dial. I'd been in Turtle Creek for four days. The world was spinning on its axis without me.

Mississippi P.I.

One afternoon, I flipped to the "Printer" section of the Yellow Pages and started calling. I was in luck, one woman told me. "We print in green ink only on Thursdays, and this is Wednesday. So, sugar, if you can get your order in by five o'clock, then we could have the cards for you in five business days." I thanked her and hung up.

"Mother, do you mind if this kitchen becomes a detective agency?"

Mother looked up from the pile of mail she was sorting. "No. That would be fine."

"Well, do you mind if I print your phone number on my business cards for the detective agency?"

Without missing a beat, she asked, "How should I answer the phone?"

"Hello! Just say 'Hello,' Mother!" We burst out laughing and then got into the car and sped over the dam to the stationery place.

I wanted to name it Chameleon Investigations, but nobody in the store knew how to say it. *This is called market research*, I thought, grinding my teeth. If nobody can say it, then it's not a good name. Five people thought it was "SHA-me-lee-ON," but one man at the counter argued with dogmatic certainty that the "ch" was pronounced like the "ch" in "chocolate." No wonder Mississippi is constantly fiftieth in everything, jockeying desperately with Alabama to be forty-ninth.

"Okay," Mother said brightly. "Think of something else."

"I don't have a second choice. That was it, Mother." I sighed. We stood at the counter, flipping through logo sample books. "Well, it doesn't look like they have a picture of a lizard wearing a fedora and a trench coat in stock anyway."

"No, sugar," the clerk said sympathetically. "I don't reckon we carry that."

Mother and I brainstormed possibilities. Nothing was right until Mother said to name it after my tattoo. Green Star Investigations.

With the cards in the works, I felt a sense of accomplishment. The next morning, I opened the Yellow Pages under "Investigators" once more and started punching in numbers.

"Yep. This is Lyndon Investigations. This is Lyndon on the line."

We talked. I liked his voice. I hung up and jumped around the kitchen. "Mother, he sounds nice! And not flirty! Normal! And..." I was already running down the hall. "And he said to come to his office!"

God, it was hot. I leapt into the shower, leapt out, dressed quickly, and instantly started sweating again. "He told me to telephone just before I came to make sure he hadn't been called out on a case..." I was on the kitchen stool, dialing. "What do you mean, Out all day?" I was stunned. "But I just talked to him eleven minutes ago." Suddenly I knew the receptionist was lying. "I know he's there. May I please speak to him?"

I was put on hold, and he came on the line. "I've...uh...

had second thoughts, and I'm not hiring anybody. I don't need anybody temporanious."

I managed to say, "I understand," in a tight voice and, "Good-bye." I hung up. Then I exploded. I was gnaw-on-the-furniture mad. Mother seldom lost her temper. Sometimes I thought I was an Italian mysteriously born to an Englishwoman.

"Mother! How dare he not see me? How dare he change his mind!" I shouted. "Look at me! I took a shower and I'm wearing mascara! In this heat—I am wearing mascara! How dare he have second thoughts!"

Mother never looked up from *The Clarion Ledger*. "I'd go anyway."

I grabbed my résumé and Vinny's letter of recommendation, jumped into Mother's station wagon, turned the air-conditioning to arctic, the radio to sonic boom, and screamed curse words all the way down Interstate 55 to the Pearl Street exit. Words I didn't know I knew. Words I think I learned in Vinny's office.

I pushed open the glass door with a vengeance and charged through the little lobby. "Lyndon Investigations" was written on the open door of an office. A trim man in his forties was standing beside a desk, talking to a secretary. He was wearing a short-sleeved polo shirt and khakis.

"I just talked to you half an hour ago. I came anyway."

He took a long, cool look at me. I was out of breath, with jaw clenched, still mad as hell. "I admire persistence. Come on in."

I followed him into another room with a desk, a phone, two chairs, and maps of various counties covering the walls. "I don't want to take up any of your time, but I thought I'd drop off my résumé." I was in a state of scarcely suppressed rage.

He motioned for me to sit down, and he looked so nice, so

calm, he had such good manners, that I did. In three minutes
I was getting six dollars an hour and twenty cents a mile. In
four minutes I had a case.

I was euphoric. I liked Lyndon right away. He was one
of those southern men who always look as if they've just
shaved, just left the comb marks in their just washed hair,
just gotten dressed. Everything pressed, clean, trimmed, and
polished. I guessed that he would look exactly like this after
a really ratty day. He looked unflappable. There was a small,
neat bullet hole in the window right behind his left ear.

Many might not see this as a great career move but I did.
Even though I was full speed in reverse financially. Vinny
had started me at eight dollars, praised me and given me ten,
then taken away my hours, and now I was at six dollars an
hour. "I know you could earn more bagging groceries at the
Jitney, but this is all I can afford to pay ya right now." It was
settled. I never made the tiniest squeak of protest.

Lyndon had been a homicide detective with the Jackson
police force, and he knew his stuff. I was delighted to be his
student, and he was a good teacher. Lyndon was from the
south part of town and I was from the north; we'd gone to
rival high schools. I'd never known a policeman or met anyone who wanted to be one. Except Nick in Vinny Parco's
office and Bo Dietl, if you count half an hour of watching
him ignore me.

That first evening, we met at a shopping center in front of
the dry cleaner's. I pulled in right next to his car, and before I
could get out, he was slipping into the front seat. "This your
momma's?" he asked, and I nodded. "Great," he breathed.
"It's the perfect surveillance vehicle." I loved telling Mother
that she'd been driving around in "the perfect surveillance
vehicle."

Lyndon tossed guns and flashlights and enough camera
equipment for a network news team into the backseat. Then

he picked up a gun and got into the front seat. "You drive," he ordered, and I pulled out of the parking lot. We had to get gas, and we were talking so much that I left the top to the gas tank off and we had to go back and look for it and it was gone. Lyndon told me he'd get another one for me and not to worry. We Saran-wrapped the hole and sped away. Lyndon directed me to drive around for a couple of hours. He showed me some of the joints with bands and dancing and some of the apartment complexes where certain subjects were. He taught me a shortcut to the highway, how to use a walkie-talkie.

The next day, he called and we arranged to meet at nine in the evening for a stakeout. Mother and I watched Tom Brokaw and then ate fried chicken out on the terrace together and pretended we weren't watching the clock. We drank wine even though Rankin is a dry county. I nearly died when Mother bought a house in a dry county, but you just go to the liquor store in Hinds County, then bring the bottle into Rankin. The sheriff wouldn't ever bother you about it.

Lyndon had rented a car because his was getting too known. "Once they've seen the car, that's all they see." In the middle of a tail, all you could do was vary the silhouette. Lyndon had a baseball cap with a built-in ponytail he could slip on, and I always had several different hats and rubber bands to change my hair. I thought about buying a wig but decided that my greatest fear would be to die of heatstroke in a parked car wearing a cheap, ill-fitting wig. Second greatest fear was being found wearing the cheap, ill-fitting wig only half-dead. Half-dead could be better or worse than entirely dead: I'd have a chance to redeem myself *or* I'd never live it down.

I was absorbing everything Lyndon said. The high point came hours later, racing down Pear Orchard Road behind him in the perfect surveillance vehicle, conferring via walkie-talkie. I'd nearly been born on that road, when it was gravel, during a January thunderstorm, and before I could walk, I'd ridden on it in front of Mother on her favorite horse, Miss Pointer. Later, Mother had named the road when we were the only white family living out there on the farm. Now, here I was, a private detective, in midnight pursuit of a blond adulteress.

Later, driving home, I went down Pear Orchard again. The windows were open, the warm wind rushed in, and I could smell my past. I could imagine the long-gone house at the end of the long driveway, in the lee of the tall trees behind veils of Spanish moss. The white fence with the roses, the kitchen doorway surrounded by the blue morning glories. In old black-and-white snapshots, the house on Pear Orchard Road looked like an enchanted cottage. So why did I remember only rooms of shadows?

I crossed into Rankin County and then went over the dam, and twelve minutes from there I was pulling into Mother's driveway.

I marveled at how the geography could pull me back into feeling like a little girl. *I'm grown up*, I told myself, trying to fall asleep. Two hours later, I remembered the paraffin earplugs and fumbled in my suitcase for them. Was I the only person in the world who had to shut out the song of the crickets, hoping to quiet the pounding of my heart?

Southern Summers

I'd spent my whole childhood wanting to be anywhere else—away from that dining room with the pale blue wallpaper covered with Chinese figures serenely suspended in space, away from the Old Canton Road house, away from Mississippi. It wasn't only Daddy, it was the sixties. It was the all-pervasive threat of violence in the very air we breathed. People used to say, "It's going to be a long hot summer," and they weren't referring to the weather. Mississippians were a society under siege, bracing for trouble, ready to defend, at all costs, "our way of life."

There was talk of Mississippi seceding from the United States.

I remember the summer when the three civil rights workers were murdered and buried in the dam in Neshoba County. The state wouldn't bring murder charges against the sheriff and his deputy; the federal government had to step in and prosecute them for violation of civil rights. Mother and I dared to sneak into the courthouse for their sentencing. She wriggled through the crowd and sat with the Klan women, who favored spike heels and hairdos that could have gotten caught in ceiling fans. Mother put a whole pack of Juicy Fruit in her mouth and squeezed right into the first spectators' bench.

This was a time of the freedom riders. Medgar Evers was shot to death in town in his own garage. The Citizens' Council. The Sovereignty Commission. The Klan.

And through it all, Mary worked for us six days a week when she had six children and a husband at home. She had her own drinking glass and her own bathroom in our house, but she cooked our food, knew every detail of our lives. She could take her children to the public zoo and could buy them hot dogs, but they weren't allowed, by law, to sit on a bench to eat them. It was as if she were unclean. Mother and I agreed that it wasn't right, but we couldn't talk about our feelings to anyone.

Boys and girls I liked in school, even my teachers, would sometimes say "nigger," and I would cringe. Mother said to never say it, and I never did. Daddy did, Aunt Frances did, and then people started saying "niggrah." From the time I was five, I was always aware of feeling different, of being like Mother. It meant keeping quiet, required constant vigilance.

One morning, about five or six of us were waiting for the bell to go inside. We'd been assigned *Uncle Tom's Cabin* for English class, and I dared to say something deemed too sympathetic to slaves. Suddenly surrounding me was a circle of faces I scarcely recognized.

"Nigger lover!" they sneered.

"Guess you wanna go ta school with niggers who have flies in their hair!" a girl shouted at me.

They were my friends, I'd been to all their birthday parties, had known them all my life, but now I was under attack because I'd let it slip I wasn't like them.

Mr. Hunter, my journalism teacher, told our class in tenth grade to bring in two dollars that Friday so that we could each have a subscription to *Time* magazine. He said it was an example of excellent writing—I suppose he was saying, in effect, that *The Clarion Ledger* was not. The next day, about half the class said their parents refused "ta pay fer some liberal

Yankee rag." The following Monday, there were bullet holes in the classroom's big plate glass window; the gunfire had strafed Mr. Hunter's podium, too. He shrugged and started assigning articles for the school paper. The glass was replaced, but Mr. Hunter's classroom was shot up again the following year. He came in, small, thin, in his drip-dry white shirt and skinny black tie, surveyed the broken glass and the new bullet holes in the walls, and shrugged. "Was it something I said?"

North Jackson was the wealthiest part of town and Jackson was the capital city so it followed that Murrah in north Jackson was considered the best high school in the state. When the news came during lunch hour that President Kennedy had been shot and killed, cheers and applause rang out. Students jumped on desktops, shouting, "Now we'll have a southerner as president!" Rebel yells echoed up and down the hallways.

It was a time of two drinking fountains labeled "White" and "Colored" and four restrooms. When I arrived in Johannesburg years later, I thought: I know this place. Daddy, born in Vicksburg, had grown up in this society. So had I.

THAT SUMMER OF 1994, Mother and I talked endlessly about politics, about our marriages—mostly hers, since it had lasted eleven times longer than mine—and about Daddy, about what had really happened.

"Money," I said. We were eating pastry in a booth at the Olde Tyme Delicatessen. "You didn't care about it, and that in itself infuriated him." I'd grown up with a mother who said, as we arrived home from shopping, "Wash your hands, you've been touching money," and a father who worshipped it.

"Conniving," said Mother as she bit into a bear claw. It was her favorite word to describe the McNairs.

The McNairs. There had to be exceptions, but the ones I know best never miss a chance to announce self-righteously that they are "good Christians." Duplicitous and avaricious, they did things Mother's family never would have done. When I was five years old, my aunt Frances held me over my grandmother and commanded, "Kiss Big Momma good-bye." She'd been in her coffin.

I shuddered at the memory and went on. "Uncle Angus wasn't great to his children, either." There was the story of a daughter, my first cousin, arriving at his deathbed after years of exile to beg forgiveness for marrying a Catholic. Uncle Angus turned his face away from her and died. He hated Catholics.

Daddy hated Catholics and Jews, Episcopalians, Italians, liberals, the Irish, everyone who lived in New York, the French, the Pope, desegregationists, Mexicans, anyone who held office in Washington, the Japanese, everyone in California, Arabs, chiropractors…the list was colorful and endless.

On the other hand, Daddy's father had been a gentle, kind man. He'd worked for the railroad, and his father had been a doctor at the siege of Vicksburg. When the war was over, my great-grandfather had become a hero by quelling a yellow fever epidemic. Grateful, the survivors changed the name of their town. Mother and I had driven there once. McNair, Mississippi, was a filling station and a little run-down general store with a sign that advertised RC Cola.

"So much of it with your father was money, was status," said Mother, who treated everyone the same. She sipped her iced tea.

Money. Daddy was as tight as the bark on a tree. A new winter coat for me would be brought into the house and put away, the tags, the box, and tissue paper immediately put outside in the garbage by Mary, who knew the drill. All the fun of picking out anything new in a store was replaced with a sense of gloom as we pulled into the driveway. Even now, if anyone compliments what I'm wearing, my first instinct is to deny that it's new and my second one is to swear it was on sale.

How we all dreaded the department store bill's arrival. Mother would stand before Daddy as he sat in his red leather chair and would make her case for this outrageous show of extravagance as he would scream, "Whaddya think? Ya think Ah'm made a money?" I would huddle on the staircase, cringing on her behalf, as he tore her to pieces, attacking her intelligence, her background, accusing her of being spoiled and pampered. My sister did her homework through it all; I think she could deal with algebra as flames licked the legs of her chair. When I could endure the shouting no longer, I'd clump into the kitchen and bang pots around, making popcorn, giving Mother an excuse to "see what Cici's doing."

Though Daddy claimed he wasn't "made a money," he did have all his shirts made by hand in Hong Kong with tiny initials on the pocket. I remember sitting on the floor of his closet, staring in awe at his alligator shoes from Argentina. He always looked impeccable. Mother and I would stand smiling at command performances beside the elegant, popular, handsome eye surgeon, then all the way home in the Mercedes we would be belittled and berated for some imagined transgression. Long after he'd gone to bed, Mother sat at her desk working, sometimes past midnight. She balanced all the checkbooks, oversaw all the accounts for Daddy's medical practice, for the office buildings he owned, for his investments. I asked her why he didn't hire somebody else to do it, and she said, "Because your father doesn't want anyone to know how much money he has."

Secrets. I grew up behind enemy lines. Anything divulged to Daddy could be used against me. Melinda, my best friend in eighth grade, was bright and funny, and I adored spending the night with her. When Daddy learned her identity from me during one of those achingly uncomfortable drives to school, he shouted at Mother that I was not to see her again because her parents didn't belong to the country club. I did, of course, but Mother arranged it so that Daddy never knew.

Daddy demanded, threatened, taunted, and bullied as we survived quietly with backup plans and strategy behind a veil of secrets—like some female Resistance army.

THOSE WERE SUCH LONG years, but Mother always pretended everything was fine. Maybe it was pride, never admitting that she'd married the wrong person and moved across the country and had five children with him. Life in the Old Canton Road house went on. We endured. That's all we did.

Mother and Mary and I banded together for bouts of hilarity in the kitchen, taking turns mimicking Daddy, mocking him to make ourselves feel better. My sister never joined us. "But I don't understand why you're so upset, Stirling," I would say in Mother's calm voice, and then revert to Daddy's: "That's 'cause you're stupid! If you don't know why by now, you never will!" We did the chandelier skit, standing under it in the dining room, turning it off and on, pretending one bulb was dimmer than the others, howling with laughter. Sometimes Mary would laugh so hard, she'd have to wipe her tears on her apron.

I begged Mother to get a divorce, I begged to be sent away. No and no. I couldn't be sent away to prep school, but I could go away to college. She wanted him to pay for my college.

I thought of killing him, but I had no idea how, and then I worried I'd be caught and would end up wearing black-and-white stripes and ankle chains, cutting weeds by the road in the blazing sun, shackled to a dozen grown men dressed the same way, doing the same thing with big, heavy scythes. I probably couldn't even lift one. What would happen to a little girl who murdered Dr. McNair? Would they send me to Parchman? Would it be worth it for me? Then I would really be stuck in Mississippi for the rest of my life. Unless I got the electric chair. I wondered if they'd have to put a pillow on it for me to sit on, to make me high enough to strap in. My arms were so skinny, they'd have to put new holes in those leather straps.

I kept trying to think of how to kill him, and then I decided to let God do it. A few years before, I'd had a prayer answered: The Tiny Tears doll was under the Christmas tree just as I'd requested. Now I prayed that Daddy would be struck by lightning on the golf course. I told God there was Wednesday afternoon and all of Saturday and most of Sunday. Plenty of time. Lots of chances. Every night I wished on stars and prayed and I watched the pine tree grow taller outside my bedroom window.

BEING IN MISSISSIPPI, BEING with Mother, made it seem like yesterday. Now I was an adult with two brothers and a sister. Occasionally, that summer, I spoke to my Texas brother on the phone, and it was strained but pleasant. My sister didn't call Mother once so I didn't speak with her; however, I did see quite a lot of my Mississippi brother. I was genial but wary, rather the way I'd be in the presence of a large, unpredictable dog who had bitten me several times in the past.

The year before, Mother had mentioned on the phone that she'd see me in Florida soon. I was confused, then horrified. One of my brothers insisted she had Alzheimer's and said I was not to believe a word she said. I had not believed *him*, as I spoke to her nearly every day. Mother was specific, gave me the dates, said it was a family reunion in Destin for five days, that we would all be together in condos right on the beach. I hung up very worried. Later, I found out that my two brothers, my sister, their spouses, my nieces and nephews from Texas, Oklahoma, Mississippi, all over, and Mother had, in fact, gathered in Destin. They'd kept it a secret from me. I was shocked. *My God*, I thought. *It's like a one-liner from a stand-up comic: My family had a reunion and didn't invite me.*

The Season of Endless Talking

That summer, Mother and I had our rituals. At half past five we were often crossing the dam, with Mother exuberantly singing a St. Andrew's hymn, on our way back to Turtle Creek for the news. She and I quite liked having a glass of wine with Tom Brokaw.

Sometimes we'd go to a Japanese restaurant and order appetizers on little wooden sticks and drink Kirin beer. Once in a while, we'd pick up pizza on the way home from errands and have it out on the terrace in the dark. One night, I had on my harpsichord music loud enough to hear through the screen door. It began to rain, but we kept eating pizza under umbrellas, hearing Scarlatti's notes along with the *shhhhhhh* of the rain in the tall pine trees.

Mother and I were fine living together; she never seemed to need the car when I did, and we had no conflicts whatsoever after she stopped the "get in touch" with so-and-so campaign. I found it delightful—and astonishing—that she kept my secrets. No detail of a case or even Lyndon's name was ever uttered by Mother, which was amazing for a woman who had once regaled an entire table at the yacht club with the story of my failed marriage. Mother wanted everyone to understand that her daughter's bad choice of a husband wasn't her fault. This detective stuff was entirely different. Discretion was Mother's middle name.

She never said no to anything, loved to be driven, and wanted to ride shotgun with me no matter where I was going. It was the same enthusiasm she'd shown astride a camel at the Pyramids. Hattiesburg would be regarded with the same curiosity she'd exuded visiting me in Rome. Istanbul or Natchez, Mother was delighted. Sometimes Lyndon would give me an assignment and an address a hundred miles away, and Mother would say, "Let's take the Trace," and off we'd go. The lush green landscape met the clear blue sky ahead of us as we proceeded through the middle of the chewing-gum-gray road, like a bug crawling across a painting.

We might end up in a town with one traffic light and a statue of a Confederate general in the town square. Calling out the window, we'd get directed to the courthouse and I'd do the research, get the papers Lyndon needed. Afterward, Mother and I, hoping for a murder trial, would slip into the courtroom and listen to the testimony. We adored court-rooms. It was theater.

Mother was the consummate good sport, the happiest person in any café, the best companion for a tense ride to pick up documents at two minutes before five o'clock. We never stopped talking. It was a parlance peculiar to the two of us, with half sentences but whole thoughts, interrupted by traffic conditions, phone calls, waitresses or entire days then seamlessly resumed like recovering a dropped stitch in knitting. We talked over biscuits and fried chicken, over catfish and corn bread. We talked in diners, in country stores with one table in the back, on porches, in bars, on the yacht club deck, in ice-cream parlors, and in juke joints. That summer, Mother drank a lake of iced tea and I must have eaten an acre of brownies.

Wherever we were, we never stopped talking. We were constantly, relentlessly trying to make sense of the past.

*   *   *

I REALIZED THAT NOT only was I very much like my mother, but that she was like me. We were taking care of ourselves, without men, and we agreed on what should be in a refrigerator. The good manners, the "doing the right thing," the necessary grace of a thank-you note, had come to me from Mother, and I suddenly appreciated all of it more than ever. But Mother could be remarkably uninhibited. Years before, when we'd come back from a trip to Haiti and I was visiting her, she put her bag of groceries right on her head in the Jitney Jungle and walked, with her perfect posture and great dignity, out to her car. That visit she carried all sorts of things, including her pocketbook, on her shoulder, but she really liked using her head. Mortified, I ran alongside her, pleading in a wild whisper, "Mother! Mother! Mother, put it down! Please!"

The summer of 1994, I realized that nothing Mother did or said would ever embarrass me again. Maybe I had grown up.

I saw her independence as very brave after thirty-three years of marriage. At my age, she had five children and was running a large household. For a tyrant.

Mother found her fulfillment away from Daddy, out of the house. She played cello in the Jackson Symphony Orchestra, she was a force in state politics; the Sierra Club gave her an award. She taught art at the state mental hospital. For years, she wrote, in her handwriting, which was nearly calligraphy, all the birthday cards for St. Andrew's Cathedral and she never missed choir practice. The Jackson Yacht Club, the Caledonian Society—she was involved and people loved her. But once she arrived "home" she was badgered and belittled without mercy.

I never heard her ever say "what if" or "if only." It took

very little to make her happy. Mother was endowed with joy the way somebody else might have curly hair.

Maybe she was the source of pretty much anything that's good about me. Mother is a key reason I walk quickly, learned to sail, love to swim, can go around the world with a carry-on bag.

Mother believed in doing what was natural. Though Daddy was a doctor, it was honey and vinegar for a sore throat. Some of her convictions may have come from a European nanny. Water used to boil an egg is poison, and one should never drink it. I have always wanted to, but I haven't. Maybe I'm afraid I will slump to the floor in the ultimate "I told you so" moment.

"Hair dye" would go through your scalp right to your brain. If you never used a hair dryer, then your hair would never go gray. Mother herself was an example of never using a hair dryer, never having gray hair. That summer, when I was drying my hair, Mother would back out of the room the way they do in the dentist's office when giving you an X-ray.

"But, Mother," I insisted, "it's genetic. Big Tom didn't have gray hair, either."

"Of course he didn't," she said. "He never used a hair dryer." It was like reasoning with Gracie Allen.

"Don't eat the pyracantha berries, they're poison." Of course, I had the urge to gobble handfuls of them.

"Never sleep without opening a window."

"Don't talk on the phone in the bathtub."

I have my own primitive sense of order. I never walk near a bed in bare feet and actually give a little leap getting in at night. Can't sleep with a closet door open. Worry if I can't write in green ink. I don't discount the existence of werewolves and I believe in love at first sight and extraterrestrials. Plus, I seriously wonder if we are all dead *now*.

I admired my mother. A few months shy of her eighty-fourth birthday, she'd get into her beloved Cape Dory, wearing her blue sun hat on a hellishly hot day, and row out into the middle of the reservoir for a few hours. She thought of it as just getting some exercise, but I would have alerted the media if I'd been able to do it.

Sailing in my teens may have saved me. Mother and I would spend Saturday and Sunday afternoons at the first yacht club on muddy little Lake Hico before the reservoir existed. I loved being sopping wet, not caring what I looked like, in contrast to the fierce and unforgiving competition of clothes and hair at school. My friends were driving around in convertibles on Saturday afternoons, their hair in giant pink rollers, to announce to the world that they had a date that night, whereas I was in shorts, wearing sneakers, out on the water, possibly fighting with a spinnaker.

Mother taught sailing; I remember learning to race Blue Jays. Sailing with my brother Stirling. I remember turning the Biloxi Skate over again and again with Bette Phelps and her brother, Bud. All of us gasping with laughter in the coffee-colored lake, up to our hips in cool, slick mud, more worried about water moccasins than drowning.

If I'd had another kind of mother, none of that would have happened to me.

In between errands or after lunch at some little country place, if I wasn't tied up with a case, we'd go for a swim. Sometimes I wouldn't get home till midnight, and if she was still up, we'd pull on suits and get into the car and drive to the yacht club.

Years ago, when Mother first bought the little house, we used to walk down to the point every evening before the news and jump off the dock. But then a couple of dogs disappeared and some men went out in a boat with flashlights tied to their hats to find the alligator. He was moved to the Pearl

River, which is fine, but I've always worried that he might have left a friend behind.

Anyway, now we swam at the yacht club. At night, after it closed, it would be dark except for the underwater lights in the pool and the reflection of the stars and maybe the moon over the reservoir, which was a big, shining, silent vastness out there over the lip of the hill. The two of us would stumble down the path, talking in low voices, as if we weren't supposed to be there.

I wrote in my journal that there were three full moons that June and now I don't know how there could have been.

Working for Lyndon

Working for Lyndon wasn't like working for Vinny Parco. Nobody was going to ask a Mississippi detective to take care of a problem in the Bahamas; Lyndon wasn't getting any calls from Schlomo in Israel. There were assignments, lots of papers to get signed, lots of property searches and record searches at the courthouse.

A lawyer hired Lyndon to gather background on the plaintiff for a sexual harassment suit. I kept following her to the Jitney Jungle, where she worked, and lying down in the front seat when girls I went to school with would walk past pushing grocery carts and leading children—grandchildren. I'd think how different our lives were.

There was the case of the sweet man from Picayune who was about to lose everything because of a scam. We got all we could on the scammer, hoping to save our client's house and furniture business, and we did. At least, the last I heard, he had a court date and some ammo and a fighting chance.

Things could get slow, I was warned. Mother told me she'd heard that a neighbor was being questioned by a private investigator. The case concerned dirt that had been dumped on someone's property and the chase was on to find the source of this dirt. I rolled my eyes and sighed.

"But wasn't it really exciting to be a homicide detective?" I asked Lyndon one day. "I mean more exciting than now?"

"Nah." He shook his head. "Cuz once you get there, everybody's dead, nobody's doin' anything. Nothin's happ'nin'."

I asked Lyndon questions all the time, on stakeouts, in his office. He told me he wasn't going to have anything to do with "those Alabama detectives."

"All they think about is money money money. And they're stupid, too. Couldn't find their ass with both hands and a flashlight." He waved a manila file at me. "Cost me five hunnert dollars ta git 'em to find out if Vaughan Carter's married, and then"—his voice rose in outrage—"they decided he's real dangerous cuz he's got a black belt in karate so they gotta have two men surveil him!"

It was noon one day when Lyndon and I got in his car and drove to a salvage yard. The biggest in the state.

A man in a sweaty T-shirt waved us onto the property, which was mowed grass at least the size of a football field. Lyndon parked and we started walking up and down the rows of twisted metal until he found what was left of the car we were after. It was metallic blue and chrome, shining in the sun, but it looked like a foil candy wrapper that had been crushed in a giant fist.

"Lawyer's hired me to do an accident reconstruction. Lady killed on her way to the coast, and they might have a case against the truck driver who hit her. Head-on." He was getting a camera out of its case as he talked. "I gotta decide whut happened, be able to prove it, and testify in court."

Sweat was running down under my shirt, and I kept wiping my upper lip with one finger the way you get rid of a milk mustache. Lyndon had one single bead of perspiration at his temple. I peered in the bent frame of a window, saw bloodstains on the front seat, and felt a little woozy. I told myself I really should be wearing a hat out in this sun.

"I kin measure skid marks on pavement and tire tracks on the shoulders of a road and compute how fast the vehicle was traveling when it left the road. Kin tell at what speed the brakes were applied. I kin determine whether it stopped at the last stop sign and if it did, how fast it accelerated before it met with another solid object." He was looking at one of the tires. "I kin figure how fast the other vehicle was traveling when it hit." He walked around to the other side and started snapping photographs.

"But how can you do that?" I asked.

"The formula is so big, it would take up an entire windshield to write it all out." He sighed, looking at the shattered rearview mirror. "But it works."

The searing heat, the smell of the grass, the white hot sun blindingly reflecting on the acres of torn metal—it all felt surreal, macabre, like a bad dream. Lyndon worked in silence for half an hour and then suddenly pointed to a green van with a shattered windshield. "Ya know what you kin tell from that?" I shook my head. "This one was prob'ly hit by an eighteen-wheeler, but this other one was prob'ly hit by a train because the wheels are tore off. When a car's hit by a train, it gits dragged three or four hunnert yards."

Lyndon put away his camera. We waved at the man in the T-shirt sitting under a tree, got in Lyndon's car, and drove back to the office in silence. We had spent a long time in a field full of death.

Tailing the Blond Adulteress

Lyndon did a lot of workmen's comp and told me he wanted to expand that part of his business after he got rid of the domestics. I didn't say anything. He had a secretary named Arline, but I hadn't seen servants of any kind running around the office.

I learned quickly what and how awful domestics were. "This state idn't like New York or California. Ya don' have a judge dividing everything down the middle. And if a husband wants ta hire an investigator to prove that his wife is not a nice person, the judge might not award her as much as if she were a nice person." And it wasn't just money. It was custody.

Lyndon had been burned by Elizabeth, the blond adulteress, and so had his backup guy. The other two detectives the ex-husband had hired had also been spotted, so now it was my turn. I tailed her night after night, which took Amazonian stamina. She usually left work at six, then drove to her apartment to change clothes and see her little girl. That was easy and predictable. I'd do a stakeout until about eight, when her mother would arrive to babysit, which meant Elizabeth was free to leave and start prowling the pickup joints. She'd focus on somebody within an hour, hang around drinking beer with him until two or three, and then they'd go to his place.

Once she spent the night on a houseboat as I lay, hour after hour, on land in tall grass, worried about snakes.

I'd been on her tail five nights in a row, and Lyndon was delighted I still hadn't been burned. This particular evening, I was parked about sixty yards from her front door in her apartment complex and it was getting dark fast. I was staring in the rearview mirror, thinking she'd be out any second or in a half hour. No way to tell. I hardly dared to blink. I was totally focused on that door.

Suddenly someone called my name, and in the semidarkness I saw this large person with wild hair coming at me from the left. I didn't know how anyone would know my name. It was a woman. This had something to do with Elizabeth. She'd seen me, was furious, and had sent somebody. I saw the glint of metal in her right hand as she straightened out her arm toward me. I turned to water inside. This was it. Point-blank range. I'd hear the noise and it would be over.

"Hey," came the voice. "Lyndon tole me ta bring you this."

Her big silhouette was blocking out what little light there was as she handed me a walkie-talkie through the window. "I'm Sherrylynn."

I watched her walk around the hood and get into the front seat. There she was—this wide, friendly face, all smiles.

"Ya know how ta work this, don'cha? Sorry 'bout the teeth marks. It's the ferrets."

So this was Sherrylynn! I'd never met Lyndon's wife, but I already knew a lot about her. She was constantly on the walkie-talkie with Lyndon, reporting on her "chores," giving him her thoughts on the local newscast, or telling him she was going to the grocery store to buy cat food for the ferrets. I was on the radio, too, and could hear every word. A bottle blonde, she was big-boned, warmhearted, and crazy about animals—lost dogs, stray cats, injured birds, baby squirrels.

She had named the ferrets after the Menendez brothers: Lyle and Erik. Evidently, she'd memorized the courtroom testimony, all the while talking nonstop to her twin sister on the phone.

But these were "temporary ferrets" because they had "got on up under" the new sofa, gotten trapped in there, and then "et theirselves out" in a toothy escape. I wondered if all this had happened as she sat on it watching the trial.

"You know, I don' need this," said Sherrylynn, shaking her head. All that blond hair moved like a lion's mane. "A six-hunnert-dollar sofa. I don' need this."

This was a verbal woman. Lyndon said, "Sherrylynn and Jerrylynn will be on the phone for hours, and one of 'em'll say, 'Did you hear that click noise? Somebody's tapped the phone! Must be the FBI!' and they'll carry on ad infinitum about it."

My first Elizabeth stakeout was with Lyndon. Via radio, Sherrylynn was relating, in great detail, the progress of O. J. Simpson's low-speed chase. We sat in the front seat of the perfect surveillance vehicle, sweating in the dark, listening to Sherrylynn. "People are lining the highway and they're waving signs and cheering!"

She was on the radio for at least an hour, and when he didn't answer right away, she'd demand a response. I could see his silhouette in the glow of the dashboard lights, and he looked tired. I hoped he was happy with her because he was a good man. Furthermore, I was delighted he never seemed to notice if I was male, female, or anthropomorphic. I was very tan, but I was careful not to wear shorts above midthigh, and I knew I looked okay. He looked okay, too, and sometimes I thought it was wild for us to sit outside a building in the dark, waiting for someone to finish making love so we could follow them to their next stop. *It's the heat*, I told myself. *Stop it. Stop wondering if you will ever make love again.*

*   *   *

ONE NIGHT I FOLLOWED Elizabeth from work at six to
her apartment and then to a couple of honky-tonk water-
ing holes. At about midnight, still alone, she drove to The
Dock, which is really a big boat permanently moored to
shore. There's an inside room that's air-conditioned, a juke-
box, a dance floor, and a bandstand for live music on weekend nights. Outside, there's an open deck area and another
bar. If you wore anything but denim, you'd be madly over-
dressed. Elizabeth had on her signature bare midriff halter
and a denim miniskirt. I had a beer and watched her have
three, swigging right out of the bottle, throwing back her
long, fashionably frizzed blond hair, and laughing. I was
thoroughly sick of her.

By two o'clock she had made her choice: a tanned meaty
male in a sleeveless T-shirt, bathing trunks, and rubber
thongs who kept putting his hand on her breast. I fervently
hoped our client, her almost ex-husband, would get custody
of the little girl. He was a young real estate agent in town
who seemed quite decent. "She's trash, nothin' but trash,"
Lyndon had stated vehemently.

The bull paid as she went in and out of the ladies' room.
I followed her out to the parking lot, and with horror I real-
ized I'd lost the car. Mother and I did this just about every day.
We'd be talking and park, then come out of the store in a daze.
The station wagon might as well have been parked in Mon-
tana. *This cannot be happening!* I screamed silently. *Just when
I was going to be able to tail her to yet another man's bed.*

The bull got into a dusty red truck, and she leaned in his
window on tiptoe and gave him a big tonguey kiss. I prayed
she wouldn't get in beside him. Prayer answered. I followed
her to her car and then saw Mother's. The parade started.

I parked outside the trailer park and watched their silhouettes in the window until the light went out. I was almost blind from tiredness.

I fought off sleep mentally while every inch of my body begged to succumb. Cats' heads floated between me and the windshield. Then I'd see colored lights, blink them away, and the cats' heads would come back to taunt me. My body ached with fatigue, like getting the flu. "Sleep is not an option," I said aloud. I wanted to be able to tell Lyndon how many beers she drank and the brand. The toyboy's license plate, the address, the time they left The Dock, the time they went into his trailer. Now I was waiting for her to leave. "Ta finish her bidness," as Lyndon put it. I told myself the hard stuff was over. All I had to do was stay awake a few more hours and follow her home.

I broke a couple of graham crackers into portions and lined them up on the dashboard. I would let myself eat one piece every five minutes, and if I looked at my watch before five minutes were up, I had to start over. Radio on. One song. Radio off. I sang "Wake Up Little Susie" and then a medley of Everly Brothers hits. I moved on to Elvis. I pinched my thighs, realized I was making marks, decided singing was safer. Radio on, radio off.

I was still awake just before dawn when Elizabeth came out of the trailer. She pulled her stretch top into place, then bent down to fix a sandal strap. The air was fresh and cool; above the road hung gray clouds of mist that dissipated as her car crashed through their softness. I watched her make the turn into Pinewood, and then I went home and waited till six-fifteen to call Lyndon.

"Cripes, Lyndon! What does Elizabeth take in the way of vitamins? She's got a full eight hours of work ahead of her and tonight she's going to pull this all over again!"

"That's the last surveillance for a while," Lyndon said, laughing. "Talked ta the client last night and he thinks he's got what he needs. Now get some sleep. And thank you."

Lyndon's Operatives

Lyndon liked my work. He said it was difficult to get good operatives. "I don' want you to get totally pumped up, but you have complete integrity out on the street. And the aptitude, the right instincts..." I was *totally* pumped up.

Lyndon's last main man had gone off to investigate a workmen's comp at a chicken plant in Morton.

"He crawled on up under a chicken coop at four in the mornin' and jes' lay there all day in the heat and a dog bit him and now he won't come back ta work." Lyndon shook his head. "He's taken a few days off to do some thinking and his wife says he's real distressed."

That was weeks ago, and he was evidently still distressed. Lyndon said, "Ah'm not real sorry he's gone because he wuz paddin' his mileage and he wudn't too smart." I thought, *Why would you lie under a chicken coop all day and expect to be paid for it?*

We agreed there were some things I could not do. Lyndon had wanted to send me undercover to that same chicken plant in Morton as my first assignment. "But you wouldn't fit in." Since then, I had seen a couple of big old, beat-up Buicks at traffic lights overflowing with big, giggling black women wearing shower caps. Mother told me they probably worked at the plant. No. I wouldn't fit in. They had the radio on full blast and were squealing with laughter. Maybe it wasn't so bad to cut up chickens all day.

Lyndon had somebody named Josephine who sometimes worked for him. She was a hefty black woman who once paid him to tail her husband. Lyndon needed a black operative, maybe for a chicken caper, and when he stopped following her husband, he hired her.

Lyndon and I had both been through the transitions from hearing "nigger" to "niggrah" to "colored" to "Negro" to "black" to "African-American." Lyndon has always lived there, never been north. He told me he didn't want to get into any trouble so now he refers to blacks as Democrats. Josephine was a Democratic operative.

Josephine and her husband declared bankruptcy awhile back, but they seem to live pretty well. They have a huge van, a Cadillac, and some kind of little car with a sunroof. I pictured big Josephine squeezing out of the sunroof with binos glued to her face. Lyndon said, "You'd have a heart attack in the front seat with her on tails in that big black van." He sighed and rolled his eyes, then acted it out, playing both parts. "Josephine, they're three red lights ahead!"

"Don' mattuh. We ketch 'em on dat next cornuh. They be goin' jes' where they wents yestiddy."

Lyndon, with head in hands, would moan, "But what if they *don't* go where they went yesterday?"

"Don' mattuh. Then we gits 'em tomorruh." And so on.

Lyndon cracked me up with stories about the retired fireman who couldn't follow a woman two blocks to the Tote-Sum. "He'd git confused. It was jes' some kinda mental confusion."

My letters and postcards to friends were full of these anecdotes. I wrote that stakeouts were my entire social life, and I'd sign them Delta Dick or Swamp Sleuth.

Out in the Field

One day in the office Lyndon handed me a file to read, and I'd felt him staring at me and looked up. "Yore daddy the eye doctor?"

"Yep." I looked down and turned a page.

"Pretty famous round these parts."

I shrugged. Hadn't I endured this all my life here? Every single day? With every one of my teachers, the parents of my friends, kids I went to school with, even the clerk behind the counter when I charged notebooks and pencils at Brent's drugstore?

"Everybody knows his name." Lyndon was trying to get me to talk, and I wouldn't. "Hey, you gotta admit he was a helluva doctor. A great surgeon was what I always heard. He did a lot a good fer people in Jackson. Hell, people would come from all over." He paused. "No matter what, yore dad was a wonderful doctor."

I hadn't answered him. I remember hearing how Daddy had "saved the sight of Aunt Bessie in Clarksdale" and "My cousin was going blind until yore daddy operated on him." He was a god. Cynical little first grader that I was, I thought that anyone stupid enough to get a Cadillac in their eye deserved to think Daddy was a great man. And sometimes these idiots even had a second Cadillac that had to be operated on.

I hated the idea that Lyndon had bought into the myth along with all the other fools. Then I wondered what the "no matter what" meant. Did Lyndon know something about Daddy? Probably not. Daddy would walk into the house and become another person. The charmer at a wedding reception could scream for hours about a window he'd found open half an inch. "You think Ah'm made a money? You think I wanna pay money ta air-condition the whole goddamned state a Mississippi?"

I told myself to stop remembering Daddy and focused on the file again.

I WAS LEARNING ALL the time. Rural detectivery was a far cry from the world of Vinny Parco. "If you hide the car here and then creep through the woods, you can lie on your belly and watch the back door of that house," Lyndon explained one afternoon as he pointed out a good vantage point. Another domestic, of course. Lyndon would lie in the bushes all night, for Pete's sake. With mosquitoes devouring him. I could hardly imagine Vinny Parco in one of his two-thousand-dollar double-breasted suits sitting on a bench in Central Park. That would be the limit of rustic for him.

Vinny had sent me out in the field—my first stakeout was on Park Avenue—but now I was really out in the field. With both wild and domestic animals. It was 4:10, the sun wasn't up yet, and I was parked off a country road, staring at a darkened farmhouse on a hill one pasture away. There with the cattle, swigging Diet Coke and eating cold hush puppies wrapped in a paper towel. The air smelled of freshly cut hay, and a haze hung over the landscape.

At 6:31, a light went on in the far wing of the house. Then

another light went on behind a small window. The bathroom. At 6:50, I saw them wink out. A minute later, a man got into the blue pickup truck under the porte cochere and headed down the long, winding driveway on the opposite side of the hill. My heart skipped a beat, just as it had the day before when the truck went out of sight for three seconds. Then it reappeared heading toward me. I lay on the front seat as the truck ripped past, then roared the station wagon to life and tore out onto the road after him. It was a beautiful morning, and the trees lining the roads were the richest green, the woods beyond looked dark and deep. The blue truck went only a few miles and then turned into the Pelahatchie Trading Post. I drove past, did a U-turn when I was out of sight, and in less than two minutes I was back, pulling off the road and parking three trucks away from his. Just like yesterday.

The sheriff's white car pulled up on the other side of me, and this enormous character in khaki wearing a Stetson boomed, "And how are you this morning, young lady?" Just like yesterday.

"I'm fine." I smiled and thought of the expression "Butter wouldn't melt in my mouth."

I combed my hair with my fingers and tugged at my T-shirt. I had on lipstick. Putting on lipstick is about the maximum you can do on a stakeout. I lost Elizabeth once while dealing with mascara. She actually drove away as I blithely moved the little wand over my lower lashes.

The sheriff held the screen door open for me, giving me a very appreciative look.

I braced myself. Mother loved eating breakfast at odd places, and I knew this was one of her hangouts. She'd get picked up by a friend, and off they'd go for early morning *bouffes* of pastries and waffles. The settings varied from McDonald's to the Beagle Bagel to places like the Pelahatchie

Trading Post. I scanned the room. Subject was two tables off to the right, Mother nowhere to be seen. Safe. Mother would have been cool and ignored me; it would be her companion who'd get excited and call out to me.

I sat near the front window with a Diet Coke and Oreos, planning on the ladies' room once the subject's food arrived, hoping he wasn't thinking of driving to Florida right after leaving here. He ordered grits and other unspeakables. I loathe breakfast food. The stench of hot coffee stank up the room. I studied my surroundings and tried not to inhale too much. A certain provincial charm, I supposed. The kind of place where crayoned signs for "Live Bait" hung from the ceiling. A bucket of night crawlers sat ominously by the cash register right next to the free mints. Two dozen brands of chewing tobacco were displayed between the cigarettes and the cigars.

Lyndon had quit the chewing tobacco. I'd noticed he kept casually spitting into the wastebasket during that first meeting in his office. He'd open the car door and spit on the ground. I waited for him to tell me he had tuberculosis or some terrible condition and felt sorry for him. It wasn't till that stakeout at Red Lobster that I actually saw the round tin in his hand and realized what it was. That's what Mother had told me, but I thought it was just not possible. We were sweating like seriously fat people in a steam bath as he told me he was hooked, had been for years. He offered me a pinch and seemed to approve when I said no thanks. "You're right. Ugly stuff," he said as he slipped the tin into his jeans pocket. Then the funniest thing. He just gave it up.

I snapped back to the present. Suddenly the subject decided he wasn't going to finish the grits. He stood up and paid. I always paid right away so I'd be ready to move out. This time I noticed the sheriff watching me, so I hung around the cash register and pretended to consider buying some gum. The subject left, the screen door went *ka-wak*, and I even heard his truck start up before I headed to the door. He turned right onto the road in a cloud of yellow dust, and in minutes I was after him. This was not the way back to his farm. He got onto the highway as I counted to ten, holding back, then made the turn after him. Traffic joined us as we picked up speed, passing signs and exits.

Not too long later I was in Vicksburg, parked in a casino parking lot using a pay phone. Lyndon usually said stick to him, ride it out, "keep on it." But this time he said, "Yeah, he's got a job there sometimes. We know about it. Go on back home now. You did good." He thanked me—he always thanked me.

In minutes I was on the highway again, the radio playing really loud, all the windows open, tearing past all these people on their way to work. I was happy.

"I did good," I repeated. I looked at my watch. I'd been in that field since four a.m. and that was four and a half hours ago times six plus all that mileage money, so I'd already earned twenty-seven dollars and the day had just begun. But best of all, I chortled to myself, Lyndon said *I did good*.

Leaving It All

The months went by, and it was almost August. I knew I could go back to New York and stay in Greenwich Village with the Orange Boys while a friend and her husband took their August trip abroad. I talked to Lyndon about it, and he started calling those cats the Marmalade Twins, which I suspected they would like to be called.

I lay awake one night trying to imagine myself with an apartment in town, driving the car that Lyndon said he'd get for me. Was I really thinking of staying? When my entire childhood had centered on escape from this place? I remembered asking to be excused before dessert so that I could go upstairs and conduct my secret ceremony, which focused on not being where I was.

The escape. The longer you have to wait, the more elaborate the plans become. I waited year after year, getting taller and more resolute. Counting the years as the pine tree grew outside my second-story window. I read *Kon-Tiki* by Thor Heyerdahl eleven times and between its pages would tuck an envelope with initials I printed in green ink. There was money inside, a rather pathetic number of one-dollar bills. Every once in a while, I would convert my dimes and quarters, which meant it was time to tear open the old envelope, initial a new one, add the new bill, then seal it with sealing wax. Lighting the match, admiring the flame and the paraffin stamp, were part of the ritual. Then I'd hide the book at least one layer of paperbacks from sight.

The money was for New Orleans. For a ticket on the train called the *Panama Limited* I would hear in the middle of the night. It was not just money to run away, because that wasn't enough. I did not think Daddy would hire someone to come after me, but I couldn't take the chance, so the envelope was labeled, in code, "Money to Disappear."

I had heard that whores made their living kissing men, and I thought I could stand it. One kiss on the cheek and the man would give you—one dollar? five dollars? more for on the mouth? I didn't know. But whores lived on their own. If they could do it, then so could I. Somebody had called it the oldest profession so it had been a success for a long time.

I never ran away to New Orleans, I never kissed men for money. But I did escape. My first escape was when I was fifteen and decided never to speak to my father again. There were rules. I would respond to "Good morning" or "Good night" and answer questions with only "Yes" or "No." I stopped crying at the dining room table. I had set the rules and I had power, albeit known only to me, for the first time. Now I look back and think the irony is that no one ever noticed that I stopped speaking. The household was in chaos. Mother was barely holding it together with her delusional optimism.

My second escape was when I finally left that house and Mississippi and the South for a college I picked out of a catalog. Because of Mother's parents, there had been some summers in Watch Hill, Rhode Island, and my sister and I had had an August or two at Camp Wynakee in Vermont. I inhaled those times, which seemed to last a few days, and saw college as my chance to go away for good. My father screamed in a red-faced fury that I was to go to Ole Miss or Sophie Newcomb or Vanderbilt, but I never even applied. Finally he wrote the tuition check to the one far away. That was when my life began. When I began to be myself. All this raced through my mind in the dark before sleep overcame me. I decided to go back to New York.

LYNDON WAS SORRY I was leaving. He said, "When you decide you've had enough of the big city, come on back and there'll be a place for you here with me." I thought of Samuel Johnson: "When you're tired of London, you're tired of life." Lyndon made me an offer to be his partner. Unimaginably complimentary.

I said, "But you can't. You've been doing this for twenty years. You've been a homicide detective while I've been doing other things. I've just started to learn everything you've known forever."

Lyndon shook his head. Arline had gone on an errand and we were alone, sitting in his office with the maps of counties all over the walls. The air-conditioning was on full blast; the temperature outside, according to Magnolia State Savings and Loan, was 102 in the shade. Pearl Street actually shimmered with the heat. "You've taught me a few things. You kept me from driving a hunnert miles a couple a times. All you did was pick up the phone and get the job done."

"Well, I can't ever tell you how much I've learned from you." I felt sad to be leaving him and this job. There had been times he hadn't called for a day or two and I'd silently gone crazy, checking Mother's phone for a dial tone, rushing to the answering machine every time we returned from twenty minutes out of the house. This was the summer I came to know every working pay phone within a thirty-mile radius. I was like some crazed lover waiting for Lyndon to call and give me a case. When I heard his voice, I'd nearly dance with joy. I'd hang up and tell Mother I was off and didn't know when I'd be back. Who knew? I might have to follow somebody to Memphis, then stick with them for five days. Or to Biloxi and stick with them for ten days. Often she'd come, too. We'd both be entirely wired. I'd stuff a bag with graham crackers and Diet Cokes, then grab a flashlight, the walkie-talkie, a notebook, pens, binoculars, the camera, my bikini, a fistful of toilet paper. Mother would call, "Do you have the car keys or do I?" and we'd be out the door.

Lyndon and I talked for a while, and then his phone started to ring. He let the machine pick up a few times, but I knew I had to let him get on with business. Arline wasn't back yet. We laughed about her not liking me in the beginning. "Oh, I know," said Lyndon. "She jes' looked you up and down like an old snake coiled up in a corner."

"And every single time I opened my mouth, she'd comment on my Yankee accent!"

We were sitting exactly where we'd sat for that interview in June. He looked immaculate—as usual—in a blue polo shirt and pressed khakis. Suddenly I said, "Hey, Lyndon, that bullet hole's still there."

He didn't bother to glance around. "Yeah, I know. I keep fixin' ta get it fixed."

"You never told me what happened."

"Somebody took a shot at me."

"Come on! I know that! But it's in the perfect place to blow your head off..."

Lyndon leaned back in his chair, hands clasped behind his neck, and grinned. "Ever drop your pen and jes' reach down..."

We burst out laughing.

"But who? Who did it?" I insisted.

"Ya know ya git enemies in this bidness," he said in his most mellow tone.

We were laughing when the door opened to the outer office and Arline called, "What are y'all up to? No good, I 'spect." We all talked in the hallway for a few minutes, and then she threw her arms around me to say good-bye. She called me a "special lady." I hugged Lyndon and got out of there fast. It was the end of something.

I remember my last night. I pulled into the driveway at about half past eleven after my last stakeout and Mother was still up, doing the St. Andrew's birthday cards at her desk. The television was off, and beyond the screen door the night insects were singing in the pine trees.

"I'm back," I called. "I'm too wound up to sleep. I think I'll drive over to the yacht club and get in the pool." I went outside and got my suit off the line. We'd been swimming that afternoon, which was why it was on the line and not in the car.

"I'll go over with you," said Mother, turning off her desk lamp and putting her ice-cream dish in the kitchen sink.

It was about midnight when we parked and walked the steep path to the pool. The reservoir was black out there. The only thing you could see was the dark gleam of it, like a pan of fudge, and a few lights on land all the way across to the next county. I slipped into the water and watched the light play on my legs, saw that the bubbles were silver. I was floating on my back in this pastel inland sea; the rest of the world was black except for stars so bright and so close I thought they might be breathing.

Suddenly I heard a splash and a shriek of laughter. "Couldn't help it! I had to come in!" Mother hadn't even taken off her shoes. Her clothes billowed around her as we swam and laughed like giddy ballet dancers in a turquoise paperweight under a star-spattered sky.

*   *   *

THE NEXT MORNING, I was hugging Mother good-bye beside the *Panama Limited*. I got on, settled myself, then waved as the train started to move. It always scares me to see a person I love getting smaller and smaller. Sometimes I look down and stretch my legs and check my size. Wherever I am or wherever I'm going, I'm here and I won't ever be the one to get smaller.

I stared out the window. A few nights before, Mother and I had delved through big drawers of photographs. One was of the mimosa tree that I thought was magic, my favorite tree to climb. Even in black and white on shiny paper it looked delicate, Oriental, mystical. I remembered the pink powder puff blossoms. Daddy had ordered Mother to have the yardman cut it down. And she had. No explanation except, "Your father wants it cut down." I'd cried as I watched Willie with the ax, and the maid had taken me to the kitchen and let me have the chocolate icing bowl to distract me.

There were pictures of Mother's father's and grandfather's houses on the hills outside Philadelphia. Pictures of me, of us, of Daddy straight and tall in his Navy whites during World War II before I was born.

Mother suddenly said, "I remember waking up in the middle of the night and there was your father standing over me holding a pillow with both hands. About to smother me." This vignette was delivered in the same tone one would say, "We decided to have tuna-fish sandwiches." I said nothing because I wanted to start screaming. It wouldn't do any good. It would only hurt her. But the words were loud in my head: *You stayed you stayed you stayed! Good for you! Be proud of all the years you threw away! Congratulations!* But I swallowed the words in my throat and suddenly I didn't blame her anymore. It was like reaching for my wet bathing suit on the line and realizing it was dry.

It was he who finally left. The holiday with Mother after the divorce sprang into my mind. I was home from college and Mother relayed the message: Daddy said he would give any child who came to wish him "Merry Christmas" fifty dollars. I laughed. He was serious. How pathetic. My sister went.

Daddy never knew me. I was closed and silent in his presence after fifteen years of weeping at the dining room table. I was a great disappointment, of course. He had made that clear every day of my life. It was a perfect record: not one compliment, not one word of praise. I didn't even consider going so I didn't see him in his new house with his new wife and I didn't claim my fifty dollars.

A week later, he was dead.

Daddy always thought the one with the most money won the game. His game. He never caught on that I didn't want to play.

THE TRAIN MOVED SLOWLY through a curtain of green. Branches actually brushed the roof and the windows.

I thought of that first day in Lyndon's office. When I had charged into Father Borgomeo's office at Vatican Radio, insisting he hire me, confessing I wasn't a Catholic, his desk had been in front of a big window, too. Behind him, across the Tiber, looming in dark stone, was Castel Sant'Angelo. On the wall to the right was a bigger-than-life-size portrait of the Pope, to the left a map of the world. I thought again of facing Lyndon with all the county maps and the bullet hole. I thought of how he'd said, "I admire persistence. Come on in."

We were moving slowly through the southern landscape. I missed having Mother beside me, seeing this. The summer had made me realize that Mississippi was Mother's adventure. A lot of what I hated about it, she thought was original. The kudzu was outside the train strangling the trees; I imagined alligators lolling in the bayous. A turtle as big as a dinner plate slipped off a rock into olive green water just past Crystal Springs.

The train began to go faster. I opened the napkin in my bag and ate one of the Jitney Jungle brownies, staring out the window, thinking. I was speeding toward the Big Easy, having left the Little Difficult, wondering what would happen next.

PART III
A Warehouse in Hell's Kitchen

Late August in New York. There was a curious emptiness to the city, which baked in a traffic-dirty heat like Athens or Cairo. I was cat sitting for the Orange Boys down in Greenwich Village in C. S. Lewis's old writing studio, with the ceiling fan twirling day and night. The giant Marmalade Twins were quiet; the three of us watched the evening news together, but the rest of the time we kept to ourselves with great respect for personal privacy.

Vinny Parco had hired me for a few small cases, but things were slow. He asked me for dinner, then apologized for being late because he'd decided to shave his head. I knew that shaving his head twice in one day signaled romance, and sure enough, he made a tentative play for me. Right across the *spaghetti alle vongole* at Tre Pommodori on 34th Street. I don't think his heart was in it, he had never been attracted to me, had even told me so. I gave him an ego-saving monologue, and he hired me for a little stakeout the next day. Nobody's feelings were hurt.

Within days, I'd called Caro and regaled her with my tales of rural detectivery. We talked at length about the futility of job hunting in late summer, and then she suggested I call

Parker Investigations. She'd found that missing person for
them all those years ago.

That same afternoon, when Elbert Thatch said he'd like
to meet with me sometime, I said I could be there in half an
hour. He had stammered in surprise but said all right.

This was my first walk down 29th Street going toward the
Hudson River. I slowed down approaching the 500 block,
thinking this was a world away from any reasonable West
Side landmark like Central Park or Lincoln Center. In the
summer heat, the garbage gave off the sharp rotting smell
I remembered from Moroccan markets. I stepped over discarded cabbages, squash, heads of lettuce. The twenty-four-
hour garages were crowded with ailing taxis, and the street
was clogged with twenty-four-wheelers loaded with wholesale vegetables. The only parked cars had their doors open
and radios blaring Spanish music. The men were grease
smeared and overalled or wearing T-shirts and jeans and
those wide weightlifter belts. They were all nationalities.

The neighborhood was entirely new to me. On the way
to the interview, I hoped that the most dangerous part of the
job would be getting to the office.

I crossed Tenth Avenue and started looking for the number. A sign said, "These premises protected by Holmes," and
I thought, *Great. But who's protecting* me?

Number 538. I rang the bell on the downstairs warehouse
door, was attacked by a boxer dog, rescued by a small Asian
in a loud Hawaiian shirt, and directed to go outside again
and to ring the next doorbell. I was then buzzed in and
climbed a flight of wooden stairs to the second floor, which I
would later call the Executive Suite.

The windows of the huge open space let in the noise of
29th Street, and I could hear honking horns, the scream of
sirens, and the general traffic noise that sounded like the
ocean when the light on Tenth Avenue changed to green.

Parker's was a ship upon this ocean. Inside the room were the ringing phones, the intercom from downstairs, and the crackle of the two-way radios from Chinatown and New Jersey.

Elbert Thatch's office was a plywood-partitioned, windowless cube in one corner; Elbert was a rumpled man in his early fifties who looked as if he'd been wakened from a sound sleep. He sat at his desk and motioned me to sit in the only other chair in the eight-by-eight-foot cubicle. I scanned the titles of the books behind him—the *Oxford English Dictionary*, a thesaurus, several atlases, psychology texts, books on the CIA, a biography of Jack the Ripper, the complete Sherlock Holmes, books on woodworking. The desk, the shelves—it all looked homemade. On the top shelf were hats for all situations: baseball, beret, fedora, cowboy, pith helmet, and hard hat.

The interview went well. Elbert explained that the firm specialized in intellectual property, which meant Parker's went after the counterfeiters of designer goods. If you looked through a yuppie's closet and read the labels, it would be the client list. Handbags, watches, jeans, running shoes, T-shirts, sweatshirts. I kicked my fake Fendi bag from Rome under the desk as Elbert was saying that the money spent on such things funded terrorism. Later I would be told that two days after the 1993 World Trade Center bombing, the Feebs (FBI) had knocked on the door to ask if anybody knew certain players, and Parker's had files on every one.

Many Parker investigations took place on Canal Street, the largest commercial thoroughfare in New York City's Chinatown which is the largest Chinatown in the Western Hemisphere. Hundreds of stores, some really only stalls a few feet wide, are jammed side by side selling watches, sunglasses, pocketbooks, T-shirts, perfumes, and scarves. The ones decorated with counterfeit designer logos are sold for a fraction of the designer price. The Vietnamese gang called Born to Kill runs Chinatown, deriving most of its income from the illegal knockoffs and controlling its turf with the constant threat of violence—extortion, kidnapping, arson, and murder. The name Born to Kill was taken directly from what was written on U.S. helicopters in Vietnam.

"These investigations are totally satisfying," Elbert told me, "because we go after the bad guys. It's black and white. No second-guessing. They're breaking the law and we go after them." He spoke well, was educated.

His hand kept moving toward and then retreating from a pack of tiny cigars, so I said, "Go ahead and smoke. I don't care."

He stood up, grabbed the pack like a lifesaving drug, and said, "Can't do it here because the secretaries don't like it. Let's go outside." Outside was through a swinging door to a landing lit by a bare light bulb; we sat like kids on the bloodred-painted wooden steps as he sucked greedily on a skinny black cigar. "There's a seizure tomorrow. When we find at least a hundred thousand dollars' worth of counterfeit goods, we get law enforcement involved and go in. You should come, see what it's like. Stay in the background, just observe." Elbert, bearded, wreathed in smoke, had the look of a tired professor. "And wear jeans."

I nodded, wondering exactly what happened during a seizure. Jeans? I didn't own a pair. I wouldn't have dreamed of wearing them in Rome; never would I have walked through the lobby of the Beau Rivage in Geneva in them. Wool, gabardine, linen trousers, yes. Corduroys to do errands outside town, for the grocery shopping in France, or for hanging around a chalet fireplace after skiing. In Beverly Hills, I'd been astonished that women showed up for dinner parties in jeans and white T-shirts until someone told me it was to showcase their newly purchased breasts.

"Okay," I said to Elbert. "Anything else?"

"Running shoes," he said, looking at my little ballet slippers.

So I went to the Gap and tried on about eighteen styles of jeans, whirling around in front of the three-way mirrors and surveying myself with no mercy. Finally I picked a pair labeled "classic" in size eight that looked okay. Seizure wear.

The next morning, I pulled on the jeans and stared at my bare feet. There was no way I would ever wear running shoes unless I were actually running. I winced at the creatures who stalked to work in them wearing stockings, carrying their pumps in little bags. A European would keel over dead at that Manhattan career woman ritual. I pulled on sneakers, then worried about earrings. "Hoops?" I said aloud, and picked small gold ones. Nothing big enough to get caught on anything—like a trigger. Perfume? I thought of dressing down for Bo Dietl and spritzed it on defiantly.

Later that morning, on 29th Street, outside the warehouse, I faced big men with guns, all introduced to me with nods. "C.C.?" they asked. I spelled my nickname, but it never took, and forever after I was called Double C, C for Charlie, Charlie Charlie, just Charlie, or just C. We drove to a storage facility in New Jersey where we stood in a parking lot shaking hands with the sheriff and local law enforcement. When the door to the garage-size unit was unlocked and pushed open, I gasped. There were hundreds and hundreds of boxes, each packed with hundreds of handbags from Korea. All with the logo of a famous designer. We set to work cutting open cartons, counting bags. Later, I told somebody it was odd that some purses were unzipped and had razor slashes in the lining. A drug dog was summoned via radio. We stood around talking, waiting in the August heat. The men smoked, we all sweated. Radios squawked, cell phones rang. The dog was coming from Passaic. No, the dog was coming from Jersey City. Another call. The dog was half an hour away. A radio crackled. The dog had taken the wrong exit. At last a speeding squad car dramatically circled the empty parking lot then screeched to a halt before us. A giant German shepherd sat alone in the backseat like a king. The car door was opened and his handler was dragged behind him, like a man on water skis, in a frantic dash to sniff the storage room.

It was a terrific day for me. I'd worked as hard as anybody and it had been noticed. That evening on the way back to the warehouse, which they also called the barn, the men began with the questions. Did I have some kind of an accent? Where was I from? How long in New York?

Unspoken approval meant Elbert would tell me to come in the next day. He never said I was hired, but I was to join the men downstairs. Undercover, they all said. I nodded. "Sure," I said nonchalantly. "I can do undercover." I was totally thrilled and utterly clueless.

Playing Games with Men

The cases at Parker's were unlike the cases for Lyndon or those I did for Vinny Parco. One would think that a counterfeit case, tracking down the perps, ended with a seizure, but it didn't because we had to back out all the information we recovered during the raid. So the cases seemed never-ending. The "aha!" was short-lived because you were handed another tangle of leads to sort and follow.

The men came bounding in and out of the warehouse with new plates to back out, with new locations to stake out, with new characters to surveil. Additions to the files, info to feed the computer—the paper chases, the research, and the car chases went on and on.

The office atmosphere was easygoing for me. The men were much more civilized than Errol and Rodriguez and Nick in Vinny Parco's office. Someone was reading John Grisham, someone else had actually traveled out of the United States to the Caribbean, there was talk of the new Tarantino movie and constant discussions of city politics. No one ever mentioned sports. Football, baseball, hockey, golf, tennis—none of it held any interest for them.

All the investigators were retired cops except for a former UN chauffeur, a former television cameraman, and me.

Elbert Thatch had a master's in psychology and had once directed a touring theater group. Appropriate. This man lived for drama, and every move he made was theatrical. He kept a dagger with a twelve-inch blade in his boot and was always forgetting about it, creating havoc with metal detectors at courthouses and airports. There were two secretaries—one Indonesian and one Puerto Rican—and countless men on call for seizures, which often meant loading and unloading trucks after the initial storming of the location. Stripping a factory of industrial-size sewing machines bolted into the floor could go on all night. If we couldn't do it and had to hire men who knew how, then we'd have to guard the place until morning against the perps' getting out on bail and returning to remove evidence.

Mickey was Chief of Field Operations and masterminded just about anything, both day to day and seizure, and no one was more fair-minded about assignments. He and Elbert chaired meetings in the back of the warehouse, which stank a lot because of Warner, our boxer mascot. We agents all sat at a long trestle table, usually recently cleared of counterfeit goods for the occasion, facing each other on two long benches. Warner sat between two of us, as was only fitting for Agent 0.5. She was more attentive than anyone, with eyes shining, ears up, and forehead wrinkled in concentration as Elbert decided who was on what team and what vehicles we would take. The actor in Elbert was obvious; he gloried in his voice filling the warehouse and used words like *ergo* often.

I liked Elbert even though he wasn't always fair to me. He could be condescending, snide, sarcastic. Sometimes I slammed the downstairs warehouse door with extra body language after returning from little talks with him upstairs. Sometimes we downstairs felt his psych degree held him back in the common sense department, but he wrote well, he was educated, and he was our fearless leader.

When I'd been at Parker's about two weeks, a woman investigator called me at home and told me how the men there had treated her terribly for the short time she endured it. "They have no respect for women and they'll never let you in their boys' club." She'd given me phone numbers to call, saying that this man and that man were looking for an investigator and why didn't I call and arrange an interview? I thanked her and hung up. The next day, I went into the office and thought, *Nobody is being mean to me here. I like these men.* So I told them how odd it all was. They said that she was setting me up—"She's trying to trick-bag you"—so that she could accuse me of taking Parker secrets somewhere else. That was the line of thinking. I thought they might be overreacting, but the men were truly outraged. I came back from Chinatown later in the day, and a big sign was there on the wall: "C—Welcome to the Boys Club." That sign was still up the day I left.

Working at Parker's was the beginning of a new way to look at myself. I reveled in the jeans or khakis, wore socks with loafers, then lace-up boots; I wore leather belts from Rome that I'd coiled like snakes in a hatbox. There were sweatshirts and windbreakers, and one of the men gave me an oversize blue jeans jacket found in the back of the warehouse. I practically boiled it, then wore it with the cuffs rolled back.

I liked putting my feet on the desk and leaning back in my chair with castors—just like the men—and not worrying about getting dirty in the warehouse or in the van. I might be asked to go down to the cellar and count T-shirts, or to sort garbage bags full of watches, or to find a certain box of handbags that was to be presented in court. It was often

grubby, mind-numbing work but I survived the Indian summer, the autumn, being the new one, being the only woman.
Winter arrived. I realized I couldn't very well wear a long
camel coat and attacked Bloomingdale's in search of a parka.
It had to be invisible for Chinatown surveillances. I picked
the warmest one, tried on both colors in my size, then carried them both to the cash register. At the last minute I chose
the black, a practical and necessary decision. I took one last
wistful look at the cardinal red and told myself to get tough
as I handed the clerk my credit card. My clothes were to put
on and forget about, and I had to count on nobody remembering them or me, either. It was a new way to feel about
myself.

ANY NEW MALE INVARIABLY tested me. Someone new
brought in on a seizure would use bad language and look
right at me. I wouldn't say a word, wouldn't blink. Sometimes there would be a mildly flirtatious remark, sometimes
overtly crude. I was oblivious, but "my" men would be watching and might say something to the effect of "Hey, watch it."
Then the new one would back off. It was boundary hunting.
Feeling for the line. A quiet assessment of who I was, how
much I could or would take, how much I mattered.

Mickey, as Chief of Field Operations at Parker's, would
sometimes say, "You're not going back there. It's too dangerous." When Mickey said it was too dangerous for me, I
think he meant it was too dangerous for anyone. Once, as I
came out of a Broadway location, he fell into step behind me
because I was being followed. I was glad he had a gun and
was right there for me.

Mickey reminded me of James Dean if James Dean had
been pissed off instead of hurt looking. He looked older
when he'd been up all night. He was born in Greenwich Vil-

lage, though he would snort and call it the Lower East Side if
he ever heard me say that. He still lived there. When he was
about eleven, he parked cars for Vinnie the Chin Gigante,
who later roamed the streets in a bathrobe feigning insan-
ity and fending off indictments for just about everything.
Mickey had run errands for him and the wiseguys as a kid.
Vinnie the Chin would send him to buy Light n' Lively and
then slip him a fifty-dollar bill. Mickey would probably be
totally mobbed up by now, a made man, if he'd been Italian
instead of Irish. When he was fifteen, he realized he had the
wrong kind of last name. He'd been a cameraman for television news for a few years, and when they'd gone on strike
he had become an investigator while waiting it out and then
never gone back. Mickey was the youngest at Parker's but he
basically ran the show. One afternoon when we were alone, I
told him he was the alpha male.

SOME OF THE LOCATIONS on Broadway were tough,
some of them were off-limits to me, to anybody these days. I
might go up to the third floor, get off the elevator, and be the
only woman and the only white person in a crowd around
a doorway. Typical. These basketball player–tall Africans
would be laden with their counterfeit jeans and T-shirts in
black garbage bags. They might be wearing djellabas, they
might have tribal scars on their faces. It was like a bazaar
in North Africa, and I was assaulted by the colors, by their
voices, by their sheer size. They looked at me, and we all
knew I didn't belong there.

I'd take a deep breath and barge right into the crowd, saying, "Excuse me," in French, and get past them and into the
room where the selling was going on. Inside the open door
was usually a man, often in a djellaba, sitting in a folding
chair. He'd be clutching a stack of bills four inches thick;

there might be a cigar box with more money in it and a cell phone on the little table in front of him. The second he looked at me, I had to decide how to play it. First, I was a woman and he was a male from an entirely different society. Sometimes I could pick out where he was from by facial features or an accent and could talk to him, but I was so screamingly out of place, it was better to look and leave. I would literally turn in a quick circle, counting shelves, noting brand names, quantity, faces, nationalities, and square footage. Wearing a videocamera was the only thing that slowed me up. This man wouldn't have a business card and if I gave him one of mine, he'd be alarmed. These were the down-and-dirty rooms. Usually my reaction was: *Take one look and get out of here. Now.*

And I did. I'd go out in the hall and wonder if I should wait for the elevator as all the Africans stared at me, speaking Arabic, or if I should take the stairs. I'd wonder if the next white face up there would be a cop with many other backup cops next week or next month. I bet they wondered the same thing. What counted was that I got a look and confirmed that the counterfeits were there. I'd hear a radio with rap music echoing up the staircase but no footsteps, so down I'd go, telling myself it might be foul but not that dark and only five flights. If I had to pass anyone, they would stare with great curiosity, and I'd tell myself to not show any emotion at all. Often I had to flatten myself against the filthy wall to let five or six herculean Africans in robes and embroidered pillbox hats pass me. I was very aware of being female and wearing a hidden camera. Passing one man on a narrow, dimly lit back stairway was worse. Mickey would tell me at least once every month, "Don't use the stairs!"

But I thought the stairs were better than being crammed into a slow-moving, evil-smelling elevator. And I always had to wait for the elevator, in the hallway, with everyone looking at me, whereas I could scamper down the stairs and be gone. With the stairs, I also had a chance to push open the doors to the other floors and wander around a bit, so there was the possibility of seeing something else that would interest us. So I risked the stairs. But I could not stop thinking what I used to hear in my head when I traveled in the Arab countries and in West and North Africa: *You're not supposed to be here so whatever happens to you is your own fault. People will say you deserved it.* I hated to think that—it was like touching a canker sore with my tongue.

Sometimes Mickey would say, "Don't go in the building if you feel funny about it. Forget it. It's not worth it." Sometimes I'd go into a small, darkish lobby and up in a crummy elevator, and it would open onto a dirty linoleum hallway. I'd listen at closed doors for the noise of machinery or voices. Sometimes I had the room number, but sometimes I was just given the floor. I only knocked if a door was locked; otherwise I'd push doors open and go right in and walk around, among the machines, as if I might be looking for someone or were in a daze. I walked fast, to get as far into the place as I possibly could, but not so fast that the video wouldn't be clear. When I was approached, whether the man was Asian or Arab, I was all smiles.

These people won't ever say, "Oh, hello, do come in." They say, "What are you doing here? How did you find me?" in this nearly condemned building on this desolate side street in this dangerous neighborhood. "Who sent you? Who *are* you?" I was immediately put on the defensive. It might not be counterfeits they were most uptight about—it could be illegal immigrants treated as virtual slaves, it could be drugs, or something I hadn't encountered yet. It was a given that they didn't want me, or anyone, walking into their factory.

I can't tell all my secrets but I often use confusion to my advantage. A southern accent often soothes an American counterfeiter because many New Yorkers hear it and assume your IQ is sixty-seven points lower than it is. Usually I can get the perp to relax, to show me what he has, to do business with me. Sometimes doors are being closed behind me. Often I notice two-way mirrors and wonder who is watching me from behind them. Sometimes boxes are hurriedly covered with dropcloths and workers leave the room. I try not to look up for security cameras.

Since my own camera might jam or my winter scarf might fall in front of the lens, it was really up to me to notice absolutely everything. It was good to force myself—the daydreamer—to be alert on the different levels.

I use broad brushstrokes, with great good humor. I fly above suspicion; I refuse to acknowledge it. It's all I know how to do. Mickey told me once that it worked for me because deep down I felt I had every right to be there. And yes, I do think that. Sometimes I've actually gotten so drawn into my own story, I've wondered about calling Delta to confirm that Thursday flight I've mentioned. I talk a blue streak. I chat like there's no tomorrow, admire what they're making, tell them all about myself, whoever I am that day. Though I never got over my stage fright at Vatican Radio, I hear my voice now and can hardly believe it's my own. I am completely calm and entirely alive. I am on their territory and vividly "high" on my awareness of that reality.

I note the height when they stand next to me, guess the weight, notice eye color, try for the age. Any scars, birthmarks, moles, odd teeth, unusual ears, hairlines, mustaches, balding patterns. I count the workstations, the machines, and decide what they are—clicker dye, heat transfer, embroidery, whatever. I count the shelves, the boxes, the product. I count off the walls ten feet at a time and multiply length by width to get square footage. I count the people and try to hear what language they're speaking above the roar of the machinery. I may have only four seconds or maybe I'll be lucky and talk to someone for half an hour. I drink it in. A crucifix above the desk of the Lebanese. A calendar with a photograph of Lake Geneva above the desk of the Korean. Whatever is on the desk I try to read upside down and memorize. Back at the office, I'd draw a map showing any windows, stairways, and elevators, and it would be faxed to law enforcement. Sometimes it's to the FBI, sometimes to NYPD's OCID (Organized Crime Investigations Division).

I owe whatever visual memory I have to Herbert Irvine, the most famous decorator in Canada, who flew all over the world in the 1930s redoing the Canadian embassies of each capital. When I met him in Toronto and he hired me as an assistant, he was about eighty. Herbert was tall and handsome with white hair, rosy cheeks, and blue eyes. Born in Ontario but very English in his manner, he was a man of endless energy and thousands of stories.

The first morning I sat at his feet in the little Yorkville office as it snowed outside—fat theatrical snowflakes came down like feathers thrown from offstage sorting ornate doorknobs into piles on the Oriental carpet. They were glass, brass, and silver, and all had come from Venetian palazzi. He remembered their stories and the architectural details of the rooms and the doors they'd festooned.

Herbert talked incessantly, pausing only to snap up the phone to chat with a client or perhaps to deal with his favorite painter, Rhinehardt Langhammer, about a color at high noon as opposed to what shade it was under an electric light. He could talk about a dinner party held in Paris in 1935 and remember the jewelry worn by the Italian ambassador's wife, the pattern on the dinner plates, the most amusing toast of the evening, and the details of the dress worn by the hostess.

In those days, Herbert's firm (which was Herbert, Julie Lombard, and me) was retained to oversee all that went in or out of the Prime Minister's residence and the Governor-General's residence and to advise the wealthiest families in Canada as to how their houses should look. He was on his third generation of these clans and knew all the characters, their parents and grandparents, their scandals, divorces, and infidelities.

I would drive his big black Mercedes over the icy roads, white-knuckled under my gloves. As we bumped over the tram tracks or skidded a full ninety degrees making a turn, I would wonder if my Mississippi license entitled me to drive in Canadian conditions. Herbert would sit beside me in the front seat, wearing a trilby, briefing me on the pedigree of the woman we were about to meet. This might include a colorful tale concerning a second cousin, a fourth marriage, a shady business deal, plus the story of the cottage in Muskoka. All delivered with a soft voice in a breathy staccato of machine-gun fire.

I remember slipping and sliding on an icy sidewalk behind him, his camel-colored cashmere coat open and flapping, as he was saying, "She stabbed her third husband with a delicate mother-of-pearl-handled fruit knife and put him in a closet." Herbert rang the doorbell of the rather imposing stone house as I stamped snow off my boots. He didn't even inhale but continued, "Never would have found him if the maid hadn't noticed a tiny trickle of blood coming out from under the— Oh, good morning! We're here to see Mrs. Wilcox...Catherine! It's so nice to see you! I would like you to meet my new assistant..."

We'd be folded into a large living room, brought refreshments by a uniformed servant, and then I'd get out my notebook. Herbert might comment, "I notice that you've moved the Persian carpet about a foot closer to the staircase than it used to be..." It would soon be determined that he had last been in the house seventeen years before. Now, *that's* visual memory. I often wished that Herbert's aptitudes were contagious. Sometimes, in a warehouse far away in time and place from a mansion in Rosedale, I called on the spirit of Herbert to help me absorb all I could as I carried on a conversation of cheerful lies and wondered how I could possibly get into the storage room.

WE ARE TALKING MONEY here. The counterfeiters make loads of it. Tax-free. Billions a year. They might as well be printing the bills right in the factory going twenty-four hours a day. It's all illegal and they know it. I was only doing my job, which was to try to stop them, and no matter how well the scene went, I'd have to remember that they wouldn't like me much if they knew.

If I had a long conversation with orders taken, samples purchased, shipping and delivery times confirmed, I would shake hands and leave the factory or the warehouse and get into the elevator feeling as if I'd burned off thousands of calories. I would go out into the street and might turn one way and then cross back on myself to check for anyone following. Sometimes I walked back to the warehouse, but sometimes I'd head toward the prearranged corner or vacant lot or railroad bridge to be picked up. One last look around before approaching the car. Mickey would actually open the door for me, and I'd think, *I am a female, after all, and he appreciates the fact. How divine.* The car and driver was my safe harbor.

I LIKE TO IMAGINE that the men were looking out for me, but the truth was I was on my own. When the men called,

"Hey, Charlie, be careful," when I was on my way to a location wearing a wire, I noticed it. But when I was on the fifth floor of a crummy building in a rickety, unlit, urine-stinking elevator wearing a hidden camera, someone waiting in the car for me three blocks away or back in the warehouse wasn't helping me much. I knew I was the one to go in—to do it—since I could get away with it. Being a woman worked for me. I was the canary sent into the mine. I had faith that if I were gone too long, someone would do *some*thing. It never came to that.

Vinny—I would learn every New York City P.I. firm had a Vinny—once said, "C is our little sister." He was an ex-cop with the NYPD and outweighed me by sixty pounds. Blond-haired and blue-eyed, with a handsome, open face, he was over six feet tall and always wore at least one gun. I don't think he was being condescending to me; I think it was affectionate, protective.

Vinny lived on Staten Island, which was exotic to me since I'd never been there. I'd been to Lipari and to La Gonâve and spent weeks on a deserted island off the coast of Kuala Lumpur, but Staten Island was the home of Big Paulie Castellano on Todt Hill. Vinny'd worked in a funeral home after his stint as a limo driver before he became a New York City cop. He once said on a stakeout, "Yeah, we did all the Castellanos," and I wondered if he'd driven them around, buried them, or arrested them—or all of the above. Then I wondered where Big Paulie's locksmith was today. Probably still hanging around Vinny Parco's office on the East Side.

Sometimes I'm told that I'm not really an American woman anymore. I was far away during the feminist movement in this country. I want to be treated equally and paid equally, but I'm not angry. Nobody held a knife to my throat and told me I had to be a detective. It was strictly my impetuous idea. I entered a male world—without the rules of the police department or a branch of the military or a corporation—entirely on my own.

I want to be as capable as the men are, and I'm still working at it. I want to be as tough as they are and as strong as they are—but I'm not, and I won't ever be. I simply don't weigh enough. I suppose many women would have stormed out and hired a lawyer that first April Fools' Day, but I made my choice over and over again as a detective. I want to learn everything, to be able to play the game and to have the adventures.

I WAS HAPPY WITH the work at Parker's. No day was ever the same. Luckily, I liked the men, as it was incessant togetherness in that windowless warehouse, in what I called the Southern Office, with its nonstop sound track from Nashville. We were jammed together, overhearing every phone call, every remark. I will talk for hours with a woman friend about her marriage, her life, and feel close to her, but this closeness with the men was different. Maybe because we were having adventures together instead of discussing an interior landscape.

There was nothing I couldn't ask. I liked having them talk to me on stakeouts and talk around me in the office.

I was a new audience alone with a man on surveillances. Story after story unfolded. Material for novels forever. These were the war stories of men who loved the action, of being on the street, of actually being embattled. They talked, I listened. And when I got tired of it, there was always the phone booth.

Mickey's father had called one afternoon and said he'd found the phone booth down in the Village, abandoned. Two of us had roared downtown in the surveillance van and rescued it. Mickey and Bobby had been in another vehicle, parked on a little side street, guiding us to the location by

radio, guarding it until our arrival. The gray winter afternoon, the detectives in guns, boots, and hats loading the
phone booth lengthwise into the truck—it made me feel that
we were all kids and that this was happening after school.
Mickey's father stood nearby in his tweed racing cap, looking so Irish that I was surprised he didn't have a brogue when
I was introduced. We were all very excited about the phone
booth. No phone, of course, but a wonderful old-fashioned
phone booth with a door that actually slid closed and wood
paneling. I got into it often to be alone, to get away from
whatever was happening.

Of course, the men I saw in the office every day are the
ones I knew the best. The supporting actors came and went,
talking about the last trip or the next trip to Atlantic City,
which they called "A.C.," showing off their new cameras,
or just smoking and gossiping. Ronnie Dogs arrived, looking like anybody under a blue baseball cap, but I was told he
was worth a fortune. His seed money had come from betting on the dogs. Dek was one of the B team, purported to
be of royal blood, a prince, from an Asian country. Dek's
father was a king, but Elbert thought it much more impressive that Dek's uncle was a chief of police. Or so the story
went. Dek had olive skin, high cheekbones, jet black hair
worn in a ponytail, and a real job in the corporate world. He
would take the day off for a seizure or work for Parker's on
the weekends for free. His gold Jaguar was not the perfect
surveillance vehicle for anywhere other than Palm Beach or
Beverly Hills; nevertheless, I did tails with him in grubby
towns in Jersey and down in Chinatown. Dek wore flowing silk shirts that came to midthigh or would arrive at the
office in full combat gear—a wildly patterned camouflage
suit, heavy paratrooper boots—looking as if he were about
to single-handedly invade 'Nam.

We worked, at various times on various cases, with the

Feebs, the U.S. marshals, the NYPD, the cops in Jersey, U.S. Customs, the Joint Terrorist Task Force, and OCID of the NYPD. There were always ex-cops coming in and out of the office and others on the phone.

The worst of them were racist, sexist, dishonest, and dumb. The best of them had a genuine urge or even a need to be protective of others. They were savvy and resourceful, and if there's anything I ever want to be called—it's that. Their brains turned me on. In every way. But I never did more than fantasize about making love to a detective. It would have been far too dangerous for my future. Detectives are skeptics, paranoid, and gossip like mad when they're not putting two and two together on their own. But it wasn't just fear of damaging my reputation. It would have made incest look like breaking a diet.

I liked the way these men looked at all the angles and asked so many "why" and "what if" questions. I'd married a well-educated man with graduate degrees from three countries who never got it when someone was hurt by a sarcastic remark. I dated men like that. By the dozens—no, by the hundreds. Harvard Business School hadn't helped them. Law school often meant even less. Nothing would ever help them. Their being obtuse made me feel very much alone lying in a double bed beside them. If I called some signal to their attention, they might accuse me of being catty or oversensitive when I thought they were boneheaded and dim. The men of the world could be divided into two groups: those who "got" it and those who didn't and never would.

Some of these detectives *got* it. They twigged on to slivers of nuance and it delighted me. Somebody would hang up the phone and repeat the conversation to the room. "But you know what he meant . . . ," and there'd be an interpretation. Maybe three interpretations. I felt radiant with joy as I listened. A translation from the literal to the possible meaning to probable intent. The room was filled with smoke and the enthusiastic exploration of possibility.

They read body language and calibrated degrees of tension. "Yeah, he was worried all right. He didn't like what he was doing." "He knew we were on to him." "He suspects we know that he knows." I adored the way they played with scenes.

They flirted with innuendo and my heart soared like a hawk.

THE MEN SURPRISED ME, teased one another in a way women would never dare. Billy, an ex-cop, was going to have a hemorrhoid operation in the spring, which he wanted to keep secret from me, so I always had my head down reading when any allusion to his future absence was made. A few days after the operation, he walked into the warehouse and Mickey quipped, "Hey, Billy, how's your ass?"

Nearly all the men in the office fought with their stomachs. Belts disappeared under the girth, they all drank diet soda but they all ate doughnuts and French fries. So when Billy bragged about having lost weight after his operation, there was silence in the office. He even turned sideways so that all could admire his diminished silhouette. Mickey said, "That's great, Billy, but now you got a new problem."

Billy, ever attentive to whatever Mickey had to say, immediately asked, "What? What new problem?"

"Your head's too big for your body."

I wondered how the sexes of the same species could be so radically different in their playfulness.

The Company I Keep

'd been with Parker's about a month when somebody said that Elbert wanted to see me. So I went up and sat across from him and the hats and the bookshelves just like that day in August when I'd had the interview. He cleared his throat and leaned back and stared at me. Elbert could look like a young boy or like an old man. He looked like someone who never slept, but his clothes always looked slept in.

Today he stared at me and then said, "I don't want you to get upset, but I'm going to level with you." Then he waited, always the one for drama. Was he counting to ten before speaking again?

"I received a call today and was told that it is the consensus of opinion in the New York investigative community that you are not what you appear to be." He paused. I sat up very straight in the chair and thought, *Oh, no! Not again!* "There are various rumors to the effect that you are with the Central Intelligence Agency. That you are a plant."

"What!" I exploded. *If I'm a plant, then I want to be a geranium*, went absurdly through my mind.

Elbert put up his hand and continued in a deep, soothing voice, "I don't want to upset you, but I thought you should know."

"Well, this is ridiculous. You know it is, Elbert! Who told you this?" I was leaning forward.

He wouldn't tell me who, but later I talked to the secretary who'd taken the call. It was an investigator Parker's relied upon for outside research, computer database information. He was the acting president of an investigators' organization where I had been introduced months before as Vinny's protégée. There'd been dinner at an Italian restaurant, and I'd sat between a coroner and a handwriting expert. This "source" had heard it from several other sources and thought that Parker's should know that I was a risk.

I tried to be cool, but I was angry. "Well, this has happened before. It happened when I worked with Vinny Parco. It happened in Rome, in Cyprus, and it happened in London." I paused. "What do you think?"

Elbert's eyebrows were raised. "I think you're an extremely good investigator. You're too good for some people."

"Thanks," I replied glumly.

"And if you tell me you're not with the Company, then I will believe you're not with the Company."

"I'm not with the Company." My voice was cold.

Men's faces flashed into my mind.

My temporary fiancé in Rome. He had been in MI5. He'd also been certifiable, on-the-windowsill-ready-to-jump barking mad. Hilarious, destructive, and extravagant; he swore his doctor forbade him to drink anything but champagne.

Miles Copeland, who sent me all those telexes in Cyprus. At least his name was on them, but had he sent them? I'd met him at a dinner party in London. Miles was a big-deal intelligence officer. Very big deal. He'd told me colorful stories of getting on planes with suitcases full of money. Money to pay for the casual coup d'état.

Baron F. in Geneva, who invited me for dinner at least twice a week. He lived in the Hotel Richemond and I in the

Beau Rivage. Aristocratic, rival sisters sitting side by side on the Quai de Mont Blanc. He called himself a Baltic baron, was connected to the last czar, and had known the last four heads of the CIA quite well. He regaled me with their neuroses. His own past was a bit cloudy. I never understood why he kept all his Impressionist paintings in storage in Paris. Witty, urbane Baron F. being fired upon as he crossed the Gaza Strip in a yellow cab that had miraculously materialized when he raised an arm to surrender. He'd leapt right in. The story was that the shrapnel in his head slowed his speech. So many dinners at the Richemond with him and his little dog, Nixie, the Australian terrier—pronounced "terry-ay"— under the table, nibbling entrecôte from a silver dish. Once, on a rainy spring afternoon in Geneva, Baron F. hired a chauffeur and limousine to take us—all three—to see *Gorillas in the Mist* because Nixie was "exceptionally fond of gorillas." The dog sat between us, ears up, staring at the screen for two hours.

Men in Cyprus, men in London. Mad Mentor in Rome, who'd made my life miserable when I refused to see him again. His highly placed complaints that I was "un-American" and should be fired from La Radio Vaticana had led to an imbroglio between Reagan's Personal Envoy to the Pope—a not overly bright Beverly Hills millionaire in way over his head—and John Paul's Secretary of State, the sophisticated and Machiavellian Agostino Casaroli. The Vatican took my side, and the Vatican won. The mysterious CIA station chief and the story that I was his mistress—the story that wouldn't die. The articles in the Italian newsmagazines that claimed I'd been meeting in secret with Qaddafi.

Somehow, I'd always been in thick with these characters: cultural attachés, and journalists who probably really weren't, and men with money from mysterious sources who never appeared to frequent anything as bourgeois as an office. Sometimes they'd ask me for favors. Often they'd ask me for an introduction. Why were they drawn to me, why did they pursue me? Did I unconsciously send off signals?

All this swirled through my mind as Elbert stared at me. "Actually, I think you're so good, I'm giving you a raise."

Pleased, I stood up. Then I remembered that none of us had gotten last week's paycheck. "Great. Terrific. Thanks." I was in the doorway, looking back at him. I couldn't resist. "Actually, Elbert, this seems like the time to ask if I can leave an hour early on Friday."

"You going away for the weekend?"

I tried not to smile. "Yeah. Langley. They're picking me up at four...the helicopter's landing on the roof." I watched Elbert's face as I imagined myself stepping out of the chopper at the Company headquarters in Virginia.

He laughed, and I left the Executive Suite and went downstairs.

Aptitudes

Underneath all this very uncomfortable gossip about the Company were the compliments. From Vinny and Lyndon and now from Elbert. I knew I was getting things done—the research, talking on the phone, persuading people to tell me things. Years ago, I'd taken three days of aptitude tests at Johnson O'Connor and then been told the test results and the recommendations. The premise was to use your aptitudes—things you naturally did well, the talents you were born with—and to be good at whatever you chose to do.

I had been skeptical and refused to write my major in college, and I certainly wasn't going to give a hint about my interests. So I took the tests and was told, on day four, that I was a subjective personality who used inductive reasoning and was capable of this and that but did very poorly on every musical test. I sat bolt upright in the chair when told that if I wanted to use most of my aptitudes, I would be quite happy as an archaeologist. Egyptology had kept me alive while under house arrest in Toronto, waiting for an arrogant husband to sign a piece of paper that gave me my freedom. I'd taken every undergraduate course in Egyptology offered at the University of Toronto—even studying hieroglyphics—but I would have to learn German to proceed to graduate levels. Impossible for me. So I'd simply returned to Egypt and to the Valley of the Kings as a civilian, again and again. Wanting to be an Egyptologist was a secret.

I was told that I liked to be able to interpret everything in my own way, to work on my own, and that I had the ability to see a portion or a piece of something and to visualize an entirety, whether it was a broken piece of pottery, part of a map, or part of a story.

The second and third professions that would allow me to use my aptitudes were acting and writing. For every aptitude there were just as many tests with low scores, lots of things I'm lousy at. The ideaphoria was, by far, my best test result, so high that I would never run out of ideas or interpretations. The flip side of this is near constant daydreaming, which annoys me and other people, I am sure. High ideaphoria rules out dozens of professions.

I wrote my first novel standing up on a terrace in Rome with my typewriter on a stack of Italian phone books. I stood there, wearing a bikini and a big straw hat, because if I sat down I might stare off into space and then notice that three hours had passed. I set up the ironing board so that if I did reach an impasse in writing, I could come in from the terrace and iron. The added benefit was that if the writing were not going well, all my clothes would be ironed. I dreaded the day I would ask my friends to send over their laundry but that day never came. I never ironed and at the end of seven months, I had a thousand pages and an outstanding tan.

Perhaps the raging ideaphoria and the nonstop interpretation of events had something to do with becoming a detective. Going undercover meant not only being an actress, but writing my own lines. I was whoever I wanted to be, complete with research and the studying to prepare for my role. Sometimes it was actually *on* Broadway. It was fun to masquerade as an authority for twenty minutes or half a day. To dare to go back again was tough because I'd be facing an expert who'd had time to ruminate over possible holes in my story.

I needed information and they could tell me or not, but I had a very few minutes or even seconds to make them want to tell me. I didn't relish fooling anyone because often I liked them, but it was a game of pretend and daring. Cops used the badge, had power. I had only the power of persuasion. Would I go back to the warehouse and be able to announce to Mickey, "You won't believe what Sallah told me!" Sometimes it would confirm what we suspected or it could swing the investigation into a new direction.

On some afternoons when the men and I were considering the "what next," I would hear the journalist in me talking. I could hear the cop in them. Vice versa. We listened to each other, sometimes made fun of each other, but I liked the street smarts they had and I didn't.

When my father used to call me "stupid" several times a week in my Mississippi life, it hurt my feelings. Hadn't he known me since I was born, and so wasn't he the one who knew the truth about me?

Now I noticed, all around me, the angles of intelligence. Unexpected. A lot of the cops can't spell, but they can drive to a Bronx location in their sleep while reciting the landmarks from memory. They've never been to a museum and wouldn't know a David Hockney from a Monet, but they can instantly recognize a face in a crowd from a grainy photograph. They don't know a thing about the handover of Hong Kong to China, but they would if it bore any relation to a gang power struggle in Chinatown. The intelligence is there and it doesn't matter if it's expressed ungrammatically or with twelve "fucks" in the sentence or not.

Assignment: Chinatown

March on Tenth Avenue wasn't March on Madison or Park. One morning, I got off my second bus at about seven and slogged in melting snow over the curb and onto the sidewalk. Then I tried to cross at the corner and sank ankle-deep in icy water. The gunmetal-gray sky felt low and heavy; the skyline was a child's cutout of low, boxy rectangles.

This was north of Chelsea; actually, it was Clinton if you wanted to pretend to be fashionable but was more like a little piece of Hell's Kitchen if you judged it by the populace. In the past, it was an area riddled with Irish-American gangs led by the likes of Mickey Featherstone and Jimmy Coonan. The Westies. Now it was a major hooker zone. The pimps kept it safe. The girls wore abbreviated hot pants and G-strings—even in January—and shivered in their high-heeled, pastel-colored, patent-leather boots. They kept their hands jammed into the pockets of tiny jackets that exposed serious cleavage and breasts like watermelons. I felt sorry for them, curious about them, and envious of their cellulite-free thighs. I also harbored the sullen suspicion that they were making more money as hookers than I was as a detective.

I waved at Angelo hurrying along the wet sidewalk, bearing a cardboard tray of coffees and teas and bagels. He was a small man in white pants and apron under a black parka with a hood. We'd call Poppy's on the corner for this and that all day, which meant Angelo got plenty of exercise. He waved back, and when he grinned a puff of vapor came out of his mouth.

Parker Investigations liked the 29th Street location because the rent was cheap, we wanted to be hard to find, and parking was easy.

Today the temperature was slightly above freezing, which meant that the eaves of the buildings were dripping. I put up my gloved hand and felt my hair, wondering if the mysterious liquid might be a more complex solution than plain water. The sun above was pale, like light behind the frosted glass door of a dentist's office.

I hurried toward the warehouse, saluted the camera above me, and kicked open the door. I adored kicking open the door and slamming it after me. It felt good and free, like batting a baseball. Nobody cared, and it seemed right. I slammed it with gusto and walked into the main room of the warehouse.

"Hey, Charlie, what's up?" Mickey was leaning back, hands behind his neck, in his desk chair. On a bulletin board behind him were snapshots of the Nguyen family and police sketches of various Vietnamese who looked feral with exaggerated cheekbones and slanted lines for eyes. A Tennessee license plate was nailed to the wall next to photos of country singers taken on his last trip to Nashville.

"Hey, C," came from Bobby, sipping tea out of a Styrofoam cup.

Bobby was well over six foot four in the cowboy boots he lived in. He had a large bald spot but wore the rest of his dark blond hair past his shoulders. He had a flowing mustache, very few teeth, and massive arms covered with tattoos of naked women. The first time I met him he scared me, but the second time I noticed his very pretty blue eyes and how gentle he was. On one of our first stakeouts, he told me he played the bagpipes; he liked to garden, to make preserves on the weekends. Mickey called him an excellent investigator.

Bobby was an ex-cop from Pennsylvania who drove to the warehouse at two o'clock on Monday morning and spent the weeknights in a sleeping bag beside his desk. He worked all five days in the office and of course was always available for any kind of night duty, whether it was a tail, dumpster diving, or a garbage grab. Alone at night, he and Warner watched a baby TV with a screen the size of an index card. On Fridays, he drove home to his wife, Annette. There were jokes that this was how he stayed married: by staying away. Sometimes after phone calls from her he'd slam down the receiver and Mickey would say, "Leave your gun here this weekend, Bobby." Bobby'd light up a cigarette, inhale, and then shake his head as if swallowing his anger along with the smoke. His long hair would move on the shoulders of the plaid shirt.

Bobby watched me pull off my wet boots and socks. I searched my desk drawers for a clean pair. "One shelf up," he called. "The bookcase. Right in front a ya." I looked at him and then at where his hand with the cigarette pointed. Jammed in between files and a Vietnamese/English dictionary were a pair of white socks. The cuff had a familiar little cartoon face. Definite benefits to having an office in a warehouse. I pulled on the socks and turned on my computer, hoping I wouldn't be stuck at it all day.

There was a knock on the door and everyone turned to look at the camera. "Come in!" was the shouted chorus when they recognized Angelo. He arrived, small and hooded against the cold, bearing cups of tea.

"I'll get it," said Bobby and Mickey and Vinny.

"No, I'll get it." The men were always generous with each other when it came to the Poppy's tab. They vied for who would pay every single time, whereas a group of women would have carefully taken turns or divided the tip right down to the penny. Angelo patted Warner, knelt to kiss her on the head, and left. Bobby handed me my Diet Coke, and the day began.

"Hey, C!" Vinny called from the corner desk. "Did you run the DMV on that guy from yesterday?" The Department of Motor Vehicles could give us a full name and address and more from a license plate.

"I ran it, but I didn't get it. We owe them money."

The air was immediately thick with, "What the fuck is going on?" and the answer, "The same old fucking thing!" and, "Fuck this!"

Vinny was already on the phone to Mili, short for Mila-grosa, upstairs. "Yeah, the phone bill's important, but so's this!" Mili guarded the checkbook and the power that went with it like a Doberman. Vinny hung up the phone and turned to the rest of us. "She says our account is in the negative for three dollars and twelve cents! What the fuck does that mean?"

Then the others began to grouse about their expense money. They spent a fortune on gas, and Mili held back so they weren't reimbursed for months. They put rental cars on their own credit cards and prayed Parker's wouldn't go bankrupt before they got their money.

Vinny was going full speed at thirty-nine fucks a minute.

The door slammed and Mas walked in. He was Indonesian, five foot five, and about 130 pounds. He'd killed a man when he was eight years old. Shot him dead to save his uncle's life. For years, he'd driven various UN dignitaries around town—the most recent had been Boutros Boutros-Ghali.

"So what's up?" he asked, and was greeted with complaints about Mili and the firm's precarious financial situation.

"What else is new?" He shrugged philosophically. Then he fell to his knees and started talking to the dog, who lay with eyes half-closed on her blue L.L.Bean cushion in front of Mickey's desk. "Warner, what's the matter with you? It's eight o'clock. Why aren't you up?"

"She had a rough night," answered Bobby. "*Casablanca* wasn't over till two-thirty, and the phone rang at four— Oh, C…" He turned in his chair. "It was that fucking lunatic wanting to speak to you. Wants you ta call him in Jersey."

"Which fucking lunatic? They all want ta speak to her."

I scowled at Vinny, then turned to Bobby. "Four o'clock this morning? You mean Hoffman?"

Hoffman was our only walk-in client. Ever. That in itself was bizarre. He had knocked on the door last August, pink from the summer heat, with freckles upon freckles, and been admitted to the warehouse. After Warner had attacked him and been restrained, the glowing Hoffman with his orange hair had stood in the center of the room with our desks surrounding him. He appeared alight with the excitement of being able to tell his sad story, was perspiring heavily, and of course, my heart went out to the radiant Hoffman. Surely he'd been bullied and beaten up after school every day. No one wanted to take his case except me.

"Cripes! I found his father for him! Why does he keep calling me? What does he want?"

Hoffman's father had been missing for twenty-nine years, and I'd found him in two afternoons. Nobody thought I could do it because the senior Hoffman didn't want to be found. There were terrible jokes about this. Now Mickey owed me my height in Oreos, and the interest on the unpaid cookies was piling up. Ten cookies a day and time was passing. Elbert had been a creep about it and never even said, "Good work." I'd been so excited at my success. Furthermore, he hadn't even told Hoffman that I had done it. He'd let me sit in on their meeting when he'd presented him with the phone number and address of his father but insinuated *he* had found the missing Hoffman. It rankled. I started looking for Hoffman's number on my big desk calendar, which served as a blotter. It was covered in brown semicircles from everybody's coffee cup stains.

Bobby went on, "Said it was urgent. Four a.m. and it was urgent. I said you weren't here."

"Does he think we all live here together?" I sighed. "And that we work twenty-four hours a day?"

"Feels like it," somebody said mournfully.

The phone rang from upstairs and Mickey picked up. "Yeah, okay." He hung up and gave me the phone number. "Mili says he left three messages on the machine early this morning."

"He prob'ly wants you ta go with him when he confronts his father. After thirty years I wouldn't want ta face my father and say, 'You owe me a million dollars,' " said Vinny.

Mas stopped petting Warner and stood up. "He said his father murdered his mother."

Mickey laughed. "Great, Charlie. You get the good ones. He's not only a fuckin' lunatic, he's a fuckin' murderer."

I started to punch in the number, then looked at my watch and hung up. I couldn't call somebody at eight who'd called me at four. I looked up at Mickey. "Oh, he told me that story about his mother and father, too. But I made him tell me how, and it seems his father killed his mother by breaking her heart."

Everybody laughed, and Warner got up and shook herself.

"Hi, guys..." The door slammed, and Elbert Thatch materialized.

Our chief, whose middle name was Parker, was a vision in black from square-toed boots to black felt wide-brimmed hat. He wore those same boots and black Levi's, winter or summer, every single day and rotated about three black or gray shirts; there were those who claimed, rather uncharitably, that his color choice had something to do with laundry. For raids, he wore an ankle-length black cloth coat, and—with the black hat—he reminded me of a refugee from an old Clint Eastwood movie. Behind him was Tom, the paralegal turned investigator. He was in his mid-twenties, round-faced, with a cheerful sort of Spanky look under his omnipresent baseball cap.

Elbert and Tom were inseparable, seemed to arrive and depart as a pair. They took long lunches and would return looking mellow, laughing at anything and everything; their faces would be flushed red. And they were developing the same shape—stocky with a round belly. Mickey called them the Roast Beef Twins.

Warner, now fully awake, twisted herself into what was close to a circle and gyrated in sheer ecstasy with pink tongue out at one end and tiny nub tail moving at the other. Elbert put his coffee mug on my blotter and leaned on my desk as she bounded in joy between him and her cushion. He called her name in baby talk. Then she attacked Bobby with affection and then, last of all, me. I think Warner knew she and I were the only females in the Southern Office, though both of us had been given boys' names.

Mickey looked up. "I talked to OCID and they're ready on the twentieth. Do you want to call the lawyers or should I?"

Elbert was scratching Warner's ears as she stood on hind legs, braced against his knees. "I'll tell them. I'm meeting with them at noon."

As one, we hoped Elbert would change his shirt.

"Okay, Charlie, you want to go with Mas and sit on 124 and do a couple of flybys at these other locations?" Mickey tore off a notebook sheet with addresses, then glanced at his watch. "You better get out of here now in case they open early."

I took the page, stuffed it into my jeans pocket, and started pulling on my spare boots. I knew the drill. Tags, faces, watching, watching, watching. Estimating how much in the shop. Who was there, who came, who left, possible relationship. Who arrived with a delivery. Hidden doors. Back exits, storage areas. That occasional leap from the van to follow someone with product through the crowded streets. Looking for lookouts who were looking for us. Recognizing the spotters. The songs on the radio, the food from that restaurant next to the Chinese funeral parlor. Three huge servings of mysterious meat on rice. The only thing I couldn't identify all day. A dollar and a half. Eating in the van, dipping my parka sleeve in soy sauce. Diet Cokes, taking breaks to pee. It would be a good day except for the cold.

"I got the radios," called Mas from the closet. He handed me one, and I turned it off and on and listened, then jammed it into my canvas bag along with notepad, pens, a black beret, a fistful of toilet paper, and some rubber bands.

"Here. I'm through with it." Bobby tossed the *Daily News* at me, and I stuffed it in with everything else.

Mas and I were suited up in parkas and gloves and halfway out the door. "I've got Hoffman's number. If you hear from him, tell him I'll try him from a phone booth sometime today. That's all I can promise." Tales of Hoffman. We would talk, and he would tell me his father had disappeared again. I was sympathetic, advised him to cherish their brief reunion and to let his father go.

"Hey, Charlie, you and Mas watch out for Army. Don't get too close," said Mickey.

"I always watch out for Army," Mas said decisively. Army was our nickname for the Vietnamese war veteran who wore a red wool beret with a black ribbon on it. Nobody knew if he had been South or North, and nobody cared. We cared about his plate, knew where he parked his blue van, and kept an eye on his corner stall. He hobbled around on one leg, leaning on a crutch, forever scanning the crowds as they milled past his patch of sidewalk.

"He's really hinky these days," warned Mickey.

"Hey, C, watch out for the lunatics." Bobby grinned, showing one tooth.

"You know that I'm catnip to psychotics," I called back, and slammed the door.

Mas and I started across 29th Street, to Mustafa's garage. We cursed the ice, the potholes, the cold, and it made us both feel better. In minutes we were in Moby Dick, the big white van with the periscope, racing down the West Side Highway toward Chinatown.

Notes from the Warehouse

Whenever I thought of those bleak days of plodding through the Yellow Pages, I knew I had been right to persevere. But it wasn't always great. The air of the Southern Office was chokingly thick with smoke.

Sometimes things got on my nerves. One day, I'd been backing out numbers in the Cole Directory, scrawling long lines of figures, flipping back and forth in the big red book in an attempt to link phone numbers and addresses. Unhappily, it didn't demand enough concentration for me to tune out the conversation. Vinny walked in from Brooklyn, and all three, Mickey, Bobby, and Vinny, began to discuss tinted glass. Car windows, windshields, the costs of, the merits of, the darkness of, the legality of in Jersey, the legality of in New York, the safety factor, the best price, the best garage to actually have it done. Then the invariable follow-up: "I got a guy who'll give you a good price if you..." Should one remove the windows oneself, or should one allow the tinter to take care of that, therefore having to pay extra? Was it difficult to remove the windows oneself? What about the windshield? Had any of them known anyone who'd actually done it? How long should it take? The voices went on. They all possessed strong opinions covering every nuance of the tinted window situation.

Suddenly I wanted to scream. I got up from my desk, went over to the phone booth, and got in. The room's testosterone level had risen to the stratosphere. I slammed the door closed and stared at nothing through the glass panel. I heard Mickey's little bark of a laugh and realized Bobby had turned up the radio. Alone. Peace. Moments passed.

I felt the tension dissolve. The dog howled, the front door of the warehouse slammed, and I popped out, refreshed.

"Your Oreos are here," said Bobby.

"And we ordered you a Diet Coke," said Vinny.

Mickey grinned. "Feel better, Charlie?"

I nodded. Bobby threw me a six-pack of cookies, Angelo handed me a Diet Coke. I tried to pay, but the men wouldn't let me. They were sweet. They were good to me. They started talking about Canal Street. The craziness had passed.

SOMETIMES I WONDERED IF I had changed since becoming a detective or if the landscape had changed. Maybe both, maybe only the landscape. I liked being able to read what I'd always read, but now it was out in the open. I didn't have to carry around one book for the bus or to have on my desk and leave the book I really wanted to read at home. These days I was racing through *Murder Machine,* the grisly story of the DeMeos, and it delighted me that instead of "Why are you reading that?" I was asked if I would lend it out when I finished. Vinny and Mickey had already read it, and Bobby wanted to. The biographies of Giancana, Gotti, Castellano, Luciano—these were the books I devoured. We all read *Born to Kill* by T. J. English. It was a *Daily News* sort of office until Mickey started reading aloud from *The Wall*

Street Journal; I was the only one who read *The New York Times.* Once in a while, I'd ask somebody to throw me *Soldier of Fortune,* and there were always gun magazines lying around. A few of us were married, but no one had children. The uniform was jeans and there were long, involved discussions concerning where to buy the cowboy boots that everybody kept up on their desks. The sound track was country and western. Most of the men drank hot tea, Mas and I were the only investigators not on a diet, if you counted Sharif's fasting for Ramadan, and Mas, Sharif, and I were the only three who didn't chain-smoke.

Sharif was a tall, thin, elegantly handsome Mauritanian who called me on the phone at night and talked about his future. He was at Parker's by default. He didn't want to be a detective. He wanted to be an accountant. He worried about getting killed in Chinatown. When he described what he was doing and what I was doing—going undercover and lying to the bad guys on their turf, endangering their lucrative way of life by working with the cops to close down their operations, raid their factories, and put them in cuffs—it did sound like tap-dancing in a snake pit. I only saw it this way when Sharif talked about it late at night, but it never worried me enough to lose a minute's sleep over it.

Sharif was from the royal family who were scattered all over the world in exile since the latest coup d'état. He was quiet, bright, could speak to the Senegalese vendors in French and to the Arab vendors in Arabic, but he could barely speak English. He was reliable in his own way. He only worked when his horoscope told him it was a good thing.

ONE DAY, THE SCAM phone started to ring between my desk and Vinny's. All talk stopped. Even Warner pricked up her ears and froze. Everybody stared as if it were a cartoon phone that leapt into the air angrily with each shrill ring.

"Oh, please, come on, somebody pick it up!" I begged.

"I'm not answering that!" bellowed Vinny.

"You get it! Go on, Charlie! Pretend you're somebody else!" said Mickey.

We all stared some more at the ringing scam phone. My handwritten names on scraps of paper were taped all around it: "If someone asks for Stephanie, it's Charlie" and "If it's for Vanessa, it's me, C" and "For Veronica, please get Charlie" and "If anyone wants Samantha, it means Charlie."

The phone rang twelve times as I begged someone to pick up. It was the number I left with one counterfeiter after another, from Broadway to Chinatown to Brooklyn to Jersey. "I can't answer it and pretend it's some secretary and then change my voice and pretend not to be me!" I shouted. "You have to answer! Just say, 'Hello'!"

"Charlie is having an identity crisis," Bobby said nonchalantly, never glancing up from his handheld puzzle.

"Fourth one today," Vinny said calmly. All the men made fun of my *What to Name the Baby* book. I kept it in a drawer and whipped it out only when I needed inspiration.

Mas finally walked over and picked up the receiver on about the fifteenth ring. "Global," he said without much enthusiasm. He listened, then he thrust the phone toward me. "Charlie. For you."

We all looked at each other in mute despair as I reached for it. "Yes, hello." I listened, then said, "Yes, this is Stephanie." Then I listened again. "He's new here. He has a block. Can't get my name right...Oh, yes, I talked to you yesterday about the T-shirts...yes, I remember. Oh, Mr. Ali! I'm so glad you called..."

I turned to grab a pen and saw that Mickey and Bobby

were rolling their eyes. Well, I *was* glad that Mr. Ali had called. I made a face back at them and said sweetly, "Yes, I am definitely still interested. You're going to give me a good price, aren't you?"

ANOTHER DAY, MAS SAID he'd teach Sharif to drive. They left the office, the diminutive Indonesian leading the giant Mauritanian off for his lesson. The door slammed. Bobby groaned, "I don't want to think about it." Mickey turned up the radio—Mary Chapin Carpenter, one of the office favorites.

The song ended, and Bobby started talking about yesterday's seizure. I was working on the computer but all ears. I hadn't been allowed to go because there was always the idea that I'd be burned and my use as an undercover would be negated. Mickey was working on his computer, and Vinny was leaning back in his chair with his feet up on the desk next to the scam phone. I could see his ankle holster and the cute little gun in it. They all wear guns, and they all go nuts when I ask if I can "hold it," but what else can I say if I want to hold it?

Bobby said, "I saw Elbert yesterday morning and he was wearing that long black coat." I could see him: Elbert in his black square-toed boots, the complete black outfit including the black hat. He'd look like a killer. Bobby inhaled, then exhaled smoke. "It was just covered in white dust and dirt. Just filthy. It wasn't even black anymore."

Vinny shook his head, made a face, as Bobby went on. "I look at the detectives from the NYPD and the Garment Center Task Force and they are all immaculate—expensive suits—and I think, *This* is my boss? So I say, 'Elbert, what happened? You bin rollin' on the ground?' and I start ta brush him off. So then Elbert—ya know how he is, fuckin' lost in space—Elbert starts ta look around and doesn't even notice that he is filthy, and he says, 'Oh, I guess I brushed up against somethin'.'"

Mickey spun around in his chair and started laughing. "Before or after he brushed the van up against something?"

"What are ya talkin' about?" demanded Vinny.

"Elbert came over ta me yesterday at about noon and he said he didn't want ta return the van and could I do it. I said sure. Elbert told me somebody hit him and snapped off the side mirror on the passenger side. Casual remark." Mickey lit a cigarette. We all waited. "So I go over to the van and take a look, and I see the mirror is gone and the door is so smashed ya can't even open it or close it...the entire frame is bent." Mickey inhaled. "This is a sideswipe of mammoth velocity." He shook his head, exhaled, and thunked ashes off the Marlboro. "So I tell the black clerk at the rental place and she explodes, 'I knowed I shouldn'a given that van ta him! He comes in here all dirty wid his hair standing out ever' which way! All standin' up! He had fire in his eyes! I thought he was drunk. I knowed I shouldn'a let him drive!'"

We were all laughing. Elbert didn't even know he'd been hit. Or where. Or see anything at all. Mickey asked him about it, and he was oblivious. We wondered what he hit and how he could not know. We were a little bit horrified but couldn't stop laughing. I thought of him trailing around in that long black coat covered with white dust and Bobby trying desperately to clean him up in front of the cops.

The door slammed. Mas and Sharif were back. We filled them in, and Sharif and I laughed harder than anybody because we were thinking of the time I slammed Moby Dick into another van right in front of the office on the way to pick up the phone booth from Mickey's father. I was backing up and kept asking, "Am I okay? Am I okay?" and Sharif kept saying, *"Oui, oui, oui!"* until this deafening crash. Our secret. Sharif and I raised our hands and slapped palms in the air. The door slammed, and Elbert, a study in black, materialized looking dazed, which set us all off again; Warner started to bark, and the phone started ringing.

Brothers

Sometimes a surveillance story told in the front seat of Moby Dick would be passed on to the others. I was at my desk, head down, fighting with the figures for a shared cost proposal, when Bobby said, "C, did your brother really make your mother pay for her dinner on her birthday?"

I looked up, surprised. "Yes, it's true. Eighty-fourth birthday. He told her to meet him at this Italian place called Amerigo's for the Early Bird Special and then he asked for two checks."

The room exploded with "Fuck" and "Shithead" laced with threats of violence.

"Wait a minute," said Mickey. "I thought he—didn't he charge her for staying at his house?"

"That was my other brother."

"What are you talkin' about?" somebody demanded.

"Okay, here's the story. Two brothers. Both of 'em a lot older than me. My oldest brother killed himself. He was decent. He left me with the two I've now got plus my sister."

"A sister? Is she like you?" somebody called out.

"She's vice president in charge of corporate compliance for a really big—I think it's international—corporation. She's a lawyer."

"*Not* like you," Mas said decisively.

"What about the dinner?" asked Bobby.

"My brother in Mississippi pulled the birthday dinner two-check deal, *but*"—I held up one finger to the waiting circle of faces—"Mother told me that after dinner, he had her follow him in her car to the filling station and he got a full tank of gas and gave her the coupon for a free car wash." The men actually roared with disgust.

I started to type again. "What's that about staying at his house?" demanded Vinny.

"My other brother invited Mother to stay with him and his wife from Thanksgiving to Christmas. She went, and when she got home after Christmas—"

"Wait'll you hear this," said Mickey.

"—my brother sent a detailed invoice. Fourteen dollars a week for food and—"

Vinny exploded, "What was she eating? Cat food?"

"Tell the rest," Mickey insisted.

I sighed. "He put down a dollar and a half for a box of Kleenex, and he computed the electricity she 'used' when she was alone in the house from eight a.m. till six p.m. Mondays through Fridays." Disgraceful. But I thought it was really more McNair than malice.

There was silence and then a storm of outrage. "Is your brother poor? Are they both poor?" asked Bobby, swirling around in his chair.

I shook my head, still looking at the computer screen. "They're all three very bright. Very successful." That last word was difficult to say because I wasn't sure what it meant. They had houses and children and camcorders and cars and boats, and my sister had a swimming pool. "The brother she stayed with always drones on about how important family is. He's pretty sanctimonious about it." I took a deep breath. "And the brother who won't speak to her or buy her a cup of coffee if he sees her having breakfast alone, who won't buy her dinner on her birthday... well, everyone in town thinks he's a great person. Especially at his church. He just gave a million dollars to start a fund for missionaries."

The roof of the warehouse nearly blew off with these revelations. They knew my mother was in her eighties, lived alone. They knew through me that she was funny and fun, a good sport, an optimist. Most important of all: She was my mother.

These were good men. Sometimes I thought that they were my brothers.

Invisible Dog

L et's let Charlie do it."

"Yeah, she can do it." Vinny was chiming in now.

I looked up from an arrest report I was paraphrasing for a letter to a client. "Let me do what?"

I'd been stuck behind the computer too many days in a row. Once in a while Elbert would decide, to my despair, that I could write and that that's what I should be doing. These periods of detainment sometimes lasted one afternoon and never more than three, but I wasn't ever happy about it. Sometimes Vinny or Bobby or Sharif would stand over my desk and I'd debrief them about their investigation, stake-out, whatever, and tack together a report. I hated it being secondhand; I wanted to be on the scene and not passively describing it an hour later. Now was my chance. In three seconds, I was F-seven-ing from WordPerfect and pulling on my black parka.

"Maybe Charlie could walk the dog," somebody said.

"Grab the leash," Vinny was saying.

"Warner won't come with me. Are you kidding?" The dog looked at me mournfully, her brown eyes so expressive in her anguish that the whites showed at the sides.

Warner had suffered great psychological trauma as a

puppy before being rescued during a counterfeit T-shirt raid. The story was that the men had crept through the backyard of a squalid house in Queens and noticed a mysterious circle worn in the scraggly grass. They charged into the dark basement, where Mickey was immediately bitten by a pit bull. Pretty ghastly place. The darkness, the smell. The T-shirts were there all right. Guarded by pit bulls. "Sure," somebody said, "this makes sense." It was drugs, of course. In cages were three puppies too weak to stand, with empty food dishes in front of them. Destined to be warm-up acts for the dogfights. The puppies were rescued by the cops; two didn't make it, but the boxer puppy was dubbed Warner, after Warner Bros., and taken to the office, where she became Agent 0.5. Point Five.

Warner suffered from agoraphobia, so the back of the warehouse was her special place. Her adamant refusal to go outside meant that when a TV crew or real estate agent was to arrive, somebody, usually Mas, would grab a shovel and Lysol and disappear for a while. To literally shovel shit.

Warner did not go for walks.

"Grab the leash anyway. We might need it," Bobby said.

In minutes we were off in Moby Dick, barreling through the Holland Tunnel toward Jersey. Bobby was already on the radio with Mickey. Nobody said "New" Jersey and nobody said "walkie-talkie" the way I had with Lyndon. It was Jersey and it was radio. Oh, and don't ever say "Roger" or "Over" or all the men will roll their eyes and think you're pathetic. On one of my first days in Chinatown, I'd tramped through knee-deep snow to get to one of those new public phones, which are miserable for hiding a radio and pretending to talk on. And how could you ever pull on a wig in one? Anyway, I'd seen what I'd come to see and was ready to be picked up, so I radioed my location and was answered. Thinking I knew the language, I asked, "What's your position?" There was a pause, then coughing as I was told Canal and Broadway. I later learned that all the men who were on the radio at the time had heard me and shouted, "Missionary!" That afternoon in the office, I was told never to ask about positions. Say "location." I had shrugged nonchalantly, I was positive it was nonchalantly, and then, to my horror, blushed.

"So what are we after?" I asked Bobby when he flipped on the blinker for a right-hand exit.

"There's a bunch a vehicles parked behind a house and we need to get the tags. Thought you could walk a dog. Maybe we could borrow a dog. So's you could just stroll by."

I looked at Bobby, hugely tall in the cab of the truck, wearing his Stetson with the turkey feather trim. His shoulder-length blond curls resting on his red parka reminded me of old pictures of Buffalo Bill. I noted the red parka and thought, *Well, he doesn't ever do undercover, so it could be purple.* We did a flyby of the location. The streets were lined with little box houses with matching garages in back. Each house had a front walk just one person wide that led to a front door. Some of the doors still sported a plastic Santa or a Christmas wreath.

"There it is. Number One ten." A two-story house with the driveway going down the side like all the others. Neither of us could see a vehicle anywhere near it. We passed it without slowing down and took a right up a side street.

The leash was in my lap. I flipped the catch open and closed. "Wish we had a dog, Bobby."

"Yeah, you 'n me both."

Bobby popped a new tape in the little recorder and we talked about nothing, then played it back, listened, and rewound. A man walked by, head level with the window, and Bobby lowered his arm to put it out of sight. "Okay, C, here ya go." I took it. "I'll be here when you're through."

"This leash looks pretty stupid." The street appeared

deserted, which was fine with me—the fewer people watching me walk an invisible dog, the better. I clicked the recorder to "play" and "record" and jammed it into the breast pocket of my shirt under my parka. It was cold, but I'd have to leave the parka open. "See anybody?" I asked, and Bobby looked in his rearview and said no. "Neither do I." This meant no one to connect me with the van. I leaned down and recorded my agent number, the date, the time, and the address, then I grabbed the leash, opened the door, jumped down to the ground, and slammed the door behind me.

I had become Agent 186. It was on my paycheck, and it was used on all office correspondence, in reports, and on the radio. We all had numbers. I thought of Patrick Bombino's twangy musical telephone recording: "They've given you a number and taken 'way your name." Seemed like years ago.

It was a gray March day trying valiantly to be springlike. Nearly noon, though, with that pale watery light of four o'clock in winter. The sidewalks were cracked and uneven, strafed with puddles, and lined with weeds. Two kids were coming toward me with a dog. I wished I had a dog.

They looked poor; I pinched off gold earrings and jammed them into my parka pocket. I wondered if I could rent their dog. I didn't belong in their neighborhood, and we all knew it.

"Winnie!...Winnie!" I called. They stopped, and I explained I'd let my dog out of the car to go to the bathroom and she'd taken off.

"What does your dog look like?" they asked.

I described a very wonderful dog. Sleek and tan and white with luminous brown eyes. "What kind of dog is she?" said the black teenager with the runny nose and dreadlocks.

"Umm, mixed. All mixed up. This dog—Winnie—is any kind of dog you want to think she is."

I bent down to pet their scruffy German shepherd, and they

told me they'd look out for Winnie. I walked another fifty yards and saw the house twenty yards away. I started my calling at the house across the street. "Winnie!" I looked under a parked car and pleaded for Winnie to come out before I crossed to the location and started down the muddy driveway to the side of the house. The ice was only half melted because the sun hadn't reached it. The trees were leafless, pen-and-ink sketches against the paper white sky. My impression was of darkness, which doesn't make sense since it was just before noon. The driveway was rutted and my boots slipped; the crusts of ice were jagged and dirty, mixed in with mud. The house looked empty, but I didn't think it was. I was being watched.

"Winnie!... Winnie!"

I told myself that Winnie was the reason I was there and I had to keep believing it. Keep calling, keep looking for her. But I really wanted to just do what I had to do and get away from this dark, silent house. This was a game. I wasn't supposed to be here. But it was just a game.

Seven cars, four vans. Not visible from the street. Parked in ruts of mud and melting snow, with sprigs of anemic yellow grass poking through. I called, "Winnie!... Winnie?" again, and jingled the leash. I thought of my wonderful aunt Winnie, Mother's sister. Her name would be a talisman. I invoked her presence. Aunt Winnie, who arrived in Rome to visit me with suitcases and blank luggage tags. I suspected I would end up floating from country to country writing postcards, my suitcase with a little blank tag tied to the handle.

I felt vulnerable. Just me and the leash and someone watching. "Jersey. Whiskey. X-ray. Charlie. Seven-six-two," I whispered into my left breast. "Jersey tag. Charlie. Dog. Adam. Nine-one-four." The parka flopped open as I turned my back to the house. I dared to try the door of a white van. Couldn't stop myself. Locked. I wanted to get in. The windshield was cracked and looked like a giant crystal spiderweb. I thought of Lyndon and the salvage yard that summer day. I saw another van—red, with rust on the hood and a padlocked side door. Padlocked?

"Winnie!... Winnie, come out!" I dropped down on my knees and looked under a black car. "Jersey. Peter." I hesitated. "Umm. Uhhh...Underwear! Fred. Six-four-one." I glanced up at the sagging wooden back porch as I felt icy wetness seeping through the knees of my jeans. The upstairs windows were wide open. No curtains, no blinds, no shades. Black rectangles. "Winnie!... Winnie! Come on, girl!"

I stood up and swung the leash back and forth. It jingled. Again, whispering into my left breast. Two more vehicles and I was finished. I kept calling as I went up the drive, slipping in the soft muck.

I stopped to talk to a couple about my dog and her bad habit of running away. They were sympathetic and would look out for her. At last I was pulling myself up into the van beside Bobby, and he was grinning. "Ya got the whole neighborhood out lookin' for Winnie? Is that it?"

We laughed. "Ya see anybody? Signs a life?"

I shook my head. "But the house isn't empty. I was being watched."

Bobby looked at me. "Ya fall down?"

"No, I was on my knees looking under a van. You know how Winnie loves to get under things."

Bobby shook his head. "Shit. You were gone a long time. I was gettin' worried."

I pulled the recorder out of my pocket and pushed the "stop" button as he started the engine. Then I pushed "rewind" and then "play." I couldn't believe it. I watched the little wheels turn. Nothing on the tape. Dead air. I grabbed a paper from the dashboard and tried to remember a tag. Two tags. "Damn!"

Bobby took the tape recorder and with a thick index finger pointed at the "pause" button. "I'm so stupid I could die!" I had my head in my hands, bent over into my lap.

"Prob'ly happened when you put it in your pocket. What do you wanna do?" He was entirely calm.

I sat up and leaned back in the seat. "I have to do it again."

Bobby didn't say anything, but he had this look of "You're really going back?"

"Bobby, I have to. If we need the plates, then we need the plates." I was furious with myself, and I would not even consider walking into the office without what I'd been sent to get. The license plates meant we could check the registration, the owner, and the address. The information was often invaluable. "We're here. I'll just do it again."

Bobby started the van, then we did a flyby and saw that the house looked the same. We parked a few blocks away. "Ya know, C, if you have a bad feeling about this, don't do it. It's not worth it."

"Do we need the plates or not?" I asked.

He looked very worried as I rewound, pushed "start" and "record," and gently lowered the tape recorder into my pocket. I jumped out of the van again and slammed the door. This time I really felt watched. I took my time about getting there. The empty streets echoed with my cries of, "Winnie!...Winnie!"

I passed one little square, silent house after another. Finally I started down the drive again. Funny how much you notice the second time. Whether the vehicles had been moved since the last snowfall, footprints on the porch, my own prints, what must be the kitchen window—open beside the porch door. I was not alone. I whispered one tag after another into my left breast and then began my last round of calls for Winnie. I talked to her as I went up the drive for the last time, thinking it was more of an incline than I'd realized. "Come on, I can't look for you all day!"

I took another street to get back to Bobby, checking twice to make sure no one had followed me. Back in the van, Bobby and I listened to a few seconds of the tape and sighed with relief. We stopped at a little grocery store on the way to the turnpike, and Bobby came out with big turkey sandwiches. We gobbled them down in the front seat as we made jokes about leaving Winnie in Jersey. Bobby picked up the radio. "Hey, Five Oh, this is Six Eight Three. One Eighty-six got all the plates."

There was a crackle, then Mickey's voice. "Ten-four. You comin' back? Got somethin' on Broadway to check out."

They yakked for a few minutes as I swigged Diet Coke with my feet up on the dashboard. I tossed the leash into the back. I hadn't liked the feel of that house, but I didn't say it to Bobby. Maybe I was still overly concerned about being accused of being a novelist, or maybe I was still a little concerned about just being *a girl*. These men, in this office, would never say it—they were many stripes above those in the Vinny Parco office—but I didn't want to give them the chance to even *think* it. I wanted to be as good as the men were. All the time. Every minute.

Bobby and I were passing napkins back and forth and consolidating garbage into paper bags when I said, "Can you do me a really big favor?"

He turned in the big hat and said, "Sure, C. Anything. You got it." Big, good-natured, kind Bobby.

"Don't tell anybody about the 'pause' button."

He flashed me a snaggletoothed grin. "What 'pause' button?" He swallowed the last of his coffee, started the van, and in minutes Moby Dick was on the Jersey Turnpike roaring back to the barn.

*   *   *

I WAS WASHING MY hands in the bathroom, but I could hear Bobby telling Mickey that he was "fuckin' scared shitless when she didn't come back. Fuck! She went all the way into the very back of the lot, and I did a flyby but I couldn't see a fuckin' thing behind the house! Not her! Not anything! That is one long fuckin' driveway and she just—"

I came out of the bathroom. "Hey! You think it's easy trying to find an invisible dog?" I sat at my desk and rewound the tape. Everyone could hear my voice with tag after tag; I was writing them down so they could be backed out. All the men laughed when I got to "U" and said, "Underwear."

"That's the one I don't know. I don't know what you're supposed to say. Underworld? U is for Up? Ulysses? Upholstery?"

They clued me in, with much good humor. U is for Umbrella.

I DREAMED ABOUT THE house at 110 Eckton Street in Jersey City. It was shrouded in darkness. The dream was silent. My feet slipped, I waved my arms for balance like an ice skater. The worst part of it was realizing that Bobby was not waiting for me, that I was alone on a dark street in the driveway of the silent house with someone watching me from the black rectangle of an open window. It felt like my father.

THE PLATES I'D GOTTEN were run, and one came back registered to a familiar player on Canal Street. A link. A strong one. There was the usual pit work. There were stakeouts in Chinatown, some early morning flybys in Jersey City.

It was dog work. It was computer stuff, going through old

files. There were so few moments of glorious revelation, so little to get excited about. I longed for the "Eureka!" factor. There were seventeen other cases going on, a hundred other players being pursued, two hundred other leads being followed up. Sometimes they crisscrossed. Sometimes one of the men would shout as he came in and slammed the door, "You'll never guess!" and the news would be that he'd spotted certain boxes with certain labels being unloaded at a familiar address on Canal. Or an unrelated case would net the tidbit that somebody was married to somebody's sister and we'd know the whole family was deeply involved in whatever was happening at the house on Eckton.

There were scam calls when I took a deep breath and held up my arm so that everyone would know to turn off the radios, both music and two-way, and to keep quiet while I asked for people who didn't exist and pretended to be someone I wasn't.

Bobby and Mickey started doing garbage grabs at 110 Eckton at half past three in the morning. I would come into the office and one of them would be in the back of the warehouse, wearing rubber gloves and going through mammoth clear plastic bags. I volunteered to do it right along with the men, but they were very chivalrous about it, told me it was too shitty a job. I did it only once. The smell made me gag. Dozens of take-out food cartons every day and all the accompanying scraps of food, dirty Kleenex, tin cans, bottles. Everything the occupants of 110 wanted to throw out.

There is a slice of time after someone puts out their garbage and before the city comes to pick it up that is an okay period to make the grab. Some unspecified middle-of-the-night moment. We talked to lawyers on the phone and never spoke of dumpster diving or garbage grabs. It was "an abandoned property search."

Garbage grabs at the location continued night after night,

and the disgusting inspection of the haul went on morning after morning for weeks. It was late hours driving back and forth to Jersey in the van and the same early hours at the warehouse; Mickey started looking like a raccoon. There was talk of being seen, of close calls, of nearly getting stopped.

At the end of the workday, I might be pulling on a parka and counting quarters for the bus, thinking I had to hurry home to change so that I could meet someone at the Metropolitan for the opening of a new exhibit. Champagne in that open hallway with the fountains or drinks and hors d'oeuvres beside the Temple of Dendur by candlelight. Maybe a dinner party. Maybe a date. I'd strip off jeans and slink into black velvet trousers, a silk blouse, and jewelry. I'd trade my lace-up boots for peau de soie pumps. I'd leave Mickey and Bobby leaning back in their chairs and chain-smoking to the strains of Nashville's newest, waiting for their witching hour.

Once, Mickey asked me where I was going, and I told him to an art gallery. "Oh, getting artsy on us, are you?"

I shrugged. "What are you doing tonight?"

"I'm driving to another state to steal garbage."

I grinned back. "You won't believe me, but that's going to be more hilarious than what I'm supposed to do."

This was met by a raised eyebrow, then Mickey said, "Yeah, Charlie. Don't let the door hit you in the ass on your way out."

THE PIT WORK AT Parker's continued. One morning, a search of a particular bag of abandoned property netted watch parts. We'd struck gold! We'd counted on the occupants of 110 Eckton getting careless, and at last they had.

I felt a little pang when I realized 110 Eckton was a Born to Kill safe house. Nobody spelled it out, and I'd probably known it in some part of my mind from the very first but not wanted to know. These Vietnamese were tough. They dealt in arson, robbery, extortion, smuggling, kidnapping, murder. They tortured people. They ran Chinatown. They made counterfeit watches and took in millions of dollars per month. Tax-free, of course. I swallowed and thought, *God, I was naked that morning. A lamb to the slaughter while Bobby waited blocks away, safe in the van.* I'd always felt the men were protective of me. Well, maybe they weren't. Then I thought, *Hey, they think I'm up to this. Knew I wouldn't screw it up, lose my nerve, get burned. Maybe I am one of them.*

It was a day in May when a dozen of us got into vans and roared into Jersey. I won't get into the politics of what police force was there or how many men. We all wore bulletproof vests, and everyone was armed. I was carrying my Swiss Army knife. Five of us went around to the back as others rang the front-door bell. There were no vehicles today. The house appeared unoccupied, but in minutes we were squeezing past each other in narrow hallways and several frightened-looking Vietnamese were in handcuffs. I'd never seen anyone in cuffs before. It shocked me. It made me think of captured animals. The image of the thin figures being led down the rickety white wooden porch steps with hands behind them, heads down, is tattooed on my brain. String straight black hair like wet, shining ink in the sun. Helpless, arms behind them. I'd seen it a million times on television, but I wasn't prepared for what it really looked like. Prisoners of war.

My impression of the house was of it being carpeted— every inch of floor. Brown shag carpeting under our boots. Maybe to perpetuate the idea of warmth. Maybe New Jersey in the winter was truly horrible for these people from the tropics. Something mysterious with an unspeakably disgusting smell was simmering on the stove. I was assigned the task of going through every inch of the kitchen, looking for hiding places. The cupboard shelves were lined with cans of things I didn't recognize, and all the lettering was in Vietnamese. I kept trying not to inhale as the cauldron bubbled on a burner. Finally I turned it off, put a lid on it, and hung my head out the porch door, gulping fresh air.

Papers I found hidden in the refrigerator were seized as evidence. And wedged between the wall and the counter was an address book that would have to be translated; all the numbers would be backed out immediately before they could be disconnected or changed. We hoped to get associates from this—wholesalers, retailers, suppliers of parts, factory addresses, even the names of relatives would help us. I knew I'd be the one to enter all the information into the computer. The last address book from a raid had been written in pencil and smudged ballpoint. In three languages. I'd done all I could in English and French and then sat down with Sharif for hour after hour for a try at the Arabic.

Now Elbert brought in a portable photocopy machine and put it by the sink, and I fed it paper—copying page after page of documents as cops trooped in and out.

The house was alive with big men, big feet, big voices, and the crackle of radios.

I was told to go to the basement to help with inventory. Very steep wooden stairs led down to the factory itself. Dozens of workers had chairs and workstations. Not all of them lived in the house; most came in the early morning and left after dark. This explained the multitude of take-out food cartons. There were watches in all stages of completion and tiny metal parts in baskets and drawers. The counterfeit logos, by the thousands, had to be counted and bagged.

We were in the house for hours. Upstairs in bedrooms and bathrooms. Instructed not to open a drawer unless a cop was at your elbow watching you. Downstairs from the basement to the kitchen we swarmed, looking for possible hiding places. Two of the Vietnamese were seated on the sofa in the living room, being questioned. There was misery on their faces. Their English was limited. I listened and was surprised at how gentle the three police detectives were being. They were sitting down; nobody was towering over anyone. A soft voice, telling them to take their time, to tell him if they didn't understand. A lawyer was coming, a translator was on his way.

It was on the living room mantel that I saw the little Buddha illuminated by lit candles and small electric lights. They were red, blue, and green like Christmas tree lights, and I wondered if someone turned them on and lit the candles every morning or if they were an eternal flame of sorts. An eight-by-ten black-and-white photograph was propped in the nest of wires beside the statue. An ancestor? I wondered if the respectable-looking male Asian, photographed in glasses and suit and tie, had any idea what the living were up to. He looked totally IBM. Suddenly the perps began talking to each other excitedly in Vietnamese as an American voice said, "Hey, you guys, cool it. Hold on."

It felt entirely wrong to be standing in my boots and jeans in front of this delicate personal holy place. I took one last glance at the red plastic flowers in the brass vase and left the room.

A long day in what was no longer a dark house. At one point, I sat on the back porch railing in the sun and killed time with half a dozen cops. Nothing but a rutted backyard now. No vehicles. I thought of that day of calling for Winnie, the frozen mud, the pale yellow grass. The sun felt good on my bare arms in the short-sleeved shirt.

There was paperwork, frantic hurrying, and then there was the waiting—for a call on the radio or for the arrival of the translator. Everyone talked about the seizure being a success. Millions of dollars' worth of watches would never hit the street. The client was happy. We tracked the counterfeiters to their lair, found the goods, and arrested them. They knew they were breaking the law, and they chose to do it. So we put the perps in cuffs and hoped they'd get the slammer.

It's ridiculous that I still feel unsettled about it when I remember the handcuffs and the delicate little shrine with the Christmas tree lights. I wonder if I would feel less sorry for people arrested who'd had a crucifix on the wall. Or for giant blond Swedes. Immigrants. New country. Hoping for a better life. I think of Pete Hamill's great line, something about saving every penny in order to buy a bicycle to ride it in the snow delivering a pizza to a yuppie. I'd heard him speak, been moved to write him my feelings about immigrants, and he'd asked me to write something for the *Daily News*. Idiotically, so in love with being a detective, I hadn't taken him up on it.

Immigrants. The hot beds in Chinatown rented out eight hours at a time—three times every twenty-four hours—for a disgustingly high price that their fellow countrymen charged them. The sweatshops. Actually, the first one I saw was freezing, a bleak day in January, and the workers were up to their elbows in plaster and buckets of cold water. Making dolls that looked like a famous cartoon character. One Mexican woman worked as her teeth chattered. Sometimes the workers are locked in. I worry about fires. They don't speak English, are incapable of answering a phone. I feel so sorry for them.

You have to be tough, Charlie. You're here. It's an illegal watch factory run by Vietnamese. Don't forget that they run Chinatown. And don't forget how they run it. They're the bad guys and we got them. End of story.

That day was the culmination of thousands of hours of

putting details together, of following leads, of making con-
nections, of lost sleep. Not glamorous, not exciting. Plodding work measured in millimeters that might become a link
in a chain. Or the discovery of something very interesting
with no relevance whatsoever. Few obvious triumphs to do
more than grin about for that one minute, and then you put
your head down and start again.

I was sitting on the porch steps drinking a Diet Coke when
Bobby materialized and stood over me, a giant in cowboy
boots wearing his trademark Stetson with the turkey feather.
He was grinning. "Nothin' like an invisible dog, huh, C?"

My Own Bad Guys, Good Dancers

The bad guys. Elbert said it was cut-and-dried, black-and-white. I never felt that way. Not ever.

Generally, the Middle Easterners do the T-shirts and sweatshirts: heat transfer and embroidered. Factories with giant machines operating twenty-four hours a day, seven days a week. They also often manufacture handbags.

The Vietnamese deal with the watches. It wasn't at all what I thought at first: tiny elderly Asian grandmothers doctoring the watch faces in front of a blaring quiz show in their own living rooms as they drank tea—something for extra money in lieu of knitting. It was done in factories at a great rate, was very organized, and the coffers of the Born to Kill gang runneth over with the tax-free millions. Big business. Important enough to protect with any means possible—a threat of force, a show of force, or basic bloodshed.

Usually, the Koreans do the handbags, and sometimes there are drugs in the lining. That gets exciting. The drug dogs are pretty geared up and great fun to watch. But as somebody said so succinctly, "Why the fuck should we risk our fuckin' lives over fuckin' drugs! We're not the fuckin' DEA. Let's let them fuckin' deal with the fuckin' drugs!

We're not fuckin' paid enough to fuckin' deal with the fuckin' drugs!"

I wasn't paid enough to afford to go to the movies, but I was alive and I told myself I had finally found what I wanted to be. I wasn't in this for the money. None of us were.

Bad guys. I was in court one morning, wearing a disguise, as two Born to Kill leaders were sentenced. A husband and wife. The woman was wearing a jade green silk pantsuit and beautiful jade jewelry, and the man looked like a well-to-do businessman in a suit and tie.

I was told in the office, "Don't look like yourself or you'll be burned for Chinatown," so Mas tossed me Barbie's wig. Barbie was his actress wife. It was quite orange. I couldn't imagine Barbie wearing it. There was no orange in nature like this, no sunset in history to rival it. I'd been pulling it on as Mas sped toward Centre Street in rush-hour traffic. "How's this?" I'd turned at a red light to ask.

Mas shook his head. "Still look like you." I was dealing with a rubber band and a ponytail that wouldn't lie flat and had the ominous appearance of a brain tumor.

"Now what do you think?" I gave the wig a fierce downward yank and put on my big round reading glasses as an added barrier between me and the real world.

"Still look like you," said the Indonesian, calmly flipping on his blinker.

"You're lying to me!" I exploded. I was up on one knee and trying to look in the rearview mirror. Then I saw him smiling as he jammed on the brakes in front of the courthouse.

"Now, go!" he shouted. "You've got two minutes!"

I jumped out and ran up the white steps three at a time, hurried my way through a metal detector and a handbag search, and ran to the courtroom. The room was hot, the translators mumbled, and I kept leaning forward to hear. Several people turned to stare at me, but I thought it was because I—along with someone from customs, the lawyers, and the judge—was the only non-Asian in court.

The wig was in the style of Carol Channing's with the doorknob pageboy and the thick bangs. At one point I reached up and didn't feel any bangs, which was a cause for concern, but I had to keep taking notes. When recess was declared, I literally ran out to the ladies' room and gasped when I looked in the mirror. The screaming orange wig was as high as a Buckingham Palace guard's hat, way above my bare forehead. I looked like a very surprised woodpecker. One more leaning forward movement and it would have sprung right off.

The man from customs must have called Elbert because Elbert stared at me, brown-haired again, in the office later and said, "C, maybe the next time you go to court you could try to be a bit less conspicuous."

So these two leaders of the Born to Kill gang looked far more reasonable than I. Far removed from the black-garbed, tattooed, teenage tough guys of Canal Street. Their lawyer spoke about sacrifices made during the Vietnam War and the difficult decision to come to this country for a new life. Hardships. Struggles. I knew from Parker's research that they had vast property holdings and at least two enormous companies back in Asia. They were worth millions and millions of dollars. We at Parker's were afraid they'd just get on a plane to Hong Kong and be gone. No matter how high the bail—it was expendable. The black woman judge listened to their Jewish lawyer and was sympathetic enough to postpone the start of their very short sentences until after the Lunar New Year.

The Vietnamese couple did look civilized, attractive, law-abiding. Their clean-cut teenage son and daughter sat directly behind them. Were they honor students, or did they torture small animals? I stared at the small-boned, elegant, well-groomed woman and wondered if she was standing by her man because she loved him no matter what he did. Or did they have constant fights because she wanted no part of his criminal dealings? Was he forcing her to support him publicly? Elbert would later tell me that she was the mastermind, the really tough one who called the shots. On the bulletin board behind Mickey in the office there was a photograph of them drinking champagne, in evening clothes, beaming at the camera. Her hair was spiky short and glamorous, and she was wearing what looked like diamond earrings. But according to Elbert, their house in Jersey had blood on the walls. He'd seen it during the raid. On their bedroom walls.

Parker's lowest estimate of the couple's take from counterfeit watches was four million dollars a month.

THE ARABS COULD BE charming, and I could be charming right back. I'd been to Beirut, Damascus, Cairo, Tripoli, Algiers, Tunis—all over those countries and Morocco, too. I wore a hidden camera one morning as Chiefie waited in the car for me. One location after another. After the last one, I came out with a Cuban cigar. The Leb had taken it out of a drawer in a plastic sandwich bag and presented it to me. We'd had such a delightful conversation. I hated myself for having a good time with him, for taking his last Havana—as I photographed his face, his stockroom, his office, his shelves of samples, and every face of every worker.

"His last Cuban." I winced getting in the front seat beside Chiefie.

Chiefie was rather quiet, with a dry sense of humor, not seeking attention, and had lost about one and a half lungs to cancer. He knew the entire cast of characters, had worked for Elbert in the past, but was taking it easy now after the operation. Mickey trusted him, and somebody told me Mickey was the one who went to visit him in the hospital every single day.

Chiefie put down his own cigar as I handed him the camera. I let him take care of pushing the "power" button off and dealing with the battery pack as I lit up in the front seat behind the tinted windows.

THERE HAVE BEEN TIMES when I felt seduced by the very air I breathed—on a boat slicing through an ocean under a star-spattered sky or talking all night in a café—perhaps in English, which only the two of us understood—while the rest of the country slept the precious hours away. There've been times when I would feel— not think, but feel: *Oh, this is easy. I could live this way, with this man, could forget everything before yesterday afternoon.* But some barometer would swing wildly inside of me, and I'd feel my feet touch ground again. I'd realize I was wearing shoes after all, I'd thrust my hand into my bag and let my fingers touch the edge of my passport. The bad guys were a big part of all this.

The bad guys came with the territory, with my traveling alone. The adventure and the romance were tangled like perfumed silk scarves in a bureau drawer. Was the very foreignness of the terrain the romantic part, or were they? Which was the adventure? The bad guys were part of the kick, but being drawn into their world far away from mine was another segment of it. The sheer, fall-off-a-cliff excitement of possibility.

This is my temptation—the sweetness of the unknown, the slightly dangerous angle. It's alluring; I'll seek it out— like chocolate mousse on a menu.

One evening in Florence, a very handsome Italian invited

me for ice cream. I liked him, so I accepted his dinner invitation for the following evening. Marco traveled a great deal and was full of stories told in a halting way with a strong Italian accent. Mother taught me how rude it is to ask, as all Americans constantly do, "What do you do?" so I did not. The evening wore on. He suggested we drive to a special place for champagne. I had a pang getting into the car with him and tried to relax as we wound back and forth up the hillside in the dark. The lights of Florence were so far away that there were clouds between us and the city.

"Are you in town for the convention of designers?" I asked. His suit was elegant, his shoes, his tie. Florence was crowded with refugees from fashion shows.

"No. I am not."

The car was still climbing away from town. I surrendered. "What do you do? As an occupation? I know you travel."

"I sell. I sell things. I am a salesman."

"Oh! What do you sell, Marco?"

There was a long silence.

"Arms."

"You sell—arms?" What an odd way to put it. His accent. Had I heard correctly?

"*Sì*. Arms."

I dropped the subject. Poor man. No wonder he was reluctant to talk about it. Embarrassed. But the world certainly needed artificial limbs. This accounted for his spending time in places like Zaire, like Cyprus. Beirut. Cuba. Wars. Amputees.

Marco stopped the car and took my hand, and we walked for a few minutes through dew-covered grass to a clearing looking down at faraway Florence. There were two chairs in this open field and colored lights strung between poles; a white-coated waiter materialized once in a while from the trees behind us. We sat alone in the grassy clearing.

At one point, he began to tell me how arrogant Mobutu Sese Seko was. We laughed over the translation: the Cock Who Leaves No Hen Untouched.

Marco talked about Cuba, about Castro. Castro as a person, not as a political figure. Arms. Guns, weapons, bullets! Forget pink plastic arms. I stared at him straight on and sipped the champagne. Marco had sold weapons to everybody. He wasn't on anybody's side, not really. I asked him about Haile Selassie and Ethiopia. Had he sold arms to the Eritrean rebels? Oh, yes.

Marco and I had plenty of stories. I had darted away to Africa with the money my father had left me: a thousand dollars so that I could not contest the will and be given a child's share. Daddy'd thought it out carefully. He was in the habit of changing his will on prescription pads. Tuesday you were in, Wednesday you were out. Mississippi roulette. A slap from the grave, a sneer from the coffin. I didn't care. My ticket to Johannesburg cost nine hundred dollars. I happily quit my job with an advertising agency and broke my lease on the tiny 81st Street apartment and flew away with someone I'd fallen in love with a month before. We'd later split up in the Congo and I'd proceeded onward on my own. Marco had never been to West Africa and asked me to tell him about it. It had reminded me of the photographs of India in *Life* magazine I'd studied as a little girl. Sometimes in a squalid little flyspecked café, I'd see a brown claw plunge into my rice and then realize it was a two-fingered hand and that something was bumping my legs under the table. There'd be shouts as the *patrón* would sweep the lepers, scuttling on elbows and knees, out into the street with a big broom.

The night sky cleared but the air had a chill to it, so Marco gave me his jacket to wear. We looked up at the stars, drank champagne, and talked nonstop. It was nearly dawn when we went to his apartment so that he could make phone calls about his trip. Would I come with him? he asked me over breakfast in an elaborate art nouveau dining room as waiters hovered at our elbows. He was driving to Yugoslavia to make a delivery in a specially fitted Mercedes. "I am a king when I arrive in Belgrade. You will be my queen." They had wonderful ice cream there, he insisted.

I declined. I imagined being questioned by some grim Slavic authority under a bare light bulb. I could hear myself insisting that I thought this handsome raconteur sold artificial limbs. Or maybe we'd never get that far. Maybe the Mercedes would blow up, and so would we, gunrunning royalty, on some lonely stretch of road. Marco was sad. He gave me a box number to write to him but I never did.

I WAS ATTRACTED TO a tall, blond German in Kabul who went back and forth to Berlin on mysterious errands. He was a smuggler. We had picnics in the desert to get away from everyone because it was Ramadan and we were embarrassed to be the only people eating in the daytime. Fancy food catered by the chef of the capital's best hotel. We drank bootleg Scotch and danced all night in dark, fabric-draped tentlike places.

Years later, in Italy, Prince Alexander of Afghanistan would come into my apartment and leave notes on my mirror when my cleaning woman was there to let him in. His father, the deposed King, played backgammon all night in a villa outside Rome with a retinue of loyal Afghan courtiers. He was waiting to go home. I wondered where all the lines connected.

Gunrunners. I used to have dinner with one in Haiti at the Grand Hotel Oloffson. He was part black, part Cherokee, and wore white silk shirts open to the waist to expose his smooth, hairless, mahogany-colored chest festooned with gold chains. He played backgammon with Al Seitz, the hotel owner, under a palm tree by the pool all day. When he wasn't hanging around the palace waiting for an appointment with a Duvalier or a minister.

He also hung around a small, dapper intellectual who carried a walking stick and wore white linen suits that contrasted with his very black skin. Aubelin Jolicoeur. Aubelin hung around me. That was the trip when I wore only white dresses since it was the only suitcase of summer clothes I could find in my late night scramble to pack. I thought, Oh, how boring, but people assumed it was intentional and that I was making some sort of fashion statement. I liked Aubelin's quick wit, his elegant manners, his feathery kiss on my knuckles. He had a finely shaped head, high cheekbones, the whitest teeth, the blackest glittering eyes, and a tiny black centipede of a mustache. He'd lived in Paris, traveled everywhere, was sophisticated, a writer, a reader, a raconteur. Graham Greene had immortalized him as Petit Pierre in *The Comedians*. One evening after dinner on the porch of the Oloffson, I took his walking stick and twirled it like a baton as everyone, clutching drinks in their wicker chairs, applauded. The next morning, I was told in whispers by a Frenchman who'd lived in Haiti for years to please never do that again.

"Eef you 'ad dropped eet, bang! Eet contains one shot. Jolicoeur was close weez Papa Doc and now weez zee Bebe. Zair are many who would like to keel him."

I was told that Pierre, Aubelin's faceless driver, who lurked behind dark glasses and never smiled, was a bodyguard and Tonton Macoute. Papa Doc was gone, but his personal militia still existed, with carte blanche to terrorize. Pierre would materialize as I walked through the market. Sometimes I'd see his big black forearm and a scrap of his blue shirt as he raised a newspaper over his face or moved behind a woman with a basket on her head. I saw him everywhere though I never caught him looking at me. Aubelin laughed and said, "Absurd!" Of course he wasn't following me. Then in the next breath, he added, "I must be sure that you are very safe." I heard gossip, a few not so nice things about Aubelin's political past (or was it past?). He often materialized in the living room of the Oloffson, and there was music, dancing, and bantering as we stood at the bar.

One afternoon, when I had a cold, Pierre picked me up at the hotel and drove me to the big white house of Aubelin, which was up a steep hill above Port-au-Prince. It was filled with Haitian paintings. I was greeted with an embrace, a rum concoction, and much good cheer. He immediately offered to make love to me, but I told him I didn't think that would help my cold. He laughed then disappeared for a few minutes, returning with tiny bottles and carved wooden boxes. He put them all out on a low table. Aubelin was chanting to himself in Creole, and when I tried to speak he shushed me. He was convinced he could cure me with a little potion that he rubbed tenderly on my arms. I told him it smelled exactly like Johnson's baby powder. "It isn't," he assured me as he murmured incantations.

My cold was gone within the hour, and Pierre, silent behind the glasses like a black robot, drove me home. Tonton Macoute, I thought in the backseat as we wound down the hill lined with fuchsia bougainvillea. Every taxi driver was. Their currency was information, secrets. I clutched the bouquet of orange and yellow that Aubelin had given me. Haiti: a country of bright colors that lives at midnight all the time.

From the windows of my room at the Hotel Splendide one morning, I saw a small white house barely visible, nearly buried in vines and flowers, on the edge of the hotel property. I asked the maid who lived there and then asked a boy from the hotel to take my note to him. The boy returned with a note, in English, from Monsieur Alberti. I'd heard of him, late at night, over drinks at the Oloffson but had never imagined he might still be alive. The lined paper, folded twice, contained an invitation from him—a man who had escaped from Devil's Island fifty years before. Mr. Alberti was still incredibly handsome, even in his pajamas, even in his late eighties. The Corsican and I drank straight Scotch in the morning in rather dirty glasses in the semidarkness of his living room. We surveyed each other across a chess-board, which was the only bare surface to put the bottle on. Leaves grew over the open windows and blotted out most of the light; tendrils were creeping into the room and coil-ing around the battered furniture. It was as if nature were quietly plotting to one day consume the very house. There was that smell of bad housekeeping in the tropics: a mix of mildew and sweet green grass. Scarred, coming-unwoven wicker should have a scent, but it doesn't seem to. Half-filled cups of black coffee had been put down here and there and forgotten. Issues of *National Geographic* were piled nearly thigh high; their yellow spines were bright in the gloom. Books were everywhere. This broad-shouldered, white-haired man, with the profile of John Barrymore, had been to places I hadn't. I was on my James M. Cain glut and he'd read most of them, borrowed the ones he hadn't. When I left the island, we wrote back and forth by return mail and he sent me tiny black-and-white photographs from the 1930s. I cried in New York when he died some months later. The story was that he murdered someone. Several someones. A long time ago.

I thirsted to know what these men were like. What sort of man would murder someone? Could you ever forget you'd done it? Perhaps it was with you always, like a scar you glimpsed every time you changed your clothes.

*   *   *

I MET A TEXAN upon my arrival in the Tehran airport at five in the morning, and that evening he took me out for so much caviar that I finally had to push the shining black mountain of it away. Later, I had to push the gunrunner away. Those little silver spoons, me, Vodka, the arms dealer from Houston, and that fierce Iranian general across the table. How could I have known they would sit there and make weapons deals?

I didn't know those men were gunrunners—not in the beginning—and I don't recommend them as a category for dating or love affairs, but they do travel a lot and deal with the top people, and they will always offer you champagne. I would ask about morals and right and wrong during some stage of the evening but it did seem to be strictly business with them.

BAD GUYS. YOU NEVER know what sort of heart is beating under the expensive suit. I'd been living in Rome about a month when Paolo Venturini called and asked me to a party at his nightclub called Cappello a Cilindro, which means Top Hat. It was near the Tiber, tucked away in a narrow alleyway, elegant with a dark, beamed ceiling, a piano, and candlelight. I told him that three friends and I were celebrating my Australian friend's birthday, and he said to bring them.

I spent all afternoon in bed with a dictionary writing a script so that I would be able to say something in Italian. I had been sick and had my fingers crossed that my fever would go down. I did, in fact, feel much better as I knocked on the heavy wooden door. A little peephole was opened, and a brown eye looked out. Very speakeasy. The door swung open.

We four walked in, glittery and chic, which was a bit short of miraculous since we each lived out of one suitcase. Lea was blond, tan, and looked as if she had spent her life on a beach; Rona had copper-colored hair and was quietly pretty like Julie Andrews; and Lynn and I were the tallish brunettes. We were met with adulation as we entered the candlelit room, and I was amazed and delighted to be picked by the best-looking of all the men. John was Brazilian, with an English father and a Portuguese mother, over six feet tall in a pin-striped suit with dark hair and a dazzling smile. He was the guest of honor; it was his party. He said he was a diamond merchant and told me his father had offices in Rio, Johannes-burg, Paris, London, and on 47th Street in New York.

John spoke very good English—until the alcohol hit him—and was very accommodating when I asked if he had any diamonds to show me. He fished in his pocket and brought out an emerald the size of my third fingernail. Then he reached into his other suit pocket and brought out two square-cut diamonds and murmured, "They're so white. *Bianco*." I gazed down at them in his palm, breathless. John said that they were four carats each and then said something about points I didn't understand. I asked if I could hold them and felt the same sort of awe that you feel when a boy lets you hold his white mice for the first time. We transferred them gently from hand to hand in the semidarkness with everyone chattering around us and the band, called Mandrake, play-ing this really loud Brazilian music.

I'd been fighting the flu for four days and had an almost irresistible urge to pop the diamonds in my mouth and wash them down with champagne the way I'd been doing with aspirins every few hours. Instead I said, "Oh, please, drop them into the champagne and let's see what they look like. Oh, please!" But he wasn't as drunk as I thought and put the stones back into his pocket.

John and I flirted outrageously; he proposed to me in several languages between the news that he was the subject of an assassination attempt and this was why he had brought his avocado. I know "lawyer" in Italian is *avvocato*, but I always think of a bright green shining avocado, so I was drinking champagne wondering what good an avocado would do you in the event of an assassination attempt. John had a grip like iron and kept leaning behind me, with one arm around my waist, to confer with his "brilliant, intelligent, wonderful, genius" avocado, who was handsome but minuscule, with a wonderful suit and a hair transplant. John wanted to know if he and I could be married immediately—before dessert. These desperate conferences went on and on as Lea and I rocked with laughter. Meanwhile, the microscopic avocado was flirting with Rona. Men were in line asking us to dance, and we were waving them away.

John would hardly let me eat, so intent was he on holding my hands and proposing marriage amid declarations of wild attraction. He pulled me onto the dance floor where I faked the samba. I kept feeling how strong his hands were around my waist and telling him I couldn't breathe. We were laughing, we danced well together. Probably because I had no choice but to follow him.

The evening ended with too many of us squeezing into a tiny yellow Fiat taxi in a thunderstorm as I tried to disentangle myself from John. Alcohol had pushed us beyond silly but he seemed sober when he said he'd call me the next day for lunch.

But he didn't. I was invited to have lunch with Rona and Mariano, the microscopic avocado, who had turned out to be a very civilized, nice man. I asked, "But is he involved with diamonds, is he Brazilian, is he who he says he is?" And, "Are you his brilliant, wonderful, genius lawyer?"

"*Sì, sì, sì*. What did you think of him?" asked Mariano.

"I liked him, but…there was something I can't quite describe. He's a terrific dancer. But something about him almost scared me. Maybe it was because of the champagne." I didn't know how to explain it. "It was his intenseness." I thought of how he'd kissed me. "He held me so tightly, he was nearly hurting me."

Mariano poured the wine and we ordered. Then he looked at me and at Rona and said, "For the last forty days he has been in custody in prison in a small city on the Adriatic Sea."

"What!" Rona and I chorused, levitating off the banquette.

"But he had a wonderful, intelligent, brilliant, genius lawyer—"

"Mariano! *What* was he in prison for?" I insisted.

"Do you know the Rothschild murder case? They suspected that he murdered the two women."

Murder? I could scarcely breathe. The first week I'd been in Rome, I'd bought magazines that were full of only two stories: Natalie Wood drowning and the Rothschild murder. I'd sat for hours in my apartment flipping back and forth in the dictionary, trying to understand. I remembered photographs of the two women—one was divorced from a Rothschild, and the other was her companion. The car was discovered in the countryside. Then the bodies. Strangled.

Mariano took a sip of his wine just as something crashed to the tile floor. He dived under the table and retrieved his revolver. Rona began to scream, "What are you doing with a gun?" and he was explaining that he had permission because he was a criminal avocado. Mariano was constantly dropping his gun in restaurants. He hated putting it on the chair next to him while he ate, and it was always a problem for him.

"Why did they think he did it?" I practically whispered.

"Because a woman friend of his went to the police and

told them that he had told her that he killed the two women."
Mariano was calm.

"But I thought he lived in Brazil."

"No, he lives outside Milano. He cannot live in Brazil
because the police want him there for something else."

"What else!" I hissed as food was placed on the table.

Mariano took a bite of the prosciutto. "For a transition."

This turned out to be impersonating another person. I
couldn't reach for my fork, and Rona was still speechless
over the discovery of the gun. I could only think of John's
hands, his grip. "But was the party in honor of him?"

"*Sì*. He gave the party for himself. It was a celebration of
release."

"Where is he now?" asked Rona.

"He left for Brazil this morning."

"But you said he couldn't go back to Brazil!" This was
getting impossible to understand.

"But he did go back." Mariano put his crossed wrists on
the tablecloth. "With the *polizia*."

"Oh," Rona and I gasped, practically rising off the banquette again. "In handcuffs!"

Mariano said, "In Brazil he gets six months for the transition, and here he will get at least thirty years for the murder." He swallowed wine. "Six months is better."

I leaned forward and breathed, "Then he did it! You mean
he did it!"

The microscopic avocado closed his eyes for a count of
three, then opened them and sighed with immense dignity.
"I can discuss this no further."

Rona and I were silent for a moment, absorbing all the
news, and then she turned to me and said, "At least you
know why he didn't call you."

The Crow's Nest

After a thousand nights of couch surfing, I signed a lease for an apartment on the Upper East Side. In the past three years, I'd lived on Fifth Avenue across from the Met, at 1000 Park and at 1100 Park, in Murray Hill on Madison Avenue, just off Fifth on 12th Street in Greenwich Village, in the oldest hotel in the Western Hemisphere in Santo Domingo, and in a lovely blue-and-white-tiled house in a Portuguese fishing village. Three countries. That's leaving out Turtle Creek with Mother, which seemed like a fourth country. Signing a lease was a commitment because returning to Rome was always in the back of my mind. Now I would live in one room and sleep on the floor, but it was *my* room and *my* floor.

Two detectives helped carry my few belongings up the three flights of stairs, and I called the warehouse in Italy and wiped away tears as I told Signora Oriana to send my possessions by ship. We were both sentimental. For me, it meant giving up the fantasy of another penthouse overlooking the Tiber. She said, "Oh, we will miss you!" with a catch in her voice. I was told that they used to scream in the office when an envelope with green ink arrived, and they'd pass it around and read the note with my storage money. This had gone on for seven years. I always sent currency in the country of wherever I was: British pounds sterling, Cypriot pounds, pesos from Santo Domingo, escudos from the Portuguese fishing village. And the money never got lost.

The following month, all my books and diaries, seashells from Capri, Haitian paintings, and lamps with the wrong plugs arrived, and I was settled and happy up in the crow's nest.

The sleeping bag itself I did not consider a hardship but saw it as a practical measure. It was because my books and paintings simply took up so much space. Even though I'd double-backed my books on the shelves, the walls were literally closing in. I'd had a few parties—one a birthday party for Casanova—and most people assumed that we were standing in my living room with a bedroom or two beyond. Sometimes I moved the bag under the window and fell asleep beneath the moon that showed itself between the tall buildings on Third Avenue. Sometimes I would lie under the Venetian chandelier and pretend the twinkling pendants were stars and that I was an Indian on the plains or a cabin boy a hundred years ago, crossing the Atlantic sleeping on deck, two days east of Newfoundland. Sometimes I fell asleep imagining I was on the all-night Geneva-to-Rome train and would waken in Italy on a bright yellow morning or that, more realistically, I would be prodded awake at Domodossola and have to fumble for my passport. I picked my countries and the cities I might wake up in, so I seldom minded the sleeping bag and resisted all efforts of friends to give me beds, futons, or foldout contraptions. In the summer, I discarded the bag entirely and slept on a woven mat from Canal Street, the sort of thing one uses on the beach. I was so comfortable on the wooden floor that when I was sent to hotels on a case, I'd end up on the carpet, like a puppy, beside the queen-size bed.

The building was narrow with high ceilings and very crooked stairs, occupied by three male tenants and me. My friends said they always felt they were visiting me in another country.

Hayko, an Armenian from Istanbul, sold and mended rugs on the second floor in space overlooking Lexington Avenue. Stephan, who was French, had the only apartment on the second floor and faced the back. Marvin, a New Yorker, had a studio apartment on my floor; his faced Lexington, and mine overlooked the terraces of the town houses on 65th Street.

Marvin was a fabulous neighbor. We never knocked on each other's doors but left notes written on little scraps of paper for each other, as in, "Did your skylight leak last night?" When I'd finished my *New York Times* every morning, I'd put it out in front of my door, and it disappeared, as did all my read magazines. Marvin was opinionated on the staircase about the latest local news but I never knew anything about his life—past or present. He was the perfect person to have across the hall.

After a long day at Parker's and two buses home, I would climb to my aerie and feel paralyzed with fatigue. Sometimes I would lie in a bubble bath until the water got cold; other evenings I would fall into a Chinese Chippendale chair and eat Carr's water crackers spread with Dijon mustard by candlelight.

The phone would start to ring. Sharif would call and tell me his dreams of becoming a C.P.A., interspersed with his latest premonition of violent death in Chinatown. Mickey would call. There was always water running in the background, the clink of glass. It was like talking to a scientist in his laboratory. Who knew what Mickey did in Greenwich Village? Mas would call. Then they'd call each other and then would call me back to say they had spoken to the others and report what had been said. They'd be calling Bobby, who was at the office with Warner. We all agreed that things were at the all-time worst regarding Elbert Parker Thatch. We never imagined things would or could actually get worse.

Sometimes, especially the night before a raid, I'd drug myself with Benadryl to sleep. I'd be too wired to even close the mud browns. Now, when sleep came to me in the crow's nest I was often in dreams doing what I did in daylight: speeding through the Holland Tunnel in a car with one of the men or pushing open the door of a factory with no idea what I'd find when I stepped over the threshold.

Sweet Talk

The warehouse was like an oven, even though the air conditioner wheezed valiantly on "high." The unit hung over the door of the Southern Office and timed its drips to splok me on the head whenever I passed under it. The room was airless, and Warner needed a bath.

Mickey was on the phone with a detective in Jersey, discussing a hijacking of designer goods. The Genovese family in New York has to give permission for any truck to get hijacked in New Jersey, so the investigation had spun off into the world of organized crime. I was drinking a Diet Coke, typing up a report, and listening.

Bobby was concentrating on one of his handheld puzzles, and Vinny was fighting with his wife on the phone. Gerald's voice crackled on the radio, "I'm goin' in the hole."

Nobody answered him because nobody cared. He was on the shit list—suspected of taking T-shirts out of the back.

Gerald was called the Polish Prince or the Frog because of his very wide-set pale green eyes and his slicked-back blond hair. He would arrive from Jersey with fanfare, always radioing ahead that he was "goin' in the hole" and then "outta the hole" so we could track his progress entering and leaving the Holland Tunnel, when radio contact would be lost. His favorite belt buckle was festooned with a turquoise the size of a goose egg. He'd get going in that raspy voice with those little green eyes darting around behind the aviator glasses, and sometimes he'd quickly swipe his blond hair with a tiny black Ace comb.

"New boots," he said once, lifting his foot and smiling proudly. "Python—$89.95. The Philippines. Can't get 'em here, but over there they're not endangered. They're like rats. They got so many uv'em. When I buy these boots I'm doin' a good thing, an envirah-mental thing for those people over there. I'm helpin 'em out."

Gerald had helped them out to the tune of three pairs, one in each color: gray, baby blue, and a pinky tan. The Polish Prince detested Elbert. One minute he'd call him dickhead, then he was numbnuts, and then Gerald would say, "He's got no balls." *Is all this possible?* I'd wonder.

Gerald is rumored to be on medication, which sounds ominous enough, but what is worse is no one seems to know what sort of medication. It was commented upon only when he forgot to take it. Everyone thinks he is crooked, would rob the wallet off a dead man, but I think anybody who stays up late the night before a seizure baking brownies can't be that bad. At seven in the morning, he'd be wearing a flak jacket and sitting, while we waited for orders to mobilize, in the backseat of a parked car with the door open and a pan of brownies on his lap, slicing them up with a dagger that looked like the one in *Psycho*. Snakeskin boots in evidence, gun on his hip, he'd complain about something in that raspy voice. His brownies were divine. I would hang around gabbing, leaning on the open door, looking nervously at my watch, anxious for action, and he'd feed me.

"Outta the hole," crackled Gerald's voice on the radio as Elbert buzzed down and asked me to come up and see him. I never knew what he'd have to say. The best would be a new case, something tricky, I hoped. The worst possibility would be preparing the next shared cost proposal, which meant that the cost of a seizure was to be divided by every client whose stuff we grabbed. Everybody but Elbert knew this didn't work.

I went up the bloodred stairs two at a time and entered the Executive Suite. It was cooler, and the air didn't smell since the secretaries made Elbert and Tom smoke in the hall. He was on the phone in his book-lined cubicle, absentmindedly pushing a skinny black cigar back and forth on the blotter, dying to light it. He hung up and we adjourned to the stairway.

"This came in today from Eagleton and Adams. It's not a counterfeit case, but one of their top attorneys asked me if we could help." He handed me a fax, and I began to read under the hanging, naked light bulb.

"So basically all they want is to find out if Allscas Countertrade and Consulting Services is okay for their client to invest in?"

"That's it. What you don't see there is what Andy told me on the phone. The client has three million dollars in mind."

"Wow." I sighed. "I'll check it out."

I went downstairs, flopped into my desk chair, and flipped open the file.

"What did Elbert want?"

"New case?"

All the men wanted to know. Curiosity in a detective, as one may imagine, is off the charts. If you didn't finish a sentence or said, "Oh, never mind," they'd go crazy until you clued them in.

"Just checking out a company for an investor." I smiled. "I've got the D&B." They all groaned, because the Dun & Bradstreet means nothing; the company itself supplies all the information.

I started with the chief executive—one Larry Rhinewald.

Through the computer, I found that his home address was in Payson, New Jersey. A completely unblemished past. He did have a driver's license issued in Missouri. A link?

The law firm had also sent a copy of a contract "and agreement of cooperation" with a Melinda B. Pugh and a Wallace Watkins as being able to perform certain commodity transactions for their client. Pugh and Watkins had the same address in St. Louis as the Allseas Countertrade firm, though that name was not mentioned. So there were two more names to check out. Watkins had a link to Florida according to another document, so I flipped open the phone book and started calling every Florida area code for a listing. No go. "Could be a nonpub, Charlie," said Mickey as I put down the phone. "Call James, see if you can rouse him."

James was in his twenties, chalk pale, rail thin, with a ponytail; a bar code was tattooed on one wrist. He looked very nineteenth century, even in jeans and a sweatshirt, and would arrive at the office, like a doctor, to specifically work certain cases since he was a whiz with the computer and the phone. People at NYNEX thought he actually worked there. The word was he'd already served time as a teenager for an amazingly successful credit card scam, but I also heard that the judge had given him probation.

James was trying to get off smack, had disappeared again.

"Call Pedro Santiago, that P.I. in Florida's pretty good. He'll find it."

The circle was widening. I put Watkins in Pedro's hands in Miami, so it was time to get closer to Melinda B. Pugh. She had to be in the St. Louis area if she worked in that office. There were two Pughs in St. Louis, but no initial "M." I called thinking I could ask if they were related. I didn't want to talk to Melinda—just find out where she lived and go on from there. Both numbers had answering machines.

I then found twenty-nine Pughs in Illinois and Missouri, at least that many in Maryland, and lots more sprinkled in several states. I called a Pugh in Cheyenne, Wyoming, when I found that the company was incorporated there. Maybe she had a house there, a vacation place. The Mr. Pugh in Wyoming had never heard of a Melinda Pugh.

It was Friday. The upstairs office was dead quiet in comparison to the Southern one. I kept waiting for the purr of the fax machine to signal the arrival of information or at least the phone number of Watkins from Santiago. Rhinewald, because he was listed as the principal on the D&B, could be the key to all this: "Born 1925. 1980–83 employed by a Saudi conglomerate. 1943–77 active as a United States naval officer."

Yet why did I feel the key player was Melinda Pugh? I kept picking up the phone and dialing one Pugh after another in Missouri. Answering machines.

At noon, Mili had paychecks ready. White envelopes with our agent numbers on the front. Everybody, including Mili, bolted out the door in a stampede to get to Elbert's bank on 23rd Street; I stayed in the office to answer the phone.

On Fridays, unless we had a seizure, the place folded early. Bobby would be in his red truck with the giant sponge dice hanging from the rearview mirror and off to Pennsylvania before two. The Roast Beef Twins had been gone since noon.

In between answering Parker calls, I dialed Illinois and Missouri.

One Mrs. Pugh mentioned a restaurateur in San Francisco. Within an hour, I had read various clippings concerning the famous fish house overlooking the Bay and then the obituary of Sonny Pugh, the owner. No widow, daughter, or daughter-in-law named Melinda.

I dialed again.

"So you think Melinda might be married to your husband's cousin?" I asked the next Pugh. "Would you give me—if it's not too much trouble—could I have his number?... Yes, it would be terrific. My sister went to school with her—oh, it was University of Missouri—they were roommates. This is a surprise party I'm organizing."

The phone rang and rang at the cousin's house, and a woman picked up. Melissa, not Melinda. "I'm so sorry to have bothered you. I just had the most delightful conversation with the wife of your husband's cousin... Yes, Sybil... Yes. She's fine. Home with the flu. Not teaching today." I listened; I was amicable. "Well, I have had such a good time talking to you. And you've never heard of a Melinda Pugh?"

I wanted every Pugh to think I was just a housewife sitting in my kitchen with time on my hands, in between dropping off kids at school, and picking them up for soccer practice and piano lessons. I was getting so involved in my own little scenario that I could squint and see my avocado green wall phone, the gingham curtains, and I was starting to smell the pot roast. Then *brrrrrrg!* The Parker's phone would ring. "Oh, Melissa, could you hold on just a minute? I'm answering the phone at my husband's office today..." I pushed "hold."

"Parker Investigations... No, he's not, but I will take a message for Mr. Thatch...

"Melissa, I'm so sorry! My husband's selling his outboard, and the ad went in today's paper. So, you've never heard of a Melinda Pugh?"

I HAD ALL MY notes at home and began again on Sunday afternoon. I watched a Hitchcock movie in between phone calls, dialing only during a commercial.

I can't remember which Pugh it was who told me about

the family reunion. Harvey, I think. He had a thick southern drawl, and I chimed right in. I practically told him I was "cookin' up a mess a catfish fer supper," and we got along just fine. It got dicey for a minute because I was no longer looking for my sister's college roommate but was now married to Jonathan Pugh and looking for a cousin. Funny that no one had heard of Jonathan. Had I married a black sheep? Well, he was adopted, I found myself saying. No one had heard of his parents, either. I had to stop doing this. *Why did I do this?* I screamed silently. My voice was calm, relaxed, but inside I was exploding with personal recriminations. Something in me loved changing the story on myself. It kept it interesting. When I got really involved, truly sucked in to my own play, I had no idea what was going to come next. It was like throwing rocks up into the air in a dark room and wondering which one would come down and hit you in the head. It was like going faster and faster on a bicycle and then deciding it was the time for no hands.

Was it the same part of me that used to start a page at the bottom, try to read it line by line going up, and guess what the beginning would be? No point to it. Idiotic. Just to do it.

Harvey Pugh asked me if my husband and I were going to the reunion. I said I hadn't heard a word about it. "You know, there are two lines of Pughs—one is in Maryland and the other is out here in Missouri and on into Illinois. We're gettin' everybody, all of 'em, together next summer for a weekend on the Eastern Shore a Maryland."

"I'll call Sharon Pugh in Evanston—you said she's the chairman?—and get the details. At least get my name put on the list... Yes, it's a good idea," I told him. "I think Jonathan would like to feel connected again. And I married into this big family and know hardly anyone! I'll call Sharon and maybe I'll see you there next summer."

I took her number and waded through friendly good-byes, but I'd already hung up on Sharon's answering machine two minutes before.

May 12–14 in Maryland. Next year. I circled the date in green ink and picked up the phone again.

I was thoroughly tired of the Pughs. I went running, took a shower, and, in a big terrycloth robe, looked over my notes again. I needed to think of something else, so I put them away, pulled on jeans and a T-shirt, and opened *The Memoirs of Casanova*. My hero, my irresistible, adorable, great Venetian adventurer. Most people just think of his liaisons with women, and he certainly devoted time and energy to women, but he was a scholar, a traveler, a gourmet, a wit, a raconteur, a diplomat, a spy, and, yes, "a victim of [his] senses."

I read for a few hours.

The man who intends to make his fortune in this ancient capital of the world must be a chameleon susceptible of reflecting all the colours of the atmosphere that surrounds him—a Proteus apt to assume every form, every shape...as cold as ice when any other man would be all fire...

Venice. New York. Chameleons. I put the book down. It was only nine o'clock, so I dared to call another two Pughs in other time zones. When I went to bed, I dreamed I was having dinner with Casanova, but a gondola was waiting and someone kept calling my name from the canal below. I had to take a last sip of wine, fold my napkin, excuse myself, and leave the table. I wakened in my sleeping bag, horrified that when I'd stood up to say good-bye I'd been wearing boots and jeans.

Monday morning, I went into the office and headed

straight upstairs. Yes, a fax from Santiago had come in early Saturday morning: "Wallace Watkins resides at 1231 Pine Lane in Vega, Florida. His telephone number is nonpublished and is listed to Darryl Hanes; the number is 555-2374."

I looked at my watch and snapped up the receiver. No radio, no dog, no jokes, only Mili arguing on the phone thirty feet away about when we'd pay the Con Edison bill. It was eerily businesslike upstairs.

"Mr. Rhinewald?" I said in a friendly voice.

"Uh, no, this isn't...uhhh," answered a male voice.

We sparred for a few minutes.

"I'm sorry, I must have gotten my phone numbers confused." Silly me. "So this isn't the residence of Larry Rhinewald? Would I be able to find him in the office of Allseas Countertrade?"

"Actually," said the male voice, "this is a branch office."

"A branch office?" That had not been in any of the papers. For some reason, this man wanted to keep talking. *Okay, but be dumb*, I told myself. *Cute and dumb.* "I'm so mixed up! Is this Florida?" I asked innocently.

"Yes." He laughed. "It certainly is. I'm looking out over a big blue ocean and the sun is out and it *is* Florida!"

"But you're not...Mr. Rhinewald."

"No. I'm Wally Watkins. Larry's flying to St. Louis this afternoon. You just missed him."

"Oh, I see. So you do know him. I'm not entirely crazy."

He laughed again. "Not entirely! I like that!"

"Well, then you know Melinda Pugh?" I held my breath. Would this be when alarms went off and he squinted and thought, *Who the hell is calling me?*

"We're partners. The three of us. Melinda's in the St. Louis office all the time, but Larry and I avoid St. Louis when we can. I prefer to be exactly where I am, looking out at the ocean."

"It sounds beautiful." We made small talk for a minute or two more, and then I said, "Do you know Darryl Hanes?" I was terrified Darryl would get on the phone, and then what would I do? But I had to know if he was part of this or merely the owner of a rented house.

I dared exhale when Wally said he didn't know him. I believed him. So throw Darryl Hanes out of this. Move on. "I'm taking up your whole morning," I said. "Do you think I could reach Mr. Rhinewald tomorrow in St. Louis at the Allseas office?"

"Let me give you that number. You won't find him there, but Melinda will know how to reach him." There was a pause. I could hear him thinking, deciding what to do. "Let me go ahead and give you his home number. This is in New Jersey. Try that. You'd have better luck."

Wally Watkins. What an affable, trusting soul. He'd never even asked my name or what I wanted! I checked the phone numbers in my notebook and smiled. He'd given me numbers I already had, but this was confirmation.

Mei Ling, our Indonesian secretary, handed me three pages. She's good, knows what she's doing. "Nothing for Wallace Watkins in Florida," she said. "No credit rating, and nothing showed up on the surname scan."

"Thanks. What about liens against Allseas?"

"Nothing. No liens or judgments against it. No litigation, no default anywhere in the United States." She paused. "You asked me to check Missouri and Florida and New Jersey, and there is no record of it in those states."

The link to Wyoming, we decided, was just that it was incorporated there.

Elbert stood over my desk and asked how it was going. The stale smell of tobacco surrounded him. "There are odd little things, but nothing full-scale hokey," I told him.

I scribbled arrows from name to name. Melinda in Mis-

souri, Rhinewald in New Jersey, and Watkins in Florida. I
asked Mei Ling to do a surname scan for each of them in
each state, then a check of judgments and liens against each
one in each state.

Nothing.

I tried calling more Pughs and then attacked the answering machine callbacks. At one o'clock, Mas and I walked
down to the Moroccans' place on Tenth Avenue and ordered
couscous. The afternoon sped by as I tried to reach every
Pugh on my list.

Upstairs, I had time to observe Elbert, to listen to his
phone calls if Mili wasn't on the phone, if Mei Ling wasn't
on the phone. Elbert had a soft, rather cultured way of
speaking. He was an actor, after all. He could handle the
lawyers but not the cops, which was what Mickey did so
well. Elbert's grandfather or great-grandfather had been a
federal marshal somewhere in the Midwest, and this plainly
fascinated Elbert. There was great romance in the man. I
found it difficult not to like him, even when he was unfair to
me and fighting with Mickey—I thought Mickey was right
and Elbert wrong ninety-nine times out of a hundred.

Demon rum was killing Elbert. He was having black-
outs, disappearing for hours, not showing up for meetings,
not remembering things. Tom was his chortling ally in this.
Elbert was married to Ada, whom I never met. She was an
artist, an illustrator of books. Once I was dispatched to pick
up a portfolio and then encouraged to look through it. I had
been impressed. Another time I had to call her for Elbert
and leave a message that he'd be late. I dialed the number he
shouted at me and got a message machine with a woman's
voice who announced that you could leave a message for
Guinivere. I hung up and asked him to repeat the number.
"Oh, she calls herself Guinivere sometimes," he explained.
"Call back."

Mickey told me Ada was a witch. She was often asking Elbert to tell one of the men to go to the "witches' store" on 17th Street to buy supplies—unusual herbs and ugly roots that came in dusty bottles with corks. Who knew what Ada/ Guinivere was up to? Who knew what Elbert was really like? He could have been good-looking if he'd cleaned himself up. He had a good sense of humor. I saw him every day, but I can't say that I really knew Elbert. There were stories he was bisexual, that he was deeply involved in pharmaceuticals, rumors he was reselling counterfeit goods we'd seized. Who knew?

The day wore on as I called Pugh after Pugh.

I lay awake that night. What exactly did Allseas do? What was it supposed to do? If I didn't know that, then how could I ever prove Pugh and Watkins and Rhinewald weren't doing what they were supposed to be doing? Sugar, commodities, futures. I knew exactly how to approach this now.

The next morning, I went into the office at half past seven, slamming the door behind me. Everybody there, the radio on, the place gray with smoke. Warner was slitty-eyed, half-asleep on her L.L.Bean cushion. Elbert blew smoke out of his nose. "How's the Allseas investigation going?"

"It's probably a legitimate company, but it's...odd. I had a long conversation with Watkins yesterday in Florida, and he confirmed that he and Rhinewald and Melinda work together. He gave me the office number in St. Louis and Rhinewald's home number. Melinda is—she's difficult to find. Mei Ling's been doing wonders on the computer, but Melinda is still eluding me." She was in the office in St. Louis, but I couldn't call her there yet. I took a swig of Diet Coke. "I was lying in bed thinking last night..."

Vinny said, "Uh-oh, trouble."

"What do you think about my calling a friend in the commodities business and—I won't tell him any names—just asking him how this company should be operating? He might know how a company like this is regulated."

"Sure, go right ahead," said Elbert. "Think he'll be in the office now?"

"He's in the office now." I hesitated. "There's just one thing, Elbert."

"What's that?"

"He's in London."

Mickey and Vinny and Bobby grinned, but I have to hand it to Elbert. He took a draw on the skinny black cigar and said, "So?"

"He used to be the head of the Commodities Exchange in London, so he knows all about this. Don't worry. I won't be on long. I won't talk about the weather..." I was nearly out the door. "I'll go upstairs."

David sounded happy to hear from me. We'd met years before, and he always let me stay in his elegant mews house near Harrods when I was homeless in London. Every January, he would track me down to wish me "Happy Birthday." Once I'd even been fished out of the studio at Vatican Radio. I had always adored him. How many London art gallery openings had we been to— from the Tate to Malcolm Innes's on Walton Street, with the garden and the Buck's fizz? How many times to the ballet? How many dinners at Montpeliano? The black-tie parties. The afternoon I had to take a cab practically all the way to Heathrow to yank an evening dress out of a suitcase in storage. What hilarious fun at the dinner dance. And afterward, past midnight, walking home through Hyde Park in the summer storm, laughing our heads off, drenched to the skin. Tigerskin rugs, champagne. His stories of the tea plantation in India. Red cummerbunds in West Africa. Cummerbunds twenty feet long ironed by fawning servants.

"So how's my favorite detective?" he teased. "Shall I call you Sherlock?"

The case seemed to appeal to him. "There are two kinds of commodities," he told me. "One is trading on the commodities exchange, being registered and regulated." I was writing down every word. "The other hinges on 'countertrade,' which is a polite way to say bartering. Eastern Europe has a lot of this going on nowadays." He paused. "Let's say steel for beans. There is no registering and no regulation for this countertrading." He stopped. "Is this good for you to know?"

"Absolutely. Tell me more."

"Okay, Charlie, as for your company...it doesn't sound like it's countertrading, so it should be registered and regulated by the Commodity Futures Trading Commission in Washington and/or the National Futures Association."

"So I can simply call them up and ask. Sounds pretty straightforward to me." I looked at my notebook and drew a square around the CFTC.

"Do that, but also—let me give you a couple of names. There's Bill Dayton of Barringer Commodities and Larry Armstrong, who is head of trading in physical sugar for my old firm. He's good. He'd love to talk to you. And...why don't you call Ian Stephenson, who's the chief trader for Marston Incorporated?"

I scrawled down all the numbers, delighted. "I'm on the right track now, David. This is terrific. You're terrific."

A happy laugh from London.

"How'm I ever going to repay you?"

Another happy laugh from London. "I'll think of something."

I saw Elbert approaching me across the room. "I'd better say good-bye. The client's paying for this. I'll let you know what happens."

We traded fax numbers and hung up.

I tried the Washington agencies and kept getting record-

ings, but at last I reached the Coffee, Sugar and Cocoa
Exchange and was told Allseas was not registered with
them. I turned to the three experts in commodities and
told one man after another that our mutual friend David
had given me their names. They were charming, delighted
to talk to me, invited me to dinner. None of them had ever
heard of the company or of any of the three partners. Bill
Dayton thought it hilarious that a retired naval admiral was
the chief executive. Ian Stephenson said in amazement, "And
you mean that two of the three partners aren't even in the
St. Louis office?"

I learned that there are only about a dozen or so companies
involved in this field. Elbert walked over to the desk I was
using and asked how it was going. "It seems that this is a very
small fraternity. They all know each other. It doesn't seem to
matter whether it's a small company or a large one—a small
one can be reputable—it's just that even a small company
countertrading in sugar would be known to them." I looked
down at my notes and read aloud. "It would be very surpris-
ing to see a company like this doing business bona fide in the
domestic or the international sugar business. They—Allseas
Countertrade—are not part of the sugar community."

Elbert smiled but said nothing. The investigation was
moving forward, or at least I was drawing circles around it. I
imagined myself homing in on the center.

I dialed St. Louis directory assistance. Should have done
this immediately. "No listing for Allseas Countertrade and
Consulting Services? Is there a listing for anything beginning with Allseas?" I was stunned.

Stuck. I still had only Melinda Pugh's name and her office
number. Absolutely *nothing* else. I closed my eyes and listened to the traffic noises of Tenth Avenue. Elbert was soothing a client, Mili was skillfully placating a bill collector.

There was no trace anywhere of Melinda Pugh. Still didn't

know what the middle initial stood for, and she seemed to
have no driver's license, no debts, nothing. That damn office
she was in wasn't even in the phone book and had two absen-
tee principals out of three!

I stood at Mei Ling's desk wondering what I'd overlooked.
She was running a plate for Mickey. "If I had her soash number, we could find her," I said, staring into space, talking to
myself.

I went back to the desk I was using and ruffled through the
pages Eagleton & Adams had sent over. I picked up the phone
and called the building manager of where Allseas rented. Yes,
they would act as a reference for Allseas. "They've rented that
space for, let's see, eleven years. Melinda Pugh is our contact
there. No problems with the company."

I confirmed that it was suite 1502 and thanked her.

"And who did you say you were?" she asked as I was making my good-byes.

"My name is Lydia Steadman. I'm calling from Clayton
Office Equipment. Allseas will be leasing equipment from us."

Oh, yes, this was fine. We hung up. Vinny Parco had
taught me to never leave anyone feeling strange. Don't let
them wake up in the middle of the night and think something was wrong with that call today. Tie up the loose ends.
Be kind.

I wanted to fly out to St. Louis, take a taxi downtown,
go to the address, and knock on the door. How big was the
office? Who was there with Melinda? The D&B said fifteen
employees. I bet not. Asking that woman for square footage
would have been pushing it just one millimeter too far. I had
felt I had to stop with her.

I went downstairs and listened to the men carp about
expenses and then walked down the street to Poppy's to get
a Diet Coke. The sun felt good on my face. I waved at the

men who shouted at me as they loaded up the trucks. That first week at Parker's, I'd decided not to be a piece of meat, so every time anybody looked at me I'd said "Hello" and "Good morning" and "How are you?" and now I couldn't take two steps without a man greeting me or waving. Only two hookers out at this hour. Was it too early or too late, or were the others getting pedicures?

I needed Melinda's Social Security number. That was the key here. I just couldn't think how to get it. She didn't have a driver's license in Missouri. Sometimes the soash was the driver's license number.

I went upstairs again and spread out the notes. Worth a try, I thought, and dialed the St. Louis number of Allseas Countertrade & Consulting Services. I'd walk right into the open jaws of it. One chance. If I blew this, it would be over. This one time had to be just right. I couldn't ever call again. And no one else could, either. Whatever was happening in that office was illegal somehow. They knew it and they were hinky on their best days. I could ruin this whole investigation with this one call. One wrong word. Phone was ringing. Once, twice. A woman answered crisply, "Allseas." A woman who sounded older than I thought Melinda would be. I pictured an elderly receptionist.

"May I please speak with Ms. Pugh?"

"She is not available at the moment. May I have her call you back?"

"Is she in the office today? I'll be in meetings and on the phone most of the afternoon so it's better if I telephone her."

"She's here but on the phone. Would you like to try again? Who shall I say is calling?"

"This is Jennifer Tyler. She doesn't know me. Perhaps it's better if I try again. In half an hour?"

"Yes, try in half an hour."

I paced around, watched the clock. It was great to work only this one case. Elbert had said it was important. Eagleton & Adams we cared about. "Hey, Charlie, it's for you," called Mei Ling. I'd been so lost in thought, I hadn't even heard the phone ring.

"Thanks." I picked up.

"Cici? Hi, it's Lisa Wright. Do you remember me?"

"Yes! It's been at least a year, though. How are you?" She was a stockbroker; we'd been introduced by a mutual friend.

"I've been great. Just back from Nantucket and— Listen, I'm not great." She sighed. "I remembered that you're a detective..."

The catch in the voice I knew so well. Oh, yes, she was supposed to be married by now. It was coming back to me.

"It's Matthew, isn't it."

"I don't know what to do. I think there's a reason he keeps postponing the wedding, but he says there isn't. He just wants 'time.'"

I felt like yawning. Time. Space. My policy was, "Please have all the time and space you want. *Ciao*." Actually, no man had ever told me he wanted that. But *if* one ever did...

"Lisa, do you think there's somebody else?"

"Yes, and I think he's lying to me about it. Why doesn't he just say it? Why all these trips to San Francisco when he never had business there before?"

"Weekend trips?"

"No. He's back on a Friday, but..." She paused. "If I knew then I would break it off and not feel that I'm hanging, not feel stupid and disoriented. I want to know."

"Where does he stay when he's out there?"

"The Sir Francis Drake. I've checked. I've called him there. But—"

It was a romantic hotel. I'd stayed there with an unromantic husband. I remembered my black Christian Dior nightgown. Terrific nightgown. Glad I liked it so much since I wore it all night. "You live together, right? Who pays the phone bill?"

"You think he'd be so—"

"You never know."

I remembered Vinny Parco's philosophy: If you think someone's cheating on you, then it's 90 percent sure that they are.

"Okay. I'm going to look at the bills. May I call you back?"

"Sure. Are you in the office now?"

"Yes. And Cici? Charge me for this. Please let me pay you."

"Hey! I haven't done a thing a friend wouldn't do for you over lunch. Let's see what we can find out. Take a deep breath, look at the phone bill, and call me anytime. Here's my home number..."

I hung up, saw that half an hour had passed, and picked up the phone. "Ms. Pugh is unavailable." Then in forty-five minutes. Then in half an hour. Every time I punched in the number, I tortured myself with the "this is it" tirade. The receptionist told me that Ms. Pugh was on the phone all day long and that her calls often lasted forty-five minutes or more than an hour. Sure they did. She was negotiating to move all that sugar from one country to another. The waiting was making me pretty tense. I had left a scam phone number for her to call me, but I didn't want her to. Downstairs was the real scam phone, but I'd given Mei Ling's phone number. Mei Ling had instructions to answer her phone not with "Parker Investigations," but with a simple "Hello," but we were both afraid she'd forget.

I took a deep breath and dialed the St. Louis number once more. "It's Jennifer Tyler again."

"I'm sorry but she is still unavailable."

"That's okay. I suddenly thought it's silly of me not to speak to someone else about this. Does she have a secretary?"

"Her secretary is not in today."

"Does she have an assistant?"

"What exactly is this about? Perhaps I could help you." There was a pause. "I'm her mother."

Her mother!

"Mrs. Pugh? Wonderful! My name is Jennifer Pugh Tyler, and this is such a silly thing. I've been on the phone all day...all over the country. I've probably been on the phone almost as much as Melinda has. I want to talk to you! Have you heard about the reunion?"

May 12–14. Eastern Shore of Maryland. It was written in green ink in front of me on a scrap of paper. That's all I knew, but I made up the rest. I have to say that it sounded like quite a celebration.

"I am on the committee to send out invitations and to confirm addresses and to get birthdays..." *Damn*, I thought. Did that sound right? Have I blown this whole thing sky high? Which rock was going to clout me on the head? "Could I just take down your addresses?"

She was considering. Seconds passed. Then she said, "Well, I can give you our addresses."

"Terrific. The invitations won't go out for a while, but we are getting under way..."

Addresses. Dictated. Written down. "Melinda is the late Martin Pugh's daughter. That's the Illinois side of the family."

I immediately claimed to be from the other branch, the Maryland Pughs. *Social Security number!* I kept screaming silently as I chattered on about hotels, hopes for good weather, chartered buses. I was nearly losing my mind. So close, so far. The hook, the fish, the phone, minutes ticking away. *Don't think*, I told myself. *Do it!*

"I'm so glad to talk to you—so happy you're Melinda's mother!" I gushed. "Okay, I have the addresses...I need...what else...let's see. Yes, birthdays."

"Birthdays?"

"What we're doing—oh, I know how women feel. Half hesitate and half say, Oh, who cares! What we're doing—just for fun—at the Saturday night party is—we're—" My voice sounded okay but I was stumped.

What were we doing? This phantom committee organizing a phantom family reunion. I knew I had to try. *Go ahead. Throw it out. One chance. What if she suddenly shouts, "Who are you?" All over. Finished. Door closed forever. Be enthusiastic. Go.*

"We thought it would be the most fun to have an astrologer do everybody's horoscope—you know, with their personality traits? Jessica Pugh—she's a Pugh by marriage, so you probably don't know her—she just got married last year—well, she has an astrologer who will do a little sketch of every person, but we have to know the date of birth and the year. No one but the astrologer will see the year. I promise. I've promised this to every single woman I've called. At the party, it'll just be the day and the month."

There was hesitation. I could hear her thinking. My mouth went dry. I waited.

"My date of birth is September first, 1925, and Melinda was born on—"

A phone rang in St. Louis. "Do you have to get that?" I tried to sound casual.

It stopped ringing. I was silently screaming, *Say it say it say it!*

"Melinda was born on June twenty-fourth, 1945."

I repeated both birthdays, confirmed the spelling of the maiden name, and thanked her. I cringed as I reminded her the invitations wouldn't go out for a while. *Like never.*

I hung up, drained. I took a gulp of Diet Coke and walked over to Mei Ling's desk. Elbert was standing there. "I got the birthdays." I grinned. "And the present address."

He grinned back. "Now we're in business!"

The address sounded familiar. It was Rhinewald's address on his Missouri driver's license. Hurrah!

But the date of birth was the breakthrough in the case. Mei Ling punched it into the computer, and there was the Social Security number and then a great chunk of Melinda Bowen Pugh's life.

The credit header listed Melinda's employment as Commerce Associates. I called St. Louis directory assistance and was told the number was 555-2742. This was one digit away from the Allseas number. I called the number, and Mrs. Pugh answered, saying, "Commerce," in her brisk way.

"So sorry, wrong number," I said in what might have passed for an English accent, and hung up.

Getting very interesting, I thought. "Mei, could you see if there's a D&B for Commerce Associates?"

The phone rang, and Mili called, "Charlie, line two for you!"

"Hello," I breathed. "Oh, Lisa? You're at home?"

She'd left the office to go and look for the phone bills. Her voice was ragged. "I can't believe it! There are all these calls to San Francisco! At two and three in the morning! I must have been asleep, he must have been in the living room!"

"What's the number?" I asked, and wrote it down. "Have you dialed it?"

She was blowing her nose. "No. I was afraid to."

"Do you want me to find out whose number it is?"

Lisa was really crying now. She didn't answer. I said, "Just wait. There may be a logical explanation." Like what? Like nocturnal conferences with an insomniac? My heart went out to her. The tears were coming in torrents. "Lisa, it's four o'clock. Have you had lunch?"

"No. I couldn't eat."

"Well, if there's nothing in the kitchen, go down to the deli and buy a tuna-fish sandwich. Have a glass of milk. Buy some Pepperidge Farm cookies."

The Wall Street banker was sniffling. "Yes."

"I'll get back to you before six if I possibly can." She was blowing her nose. "Eat something. I'll call you back."

We hung up. Mei Ling presented me with some printouts. "Look at this! Same address and the same suite number as Allseas!" She was triumphant.

"Sort of crowded in there, I guess." I was delighted. Commerce Associates was started in 1987, and listed as the chief executive and president was—Melinda Pugh. She owned 100 percent of the capital stock. I skimmed her job history. No mention of Allseas.

"Mei Ling, are there any liens or judgments against Commerce?"

In minutes, she said there was, and I had the number. I called St. Louis Temporaries and spoke with Mark Ewen. "Yes, we sued them for three thousand dollars a few years ago. They scooped one of our employees."

"What kind of business—what exactly does Commerce Associates do?" I asked.

"It's a telephone answering service. They also do paging and voice mail. Two or three people. Maybe four."

My last thing to do was check with the phone company. Yes, the billing party for the Allseas number was none other than Commerce Associates.

I was stunned. A mother-and-daughter team. An answering service. Bells are ringing. What bravado!

I presented it all to Elbert, and he told me to write it up. I did, and he took the pages and nodded, saying, "Okay, okay," as he read them. "It's in the computer, isn't it?"

"Yes, under the file number." It had been a long day. I had done it. Following threads. I thanked Mei; we were both very happy. She grabbed her tote bag and hurried off to Port Authority for her bus home.

I sat at her desk and dialed the San Francisco phone number. A woman's voice on an answering machine. I worked for a few minutes at the computer, hoping it didn't mean what I thought it did. Casanova would never behave so stupidly. Of course, he often had two women at the same time, but he'd never get caught by being careless over something as silly as a phone bill or the eighteenth-century equivalent. As I gathered my notebook and my pens, I could hear Elbert on the phone, talking to the lawyer at Eagleton & Adams. "Well, I'll tell you what I found out . . ." He never even thanked me.

I went downstairs, which was thick with smoke and loud with music and men's voices. Like going from church to a truck stop. I told them about the family reunion and the horoscope scam. They loved it. "You really got the mother ta tell you?" Bobby kept asking. "You did the whole case on the phone?"

Mickey was leaning back in his chair with his boots up on the desk. "Good work, Charlie." Then he added, "I couldn't've done that." Elbert not saying a word of thanks didn't matter anymore.

I dialed Lisa's apartment and asked her if the name Marilyn Naylor meant anything to her. "That's his old fiancée! The one he left to be with me! But I thought—he told me— she lived in Chicago!"

She sounded angry, which I thought was a good sign, but then she started to cry again. I told her to call me at home if she wanted to talk. "Or you can come over for a drink if you

don't want to be there when Matthew walks in from work."
She thanked me, in floods of tears, and we hung up.

Vinny threw me a six-pack of Oreos. "We ordered these
because we thought you'd be down. Ya want a Diet Coke?
Hey, anybody want tea? I'm callin' Poppy's." The men placed
their orders and turned the radio up louder for a song they
liked by Trisha Yearwood. Vinny got on the phone. That
accent. "Yeah, it's Pah-kuh's."

I took a bite of a cookie, feeling I'd been upstairs too long.
So much for Allseas Countertrade and the world of sugar.
So much for Matthew. Broken contracts, broken promises,
broken hearts.

Sweet talk.

Nightscape

The lights were blurred on either side of the car as we raced through the tunnel, and then we were high in the sky, nearly flying over the bridge. That hum noise of the tires was loud. I couldn't stop smiling and turned to look at Mickey. He reached forward and punched the radio on full blast. The van was three vehicles up, just where we wanted it. Manhattan was ahead of us, to the sides of us, skyscrapers lit all around us, as if we were traveling from the center of this bright star ever outward toward the moon, which hung like a pearl over the shining expanse of black water.

Wow, I thought as I opened my eyes. The Venetian chandelier was the first thing I saw. Herbert had practically given it to me and I fantasized that Casanova had flirted under it, even though it was chronologically impossible. What a dream. I turned and looked at the clock. Five. I wasn't tired, just in that melted state when my body had become one with the wooden floor under me. I was so comfortable that it could have been a featherbed.

Great dream. I'd had nightmares every night of my life, several a night, from when I began to sleep at age fourteen right up to Rome. The real horrors had stopped in Rome but

I still had the occasional dream that woke me and forced me to pace until light.

Now my dreams were more like action films. Car chases on New York streets, in Chinatown. I was happy in them. They were like clips of terrific movies, and I always felt safe, was always with one of the men from Parker's. I never even had to do the driving.

Once as I was getting wired up for a location, I overheard Mickey talking to an ex-narc who works undercover for OCID. "Charlie scares the shit out of me because nothing scares her. She has no fear." He didn't mean it as a compliment and I didn't take it as one. The truth is not quite like that. We're all afraid, just not afraid of the same things.

I closed my eyes and suddenly remembered the house dream. I hadn't had it for nearly four years. It always started the same way. I was little, just able to reach doorknobs. I was coming up the back steps, the ones that led from the garage to the back hallway of the house on the Old Canton Road. I pulled open the door, which was difficult because it opened toward me and I was standing on steps below it. But I managed and then pushed the screen door open and stepped inside. I felt a sharp dart of panic. Something was wrong, something was behind me in the garage. I pulled the door closed and locked it and thought, *It's okay, I'm in the house now.* Then I ran through the breakfast room to the back door that opened out onto the brick path and the clothesline, and I pushed the door closed and locked it. The breakfast room and the kitchen were half-dark, as if it were dusk. There were no lights on in the house, and I didn't take time to turn them on but ran through the den to push the door closed and lock it. Something was out in the garden, I could sense it. I was filled with dread. If I could just run beyond the living room to the other door that opened out back. I pushed it closed, half expecting it to be pushed back at me. I think I see something on the terrace in the shadows, but now the door is closed and locked. My heart is pounding. There is a peculiar gloom in the house, but the doors are locked and I tell myself I'm safe. I am out of breath. Had I forgotten anything? No. The doors are locked. The living room is getting darker, and a fog or mist is moving all around me, making it impossible to see. I put my hands out like a blind person and move slowly, bumping into the furniture. I am a little girl, and I keep thinking, Why is it so dark? Then I realize, nearly screaming, that the front door is open. I run to it, stumbling, desperate to get there in time. It opens inward and I am pushing it closed in the dark and it's a heavy door and moves so slowly. Then I am up on my tiptoes, straining to reach the lock with fumbling fingers. I'm using all my strength to turn the difficult, stiff lock, and at last, when it clicks into place, I realize that the danger, the horror, is right behind me. I have locked myself in the house, filled with black, swirling gloom. Whatever is most macabre—most evil—is standing, tremendous and powerful, in the dark beside me. I swallow. That's where it ends, with me waking, feeling four years old again. My first bad dream, at least the first I remember, and it still haunts me. But, I tell myself, not so much. Maybe I am growing away from that kind of fear.

WHAT IF ALL MY terrors could be put in a bottle and labeled? It would be what made me fight off sleep all those years, and it would be grayish brown and viscous; the label would say, "The House of My Father." He told me he would get rid of me—that first time—before I'd learned to tie my sneakers, just a skinny little girl with ponytails. There was no safe place for me in that big house—nothing to count on—not even my mother's goodness because I doubted her strength. So the woods and the fields embraced me; I was safe anywhere but home. I was three feet tall when I became achingly afraid I would not be allowed to live. Now I'm five foot nine barefoot, feel no sense of peril ever, feel light as air, as bright as water. I escaped. I am far away. Everything every day since leaving the house on the Old Canton Road has been a celebration.

Outrageous Fortune

Most of the time with Parker's I was over-the-moon happy. My finances were scary because even though I was getting a whopping twelve dollars an hour, it was not a forty-hour week—only billable hours to the client. I could be in the warehouse from seven a.m. to six p.m. but get only three hours of billable work. There were a few horrible days when I'd not gotten even one hour of work. I came out minus three dollars for a day of four buses, for taking the trouble to arrive, sit around, and wait. Then again, I might work sixteen hours on a seizure or spend the night on a stakeout, making it twenty-four or twenty-five hours. Elbert insisted I was part-time and would not discuss health insurance or any benefits whatsoever. There was no such thing as overtime pay. I told everyone that if I was ever pushed out a window or down an elevator shaft, to take me to Kennedy and put me on the next plane to Rome or London, where I would arrive and begin bleeding again in a country where people would take care of me. My second choice was to have them put me down like a horse with one shot to the head because there was no chance of my being able to pay a hospital bill.

The ex-cops in the office were not so concerned about the

money. They had disability, pensions. Furthermore, they lived in cheaper boroughs or, like Bobby, in Pennsylvania.

Having very little money can be terror or it can be liberation. I would sometimes give myself this little talk as I lay awake on the floor in the predawn dark.

I had enough clothes for anyone. I even paid storage for my designer evening dresses because I couldn't just throw them out. Clothes and food were easy. Around noon, when I was in the office, I walked to the Moroccans' deli on Tenth and paid a dollar for a hot lunch. Mas and Sharif complained that they were charged more, but I just shrugged and said it was a shame they couldn't talk to the man behind the counter about Casablanca, Rabat, Agadir, Fez, and the snake charmers of Marrakesh. Couscous, whatever the Moroccans spooned out onto paper plates, I ate. In the evenings if I really wanted to splurge, I knew an Italian place where they'd give me an enormous plate of *calamari fritti* to take out for five dollars, and it would last for several meals. Maybe too many. How many times can you reheat fried squid and be happy about it?

Robert cut my hair for twenty dollars way up on East End Avenue; Mara, the ex-professional volleyball player from Romania, waxed my legs; and Yolanta, the Polish woman, gave me pedicures. Nobody knows if you spend ninety-nine cents for a lipstick or go for Chanel at twenty-five dollars a tube. My favorite soap in town, and the cheapest, comes from the Pearl River Mart on Canal. I used Ginseng Placenta lotion on my face. The hilarious English translation stated that it came from "only healthy women." My personal upkeep was minimal.

Money, to me, has always meant plane tickets, taxis in the rain, new shoes, and chocolate. There was none of the first three in my early detective days, but never in my life have I ever gone without chocolate.

Women friends knew I couldn't afford to go out to dinner, so they would invite me for a glass of wine. My women
friends are in my address book in ink. Forever. Even though
several are listed first name only, as I am leery about their
marriages. Sometimes I'd get an invitation to pay $250 for a
charity ball ticket and I'd laugh as I tossed it in the wastebasket. Who did they think I was? I wasn't sure anymore so why
should anyone else know? There were cocktail and dinner
parties, but I had no time and very little strength for men
as dates, and most of them dropped away. While I was at
Parker's, there was a dazzlingly handsome Russian count,
an alcoholic Yalie, a shipping tycoon, and an art gallery
dealer who sold only Toulouse-Lautrecs, but the important
men in my life wore holsters with guns and yakked to me on
the radio. I rode around in vans with them, smoked cigars
with them. We would sit up all night staring at a doorway
to prevent a suspect from sneaking to the airport and flying off to his homeland before the D.A. presented the arrest
warrant at nine the next morning. We took turns sleeping an
hour each. A snorer was good since it helped keep me awake
during my watch.

Most of my friends thought what I was doing was fascinating and rocked with laughter over my stories. Several said
that to be a detective had always been their favorite fantasy.
Some of my friends were genuinely worried about the danger and I would censor myself. A few were a bit odd about
my new profession. I arrived at a Park Avenue drinks party
in black jeans and boots with apologies to a very elegant
Baroness von Karger, who had told me she didn't care what I
wore as long as I came. One of the guests, a Sotheby's Realtor whose links to Austrian aristocracy were highly suspect,
sneered, "Oh, there you are—in your little FBI suit." I didn't
respond but moved through the crowd. I felt lean and strong,
knew I was windburned from being on the street for hours,

and had been praised for the hidden videos I'd taken in Jersey City that afternoon. I felt I deserved a glass of champagne, whereas maybe the most exciting thing the Realtor had done all day was to use her Saks credit card.

It took me totally by surprise to elicit sarcastic responses. There were people I'd known for ages who insisted that I was "certainly only doing this to write about it," as if my being a detective were distasteful but necessary research leading to what mattered—another book. I would be introduced, quite firmly, as a writer. Being a detective, to them, was déclassé, not at all nice, not even very clean. A few names were crossed out of my address book. I never felt that I had changed. A Swiss Army knife, a little notebook with the addresses of locations in Chinatown, a two-way radio in the bottom of my bag—these were my secrets, the equipment that dealt with my "other life." I brought all this with me into the cocktail party on Park Avenue. I felt capable and physical and the jeans and the boots or the silk dress made no difference. Often I had spent the day doing things I had never done before. I was doing a job, and I must have been doing it okay or the men would have been bellowing at me, refusing to pair up with me out in the field instead of buying me Diet Cokes and tossing me Oreos.

Secrets can give the bearer amazing power. I remember wearing no underwear to a staid black-tie dinner just to pep myself up because I didn't much care for my stodgy banker escort. The first time I traveled around the world, all my good luck, I was convinced, came from a tiny tin of foie gras tucked into my suitcase. Another time, in my twenties and hanging by a thread financially, I needed a new long dress. It was the dress or a plane ticket, but I would have both. I went to Bloomingdale's and bought the most delicious black lace nightgown there was, wore it with my grandmother's pearls, and was amazed at the compliments.

My secrets, my talismans, and my rituals give me courage. Perhaps it began with the sealing wax and the envelope of money hidden in the copy of *Kon-Tiki*. I still check each shoe for scorpions before putting it on. Doesn't everyone who has read a dozen books on the French Foreign Legion and most of Wilfred Thesiger and then fallen in love with a former Legionnaire in Rome? I cannot get dressed, in any country, without giving each shoe a shake whether it's a sneaker or a black satin slingback. Sometimes I imagine that I am—deep inside—an eleven-year-old boy; that is the shining truth of it, and everything else in my life is the pretense.

Future Tense

One morning, I was summoned upstairs to talk to Elbert. "Do you have a passport? Up-to date? Valid?" he asked before I could even sit down in his cubicle.

Twak! The knife went past my head, then he stood up and walked around his desk and behind me to pull it out of the wall. He returned to his chair and flopped into it again.

"I keep it valid. It's downstairs in my pocketbook."

Twak! Elbert repeated the exercise, pulling the knife out of the wall and returning to behind his desk.

"Where do you want me to go?" I asked, thinking that knife throwing made conversation distracting at best.

"Italy. You speak Italian, don't you? Big gang over there, and we need—yeah, we need somebody to go over and meet with the counterfeiters . . ." He was carving lines in his desk like a little boy in the third grade. *That is a large knife*, I thought. I supposed it was too large to be the one he kept in his boot.

"Handbags?"

"No, jeans." He sighed, then stroked his beard absent-mindedly with the blade. It caught the light and winked at me. "Would you be willing to fly over there?"

"Sure! When?"

Elbert looked at his watch. "It's nearly eleven now, and if it's on, you'll leave tonight from Kennedy."

I grinned. "Great. Terrific. Rome?"

He looked at me and paused. Ever the drama queen. "I don't know yet."

I laughed out loud. I was thinking maybe Milan, but I hoped Rome.

"The plane'll be met when you land and you'll be blind-folded and driven to the factory. You'll be masquerading as a wealthy importer—you'll have all the papers you need—but before you order, you want to inspect the product. They'll drive you there and you'll see all that you possibly can and then make a deal. A deal in the range of forty or fifty thousand dollars."

I was silent, wondering which Italian designer it was.

Elbert gave me a few more details, very few, and we talked about a letter of credit, a fake name for fake identity papers. "I have two more phone calls to make and then I wait to hear back from the client. I'll let you know this afternoon."

I went down the stairs and back to my desk, feeling absolutely panicked. I wasn't thinking about being blindfolded by Italian counterfeiters and driven who knew where—nobody would know where—and swallowed up in the Calabrian countryside...no, not that. Not me.

It was verbs. I felt very shaky about anything but the present. I ripped off a sheet of notebook paper and quickly started to scrawl in Italian: I buy, I bought, you buy, you bought. I sell, I sold yesterday...

Then I put my head in my hands and took a deep breath. *Calma! Pazienza!* The future. Could I deal with that?

I had always ignored the future when I lived in Rome, simply using the present tense and then smiling and adding *più tardi* or *domani* for "later" or "tomorrow." Weren't we supposed to be living entirely in the present anyway? Hadn't it worked for me so far?

Elbert called from upstairs at four o'clock and said, "It isn't happening. They're scared. Too risky. Let's say it's been postponed."

It never happened, not at Parker's. Parker's was on the way out. It wouldn't be long, though, before I would have to prove that I could be a bilingual liar . . . managing at every turn, at every turn of every phrase, to dance away from the future.

Starting to Be the End

The office was a nuthouse. Someone was stealing our garbage right out on 29th Street, so now we had to shred everything. The shredder ground away like some cappuccino machine with bronchitis. All letter drafts, phone messages, the tabs from Poppy's...all of it had suddenly been catapulted into the realm of the confidential.

Detectives are pathologically suspicious and theories abounded. It might be someone who was fired a year ago who now worked for another investigative firm. "Yeah, he'd do it—he'd make a grab." But we couldn't prove it without a nocturnal stakeout and Bobby was always watching TV and most of the time Warner was sacked out on her L.L.Bean bag. The missing garbage bothered us, and then Vinny said something was going on with the phones. "Don'choo guys hear it?" He waved the receiver around over his head.

The Southern Office was pissed because though we got paid Friday, Mili said, "Don't do anything with your checks until I tell you to." When this announcement was met by actual growling, she hurried out the door and retreated upstairs to the Executive Suite.

*   *   *

ONE AFTERNOON, THE ROAST Beef Twins came into the
Southern Office grinning and loose-limbed. Elbert had it in
his mind that he should call one of the lawyers immediately,
and Mickey was trying to dissuade him.

Elbert was sitting, nearly reclining, in Bobby's chair as
Tom leaned against my desk, grinning vapidly and puffing
on a cigarette. They were red-faced, completely swacked
after a liquid lunch on 23rd Street.

Mickey said, "Bobby's doin' a flyby in Brooklyn. We can
go ahead on Friday if he sees what I saw last week."

Tom said, "I hear ya," which was his response to everything.

Elbert was holding a skinny black cigar backward, like
a German, and was slack-jawed and glassy-eyed. "Didja do
that report, C?" he asked.

"Yes, just finished. Do you want to read it now? Then if
you sign it, I can get it out this afternoon." I pulled the page
from the printer and walked over to him.

Elbert straightened up in the chair, which was a good sign
except when he moved I could smell the alcohol. It wasn't his
breath, it was coming out of his pores. Then he pointed at
the letter and said, "Hold it up! No, not like that! Come on,
hold it up! By each corner!"

I did, and in seconds he'd whipped the knife out of his
boot and had slashed the page in half. I was holding two
halves and he was making this peculiar cackling noise.

"I guess you thought it needed cutting," I said. "A little
editing." I returned to my desk and sat down.

Elbert threw the knife and it went *twak!* in the wall
behind me. Tom came over, pulled it out, and hesitated,
looking from Mickey to Elbert, then he put it on Mickey's

desk. We all, probably even Elbert, wondered if he would reach for it again. He was stinking drunk, and I didn't trust his aim. I wondered if I might have to bring up Amy Vanderbilt and the etiquette of knife throwing in an office situation, but Mickey took the knife. Elbert picked up Bobby's phone and made a perfectly ludicrous call to a lawyer, and then he and Tom ambled out, giggling.

"That does it!" shouted Mickey, furious.

The next day, he told us all he'd hidden Elbert's gun and was taking all responsibility for any repercussions. As days and then weeks passed, we waited for Elbert to mention that it was missing, but either he didn't notice it was gone from his desk drawer or he thought he himself had lost it.

The Southern Office was in a state of revolution. If we were given a paycheck, it bounced. Paranoia was on the increase. We were absolutely sure that Elbert had bugged the downstairs office and all our phones. From now on, we would only discuss Elbert out on 29th Street. This seemed perfectly reasonable to me at the time, which is a sign of how tired I was.

Often when I arrived at the warehouse at a bit past seven, the air would be gray with smoke, the radio would be on, and the men would all be there, feet up on the desks, as if they'd been frozen in a tableau from the previous evening.

Elbert might have slept on the couch upstairs, Mas didn't sleep well so sometimes he'd roll in at five, Mickey might have come in just before seven, and Bobby and Warner lived there.

I always walked in, slammed the door, and wondered what I'd missed.

It was the end of that second summer, just starting to be September, when I thought I'd had enough. It might have been that sweltering afternoon when I'd been explaining a 31st Street location and felt something pull at my hair.

I looked up to see that I was stuck in a length of hanging flypaper. My expression of total disgust sent everyone into gales of laughter until Bobby found scissors and freed me. That might have been the tipping point for me.

Blaming Elbert had become a growth industry. We hadn't been paid for a long time, and the phones were either cut off or subject to an act of God and went dead. Elbert claimed it was lightning. Whichever it was—they weren't working for a day or two, which somehow fed into the bugging theory. This limited the activity of the topflight, first-class investigative firm we were supposed to be. There was no film for the only camera that still worked, and we were refusing to use our own money to buy the film or to repair any of the others. The vacuum cleaner broke and no one would chip in money to get it fixed so the Southern Office was getting pretty disgusting. The Puerto Rican cleaning woman stopped coming, which was a relief because we all dreaded her. Mickey said, "If you turn your back, she'll vacuum right up your ass."

The dog needed a bath, and so did Elbert. One gaspingly humid day, Mickey said, "Why don't we just strap him to the fuckin' car and fuckin' drive him through the fuckin' car wash?" No one wanted to go anywhere with him. He gained so much weight that his navy blazer was three sizes too small, and the dog kept sleeping on it, so it smelled like an old horse blanket. After my last meeting with him and the Armani-clad lawyers, no one would get into a taxi with him. The lawyers were insisting, "No, no, I need the exercise."

Maybe worst of all, Elbert was drinking so much that he kept leaving the surveillance van in the wrong place and forgetting where it was parked. Moby Dick would be missing for days or until we'd get notified that it had been towed, and then we wouldn't have enough money to spring it. As Mickey so charmingly put it, "Things are really going down the shitter."

*   *   *

BOBBY LEFT. HIS CHAIR looked very empty. Vinny had been gone awhile. Elbert owed Mas for a lot of things Mas had charged on his American Express card, so Mas almost couldn't leave. Tom would never leave Elbert's side. He'd come down to the Southern Office to smoke once in a while, on his own, and he'd listen to the complaints and nod and say, "I hear ya, I hear ya," and then he'd go up and tell Elbert every word. There was talk of one of the secretaries leaving, but no one believed it until she did. Mickey threatened to quit three times a day.

Less than two years after that first April Fools' Day with Vinny Parco, I toyed with the idea of going out on my own. I'd learned a lot from Vinny Parco, had the Mississippi experience, and Parker's was dying a slow but sure death. A transfusion of funds would have saved the firm for a while, but the IRS was waiting like a shark and it was only a matter of time before it moved in with the serious teeth. Rumors were rife about Parker's demise. We all heard them. From other investigators, from the cops, even from the lawyers. There was talk of downloading the computers, an auction of equipment, but as Mickey asked, "What equipment? Slow computers, broken cameras, old file cabinets, the sledge-hammers?" The bank was attacking with urgent calls to Mr. Elbert Thatch; Ada would call three times a day and say it was an emergency. This was when the phones were working.

Parker Investigations was barely breathing. No fog on the mirror. I pictured a sort of detective/priest arriving in dog collar and shoulder holster to administer the last rites beside the front door on 29th Street as the hookers crossed their enormous chests and bowed their platinum heads.

My big incentive to leave Parker Investigations came when

a large investigative firm called to ask if I would take on a special project for them. I took the day off from Parker's and went to the preliminary meeting. The lawyers and the client looked me over and decided I would be okay. The case would involve several weeks of undercover, a completely new identity, and moving into a new apartment. I would be wearing a wire every waking minute. The fee was more than double per hour what I was getting at Parker's, but I wasn't really getting anything, as my last paycheck had bounced. The next day, I gave my two weeks' notice at the warehouse, went on my last stakeout in Moby Dick, emptied my desk drawers of old Tic Tac boxes, and prepared to fly *sola*.

PARKER INVESTIGATIONS IS NO more. I think the IRS administered the coup de grâce. And all of us? We're sprinkled around, still sleuthing, still calling each other to find out who's busy, who's starving, who's hot, and who's not.

There have been Elbert sightings on the West Side, but no one really knows what he's up to. For several months, nearly every day, I used to think I'd seen Elbert in a knot of people crossing Third Avenue or coming toward me down a sidewalk or stepping into a revolving door just ahead of me. I'd give a little gasp and then realize that the scruffy man in black wasn't him after all. It took on the flavor of an Elvis sighting, and Mickey and I would laugh about it. Basically, it's the same story: He's on our minds, but no one really knows anything about him anymore.

THERE'S A LOT TO remember not to forget.

Those car chases in Chinatown. Following the perps, like rats, through the tunnel on into Jersey. It's hard to catch them because they are DWA—Driving While Asian. You have not lived until you've been in a car chase in Chinatown.

Those all-nighters in the car. That time Mas turned on the Christian rock station at four a.m. and we nearly came to blows. The compromise of Broadway show tunes. Singing the entire score of *Oklahoma!* with the windows closed before dawn in the Queens neighborhood as the Korean counterfeiter, our subject, slept.

Everybody yakking on the radio from vehicle to vehicle. Elbert and Dek purring alongside in Dek's gold Jaguar, giving us gingersnaps in the middle of the night. We'd roll down the windows and stick our hands out.

I'll never forget the five-thirty a.m. wake-up whistle over the radio from the Polish Prince. Every day. Mickey had given me a radio and a police scanner for the crow's nest, so I endured this with everybody else.

My kick of pleasure when I realized I could operate a tremendous freight elevator and line up the doors and the floors perfectly. This cheered me endlessly at two in the morning in a counterfeit jeans factory.

That first time of walking into a dark underground parking garage with the envelope of cash. It was winter and it was night. The men were out in the field and the money had to be delivered. A disembodied voice with an Arab accent echoed, "Over here." All I saw on the other side of a concrete column was a figure wearing a black parka with the hood up; a gloved hand quickly took the envelope. I left and walked over icy sidewalks back to the barn feeling unsatisfied and angry.

"He didn't even say thank you!" I exploded to the Southern Office. The men were philosophical.

"Whaddya expect? He's scum. He's a fuckin' C.I. They're fuckin' scum. Otherwise they wouldn't be C.I.'s." Our paychecks were bouncing but Elbert was giving money to a

confidential informant. Yes, enraging us. But my big disappointment was not seeing his face. I wanted to see what a
C.I. looked like. I was destined to meet plenty of them—to
give them money, give them rides, pick them up on street
corners, at train stations. They were traitors and stoolies,
the men and I agreed. We needed them but we didn't trust
them and we certainly didn't like them. They were nothing
but cheese eaters.

The early morning Karachi Inn seizure on the West Side.
Mickey sent me out at six a.m. to buy rubber gloves, and
I'd finally found an open drugstore and returned with dozens of pairs. Twenty-five men had climbed into vans on 29th
Street, sped uptown to within a block of the location, then
waited restlessly, chain-smoking, for word to move. I was
the lookout in a van behind tinted windows, eating Gerald's
brownies. My right hand gripped the radio, ready. Seemed
forever, but at last the order came. I watched the men, like
a military operation, gloved and wearing surgical masks,
bearing sledgehammers, march across the street and into
that cheap hotel. Later, I heard how the Senegalese vendors in their striped pajamas jumped out of bed and tried
to hide their watches. They were screaming in French and
in English, "Call the police! Call the police!" and the NYPD
were shouting back, "We *are* the police!"

I'll miss those days in the warehouse on the West Side.
Those men. Sweet, neurotic Warner. The two secretaries
upstairs hurrying to cover the leaks in the walls with mask-
ing tape every time it rained. That sound track from Nashville. All those songs of lost loves, lost dogs, lost pickup
trucks. The warehouse in winter—very cold. The warehouse
in summer—very hot. Filled with smoke and schemes . . .

PART IV
Without a Net

I was a freelance operative.

On the appointed morning in December, I arrived at the building early, reached for the door, then backed away. Walking around the block, staring into space, I rehearsed addresses, zip codes, and phone numbers that supposedly belonged to an ex-husband, a father, and to me in my life before Manhattan. Ten minutes later, I was ready: The stack of papers on the Realtor's desk was like an exam I'd crammed for. Suddenly I was signing a lease with my new Social Security number, listing my new bank accounts; at the bottom of every page, I'd sign my new name.

That afternoon, I picked out furniture from a firm whose clients are often movie stars who have to live in New York for a few months and prefer an apartment to a hotel. Everything is rented and delivered and then fetched when the Broadway play or movie shoot is over. Very appropriate, I decided, for I had my own sort of performance to give. "I'll take that sofa, please, and those matching armchairs, that coffee table, and I like the big mirror I saw in the other showroom. Give me a double bed, those bedside tables, a bureau, that mirror framed in silver bamboo..."

I moved into my new and rather grand three-bedroom

apartment; the furniture arrived and was put in place. The stage was set. And the trap, too. The client had a delightful sense of humor and would call me every evening for a report. He seemed to adore my new name. The case had its hilarious aspects, and the investigation was as much fun as it could be, under the circumstances. The downside was "becoming" another person and never going home. Never going back to the warehouse, never getting into the car, so to speak. No safe harbor. Sleep was difficult because I never felt relaxed, and in the morning, I didn't feel healthy. I was at the location all the time, and the bad guys had keys to the apartment where I now "lived," so every trace of my real name had been obliterated, which meant my address book, my name on the flyleaf of a paperback, notebooks, Christmas cards, dry-cleaning slips, all identification. I had become Cecily Bordeaux Boudreaux.

I had named her, carefully picking a first name that might sound like my nickname in case I was greeted by someone who knew me, which was a very real fear in this part of Manhattan. The maiden name and married name were a mix of French wine and Cajun drama. Cecily had a mink coat (borrowed), extensive property holdings, a wildly wealthy father, an obscenely rich ex-husband, and a new "past" that evolved with every conversation. It was all for me to fantasize, fabricate, and then memorize so as not to get tripped up in my next monologue. I confess that I loved being Cecily Bordeaux Boudreaux, and the idea of fleeing the scene of a nasty New Orleans divorce for shopping and theater in New York City suited me just fine. For the first week.

Sometimes I dared to go home, avoiding a possible tail. I'd wave at Jimmy at the deli, kiss Hayko hello on the first landing, maybe chat with Marvin on the stairs, turn the key in the lock, and push open the door, and my apartment would embrace me. The Haitian paintings, the engravings from Italy, and all my books were right where they should have been. I'd sink into one of the Chinese Chippendale chairs and stare into space for an hour, and then I'd blink and think, *Now, I'm okay.* I could go back to being the rich divorcée, go back to the building, wear the wire, be Cecily.

Within the next few months, I would net seven villains instead of the two the building owner expected—all on tape doing bad things and talking about it. The client was very happy.

The firm called me again and again. Another large investigative firm called. Then there was work for another firm with international branch offices. Suddenly I had more money. I bought more file folders.

A photographer friend of mine invited me to an exhibition of photographs on the floor of the New York Stock Exchange. During the course of the evening, Paul Coughlin and I were given a behind-the-scenes tour by this hugely tall man in a pin-striped suit named Jim Esposito. He looked like a giant investment banker. Later, I would learn that he was a retired Special Agent of the FBI who was now Vice President for Security at the Stock Exchange. We traded business cards and I sent him my résumé. Sometimes we'd talk on the phone, and I soon learned I could count on him for good advice.

A couple of one-man bands called, and I did work for them. Many were retired cops who needed a woman's touch. Caro's chiropractor told her he knew "the nicest investigator in the world" and gave her his number, and she passed it on to me. I called him. Tony Spiesman didn't know Caro and the chiropractor didn't know me, but Spiesman and I liked each other on the phone and talked often. For an hour at a time. He had a rather mysterious military intelligence background and an excellent reputation as a P.I.; he'd done all sorts of things. A voracious reader and a former movie critic for some newspaper somewhere meant he became my unofficial cultural adviser. We had an ongoing discussion about which detective novels were ridiculous and which were classic, and because of Spiesman I read my first Nero Wolfe. The two of us had the same strong love of detectivery. For him, as for me, it was all about finding the truth and helping people in terrible situations. Spiesman and I agreed: It was never about the money.

Spiesman gave me some research to do, then introduced me to another investigator who used me. Then a friend of his used me. I didn't foul up anything, and I did everything right away. They called me again. I was busy.

Mind Game

Spiesman introduced me to an investigator who introduced me to the law firm I called the Boys on Broadway. He did work for them, and I'd work through him and his license when they needed me to take care of something. It might be simple—to serve process for a rather minor court case— but sometimes it was to serve a witness and the witness was on the run. I always liked to imagine that I'd have to track him down in Paraguay, but it was usually New Jersey.

The Boys on Broadway had an office on the twelfth floor of a big building way downtown at the City Hall subway stop. Jeanette ran the show. Divorced with grown children, she projected a jaded aura of "I've seen it all, heard everything, and don't even dream anything could ever surprise me." When she picked up the phone, she said, "Lore office," and I first thought, What *is that?* But it was just her accent. I'd often see her playing card games on the computer; when a lawyer approached to have something typed, she would moan loudly at the interruption and say, "Oh, *my God. What* is it *this* time?" She was bright and tough, dressed beautifully, and was once a croupier in Las Vegas.

No one in the office of the Boys on Broadway had mastered the intercom, and they were always shouting at each other, "Isaac, pick up on line three!" "Pick up pick up pick up!" "Line two, Dave! For you! Line two!" They'd run around in their shirtsleeves, stand in office doorways for conversations, and yell at each other even when they were four feet apart. The conference room table was always littered with big white cardboard boxes with the pizza crusts still in them, half-empty cans of soda, and open bags of bright orange Cheetos. I imagined mice having parties there late at night.

I really liked the Boys on Broadway. They were very no-frills, translated Yiddish phrases into English for me, and usually paid on time. Once in a while, one of them would be indicted.

"Oh, I hate this case," groaned Richard, the youngest one. I was signing an affidavit at his desk as he shuffled papers in a thick file. I knew that sooner or later it would be my case.

It took only three days for Richard to call and ask if I would come downtown. I adore new cases. I feel myself home in on the details, absorbing and assessing as I scratch down notes. It was shuffling the cards for a new game, it was getting the board out and deciding where to put the players. I am not a games person. I like poker but would never voluntarily play checkers or Monopoly; I will succumb to Trivial Pursuit only when very nearly drunk and to gin only while waiting out a monsoon. Backgammon is for Lebanon, Syria, Egypt, Greece, sunbathing, or late at night with brandy. But a new case...*this* was my game.

"The mother is my client. She wants me to start a four-million-dollar suit against a mental hospital—her daughter is or was a patient there—and she was raped."

I looked up from my pad, and Richard nodded. "Yeah,

this is the case that's been driving me crazy. See what you can do with it."

I took the subway uptown, lost in thought. Rape. A mental hospital. Off the subway, up the stairs, and out into the heat that radiated from Lexington Avenue. I waved at Eileen, who stood in the door of the deli, got my mail from David, the poet/mailman from South Carolina, and let myself in my front door. Hayko was on the landing, talking to a customer over a half-unrolled rug. I kissed him hello, stepped around the Tabriz, and started to ascend another flight. Stephan materialized in a navy blazer, carrying a bunch of red roses. This was typical. It seemed to be his perpetual situation—rushing to a rendezvous with a bouquet—whether I saw him at seven in the morning or eleven at night. Hayko and I wondered where he went, where he got all those roses, if he had dozens of beautifully tailored navy blazers. Stephan kissed me hello on both cheeks, murmured something complimentary in French, then hurried downstairs and out the front door for some mysterious assignation. I left Hayko and his customer grinning on the landing, standing over the rug.

Clothes off, T-shirt and short-shorts on, painted toenails liberated from shoes, Diet Coke in hand, and fan going full blast: I was ready to begin. My desk was cleared with a sweep of one arm and a lot of whumping noises as things fell; then I dialed Mrs. Langford's house in White Plains. No answer, so I dialed her work number. Beth Langford was eager to talk. "Jannie's caseworker, Anne Carlucci, knows everything. She talked to Jannie afterwards and she was the one to report it." Before I could ask any questions at all, Mrs. Langford told me that she knew Jannie had been raped. "The emergency room report said that penetration had taken place. They said that! They would know, wouldn't they?" she insisted.

"I'll get a copy of that report, Mrs. Langford. And I'll be talking with the local police department in Massachusetts. I wanted to touch base with you first and introduce myself. Don't hesitate to call me. I have a message machine and I check it every hour or so. I'll call you back as soon as I can."

I hung up.

Penetration had taken place. Penetration. I'd had to get over my squeamishness fast when I'd spent a year interviewing nuns and priests for a book on celibacy. *Just a word*, I told myself. *Stop crossing your legs every time you hear it.* I'd thought, after that year, that being able to ask a priest how often he masturbated and being sympathetic enough to get an answer meant I could do anything. I forced myself into the present and back to the rape case. Never would I be relaxed about the word *penetration*.

Langford seemed okay, she was well-spoken. And Green Valley was not a snake pit. It had a good reputation, and it took molto money to have her daughter, Jannie, there.

I made a list of what I wanted to know. State of mind of Jannie Albert. Medication. Her actions after the rape. When she told someone in authority. Possible negligence on the part of Green Valley. The time frame of telling and being taken to the emergency room. Location of her bedroom, her dormitory. Number of occupants. Was there an alarm system?

My first call was to Investigator Sam P. Davis of the Massachusetts State Police in Dell. I'd told him who I was and that I was an investigator asking questions on behalf of the mother of the victim. Instead of being all official and tight about his information, he treated me as an equal. I inhaled, took notes frantically, and thought, *My God, I'm really working on a rape case.*

I was fascinated, had a thousand questions, then I remembered what Elbert had told me years ago: "Get what you need and no more." But he'd said it in Latin. I needed to know everything about the security at Green Valley.

Richard called the next afternoon. "What about the emergency room records?"

"They went out to me today. Dr. Tabian called me this morning. He'd gotten the faxed permission and said, if I wanted him to, he would go over the case with me."

"You're kidding."

"No. I couldn't believe my luck. Investigator Davis, everybody, will talk to me. It's incredible."

"It's great. That's what it is. Call me when you know more."

Hour after hour for days, I made phone calls and waited for return calls and reports. Conversation by conversation, I began to understand what might have happened. I was glad that a rape kit is law in most states and was anxious to hear the results from the state police. A map of the buildings and the paths between them, previous complaints from the hospital and/or about the hospital—all of it was key. There were faxes to be sent, permission letters to be signed.

Some of my interviews made me groan with frustration. "It" happened at three a.m., but Jannie didn't tell anyone till six p.m. that evening. She took a shower and washed her clothes after the incident. Most unnerving of all was Jannie's incapacity to explain, understand, or remember much of anything. At one point, during the police detectives' interview with Jannie Albert, they asked her if she knew why she was there and she said, "I forget." She'd first said it was a boy named Peter, and the next time she'd said it was a boy named Craig.

The layout was explained to me. "They've got six buildings, all on one level, all one story. In Jannie Albert's building there is one end for boys and one end for girls. These wings are connected by a corridor; there is a living room area and a security guard on duty twenty-four hours a day."

"What do you think went wrong?"

"The kids smoke and open their windows."

I asked about security, and the police officer thought it was the best possible. "They do more than they have to, but you've got two kids at that age, experimenting."

Jannie was twenty at the time of the attack. Now she was living at home with her mother and actually going to school in a special program a few hours a day. *Good*, I thought. But when I spoke with her mother, Mrs. Langford told me that Jannie was getting more upset by what had happened instead of less. Was poor Jannie being fed the horror of rape because of the lawsuit?

It worked in my favor that Anne Carlucci wasn't calling me back because all the information I was gathering in the meantime would mean I'd be better prepared than I was when I'd made the first call to her office. Just when I'd decided she was stonewalling me, she called. My delight was tempered by her telling me she could not talk to me, but Emma Rice, a director of the hospital, could. Five minutes later, I had her on the line. Rice told me that all incident reports went to the state capital. I asked her to describe what defined an "incident" and to tell me more about Green Valley so that I could understand what kinds of patients were there.

"It's what we call a restrictive environment populated by students who have been rejected by schools because of psychological problems." She'd obviously said this many times before. She described the bedrooms, the adult always within earshot all night long.

It seemed the right time to ask about Jannie's mental condition. "She is paranoid schizophrenic, and can speak without any expression at all. She could be saying that everything is fine, but it won't be fine inside her." Emma talked about the fear that Jannie would have a psychotic break.

"Does this mean hearing voices?" I asked.

"Yes, and hallucinations. Losing all sense of reality. Jannie has been on medication ever since her arrival four years ago."

"What happens to someone like Jannie?"

"Her prognosis is guarded. She will never lead what we would call a normal life."

I wondered what a normal life was and then asked if she'd be able to live on her own.

"No. She won't be able to marry or have a job. She will always live in an institution or with her mother."

I felt sadness wash over me as I thanked her for her time. I dialed Mrs. Langford.

"I talked to Anne Carlucci and Emma Rice," I said, and then I told her I was still waiting for the rape kit analysis. She thanked me for keeping her up-to-date. Then her voice, clear and flat and demanding, came from Westchester County: "Why can't we just go in and sue Green Valley for a couple of million dollars?"

I got off the line with her and went swimming. I did laps, my slowest breaststroke, and thought of Jannie. I wished I could talk to her. What had she been thinking when the boy had come to sit on her bed in the dark room in the middle of the night? I thought of her telling him she wanted it, not knowing what it was. I thought of a teenage crush. Of true love. Of *David and Lisa*, that movie. A pearl of a girl, a joy of a boy. I thought of *Light in the Piazza* and of the beautiful young brain-damaged blonde falling in love with George Hamilton, who played the Italian aristocrat. Poor Jannie. And her mother...devastated and coping, or planning how to spend four million dollars?

I pulled myself out of the pool, dressed, walked home, then ran up the three flights to my phone messages. Sometimes I'd close the file and pick up the phone to call Mickey, who was on his own now. He had counterfeit stuff for me to do. Scam calls or visiting locations around Broadway. I would throw myself into cases with him for an afternoon.

I had written up the case, phone call by phone call, interview after interview, but was still waiting to tie up a few loose ends. Finally, Senior Investigator Sarducci called to tell me that the sex offense evidence kit had been supplied by the police and then returned to the police from the Dell General emergency room. "Then it was forwarded to the state police crime lab in Boston. Nothing was learned from it. She'd showered and changed her clothes." He told me that the district attorney had reviewed the case. "He decided it should be closed unless additional information should develop leading to a perpetrator." He sighed. "We can't use Jannie Albert as a witness."

That night I dreamed of Whitfield. I woke up remembering the way Mother and I would drive out there, one summer between my college years, after her divorce, and do volunteer work. Whitfield was the Mississippi State Mental Hospital, named after the little town it was near. It was part of the vernacular because everybody in the state was thought to fall into one of four categories: You were in Whitfield, you belonged there, you had just gotten out, or you were ready for it. Mother and I didn't know what it would be like, but the underpaid staff appeared to be kind. Every Wednesday, Mother took shoeboxes of old postcards, hundreds of them saved over fifty years, and materials for an art class. The patients would solemnly go through the postcards until a scene inspired them, and then they would copy it. That sum-

mer of Wednesdays, I was told I could go anywhere, do anything. The hospital was so understaffed that I might oversee
thirty patients while someone took a break.

I couldn't get used to the idea of shock treatments, and
I entered the lock-in wards feeling absolutely hollow inside
when the door was locked behind me. I told myself to never
forget that sound.

But it was called an "open" hospital, and most of the
patients took walks, sat on benches under trees, even went
fishing in a small pond. Some of the patients shouldn't have
been there. They weren't mentally ill but were too retarded
to make change or take care of themselves. Several had had
a farming accident that left them handicapped or breathtak-
ingly disfigured. Most of them had no visitors, received no
mail. Not ever.

Charles. My favorite patient. Thin, tan, always wearing
khaki trousers and a white shirt, towering over everyone
in the curious and excited crowd that greeted Mother's car
when we drove through the gates. They peered in the windows, touched our clothes. Charles always had questions.
"Do you know how many words Faulkner wrote? Do you
know how many presidents have an 's' in their middle name?
Do you know how many days it took to build the Governor's
Mansion?"

I dreamed of the last time I'd seen him. It was the last
Wednesday before I went back to college in New York, and
Charles had run beside the car for at least two hundred
yards down the driveway. His white shirttails had flapped
out of his trousers; he kept pace as he shouted his *Do you
know how many*'s through my open window. I was going
away and he was never going anywhere. I can still see him in
the middle of the road, getting smaller as we drove toward
the outside gate. Charles, in the rearview mirror, with that

thin, gaunt face, that shaved head, those frantically waving arms, exploding with his urgent questions.

I ADDED SARDUCCI'S CALL to my report and printed out the pages. I would reread it and fax it to Richard in the morning. I poured myself a glass of white wine, put on sunglasses for protection against spitting hot grease, and made popcorn for dinner.

Maybe Jannie still slept with a teddy bear. Maybe she yearned to be kissed and it went too far. Maybe she was all right with what happened between them until she told, and the reaction of the listener changed her memory, and maybe that was when she felt shame and guilt and panic. Maybe she liked it when it happened.

People have sex anywhere, all the time. When I was in Rome, one of the women defendants in the Red Brigades trial managed to get pregnant right in the Italian courtroom.

I wished I could speak with both boys. Maybe a pillow was put over her mouth. Maybe she'd forget it, or maybe her rapist had joined the other demons who inhabited her poor mind.

Suddenly I realized I was sitting in the dark and it was past nine o'clock. I turned on the desk lamp.

No one should have ever been able to come into her room and make her decide whether to take off her clothes. She was there to be protected from having to make a decision like that. That security guard, her mother who sent her there, and the staff at Green Valley were all supposed to take care of her.

No bars on the windows because of fire codes. No alarm system on that particular building because this is a program to prepare the residents for the community. No security guard intervened because there was no cry for help. The police report said no weapon was used. Consensual sex?

Sure. With someone who has the mental capacity of a fourth grader.

The next morning I had to be downtown at One Police Plaza, so afterward I went to the office of the Boys on Broadway to drop off my report. "Richard's in court this morning," Jeanette told me, lighting a cigarette. No one ever told Jeanette that it was against the law to smoke in the office. No one ever told Jeanette *anything*.

"Do you know about this one?" I handed her the pages.

"What's the mother going to do?" she asked rhetorically.

The office was quiet. Everyone was on vacation, in court, home with allergies.

"I worked on another mental hospital case when I was first a detective. Trying to find the niece of a client. She was lost in the system. I could get no information because they were 'protecting her privacy.' Her little elderly aunt came to the office—she was tiny, a miniature woman, and wore a hat—and she had a flower name like Rose or Pansy or Iris. She desperately wanted to find her niece." I'd felt like screaming with rage and agony when I'd heard her story.

Jeanette blew smoke out of her nose and said, "So what happened?"

"I think I found her, but not officially." Persuading an orderly to look at files and to try to call me back at a certain hour. Not being allowed to call him back because he'd get into trouble. Waiting for the call and being told that certain files had been computerized, but these hadn't and they were in storage. Multiply that orderly and that story by a dozen. The hope for news, the dead ends, the sheer outrageousness of not being able to get anyone to officially tell me! "There are state hospitals all over New York State. We didn't know which one she'd started out in, if she had been transferred, if she were an outpatient, released, or even if she were still alive. The possibilities were endless. My boss told me the case was closed because the aunt had no more money to spend on the investigation. But I'd take the file home on weekends and make calls. I couldn't stop thinking about that horrible family."

The phone rang, and Jeanette grabbed it. "Lore office! Please hold!" she commanded the caller, and then shouted, "Jacob!... Jacob! It's for you! Line three! Pick up!"

A man shouted something garbled from far away, from way down the hall.

"So what horrible family?"

"The client's sister, the girl's mother, had been molesting her own son practically his entire life. She gave him AIDS. She died, then he lingered on for years and died. Meanwhile the alcoholic, wife-beating father deserted the family. Then the daughter had a nervous breakdown and was put into a state mental hospital. She was in her teens with no guardian."

"Christ." Jeanette exhaled. "Where was the well-meaning flower aunt while all this was going on? I mean, suddenly she cares?"

"She told me she was out of the country. She never married, had a career, and lost touch."

"I had a sister like that, I'd lose touch, too."

"But she decided, after all these years, that she wanted to find her only living relative. The neighbors told her that she was in a mental hospital. She remembered the girl as a quiet eleven-year-old. Now she must be in her mid-thirties. No date of birth."

"Did you find her? Was she so damaged she—"

The phone rang, and Jeanette fixed it with a malevolent glare. She snapped it up and said, "Cohen, Stein, and Lenkowitz," as if she were nearly insensible with boredom. She pushed the "hold" button and screamed, "Jacob!... Jacob! Pick up! Pick up!"

There was an answered shout and a tremendous crash noise from far away.

Jeanette raised one Harlow-thin penciled black eyebrow, but neither of us said anything. The "hold" button stopped blinking. The phone rang again. Jeanette snapped it up and barked, "Lore office! Please hold!"

"I have to go. I'll let you get back to work." I stood up.

"Not yet! Just tell me what happened to the girl!"

"I think I found her and I told the aunt, but it had come down to getting a court order and she was the only one who could do that. She had to prove she was the closest relative."

"Did she see her? Did she recognize her?" Jeanette was smoking faster now.

I smiled wanly. "Oh, you're just like me. I don't know. I gave her all the information, the name of a lawyer to help her, and never heard from her again. I hope she found her. My happy ending would be that she rescued her niece and they lived together forever and ever."

"Yeah, but there aren't that many happy endings..." Jeanette frowned, then took a puff on her Salem. She had called me, more than once, an innocent.

I didn't tell her about Whitfield, about how much I had wanted to find that lost niece, about getting up in the middle of the night to go over my notes, about the crisscross diagrams I'd made of the bureaucracy. Departments, units, archives. Calling one office and saying I'd spoken to someone at another office. All true, of course. Then I'd say that I'd been told to call and to ask for so-and-so, who was actually whoever happened to pick up the phone. Trying to make someone feel responsible for helping me. Pretending I knew more about the record-keeping routine than I did, holding my breath, wanting to hear that the niece was alive.

"So tell Richard to let me know if he wants me to follow up on anything."

The phone rang again, Jeanette waved at me as she reached for it, and I left. As the glass door closed behind me, I heard her screaming, "Jacob! Line one! Pick up pick up pick up!"

The elevator came, I stepped in and pushed "Lobby." Investigation completed. I did what I was hired to do. I sighed. Everybody says they did their best, and yet...I think they let you down, you were betrayed. But what if it's just a case of "You lost your virginity and all hell broke loose"? What if it were all as simple as that?

I stepped out of the elevator, made my way through the lunch crowds in the lobby, and in seconds I was out on the sidewalk in the sun. Rose and Fern? Reunited? I thought of the aunt's little straw hat perched on the chignon of white hair; I thought of Charles flapping his arms in the baggy white shirt in the middle of the road as Mother and I drove away. Locked away, left behind. I suddenly felt terribly sad. Sad for everybody. It was a spectacular postcard-blue-sky day.

IT WAS JUST AFTER closing this case that I stopped in to see if Mickey had locations for me.

"I have to call my brother." I sighed. "He left messages demanding I call him last night, but I knew that whatever he told me would mean I wouldn't be able to sleep afterward."

"That piece of shit," said Mickey as I punched in the 601 area code. "How's your mother?"

"She's fine. Talked to her yesterday in the nursing home and she doesn't understand why all these people around her never get dressed, are sort of out of it. She's fine. She should be at home."

The minute I said, "Hello," the shouting started. He was

enraged. I listened to him, and then I said, "No, I'm not going to do that. It's her decision."

He was loud, furious. "Mother's runnin' outta money, and it's gonna take five hunnerd dollahs ta jes' close the grave!"

I said I had to go and hung up the phone, white-faced.

"What'd he say to you?" demanded Mickey. I told him, and he shook his head in disgust and said, "Your family is not human."

My brother wanted Mother's power of attorney and she wouldn't give it to him and I refused to persuade her. But he got it: He had her admitted to a psychiatric ward.

Mystery Lunch

W e met at a diner on Second Avenue; he drank coffee and I drank water as he looked me over. He told me on the phone he was an investigator and a friend of Spiesman's. There was some feud between him and yet another investigator I'd worked for, so this meeting and anything that came out of it was to remain secret. I had agreed. My plan was to get along with both of them. Loyal to each one quite separately. He'd said, "I want to use you on a case, but first I want to see what you look like."

That was okay with me. I know legions of New York women who would have slammed down the phone and set fire to their panty hose, but I thought it made sense. I had to look a certain way to do the case.

I wore khakis, a white short-sleeved sweater, a navy blazer, and tasseled loafers. Reed was dressed almost identically, and when we shook hands we laughed. I liked him right away. Thin, gray eyes, dark hair, my age. He told me his father was a cop and a writer. Short stories. He'd heard I wrote books and seemed to like that.

The case was super-hush-hush because the subject was the partner of an investment firm and the other partners were our client. They were obviously upset enough to consult a detective but were of mixed feelings about investigating one of their own.

The next afternoon, I met Reed in front of a downtown building and we went up in the elevator together. We were not announced but were immediately led down a long hallway to a corner office with a breathtaking view. It is in these moments, as I'm being introduced, that I think: *What on earth will I be asked to do?*

I remember Vinny Parco's hilarious takeoff on the old television show: "Your assignment, should you choose to accept it...," accompanied by excited Italian arm waving.

The secretary was told to close the door, and Brad Dutton motioned Reed and me to sit down in matching club chairs beside a low glass coffee table. The entire room seemed to float in light. The two corner walls appeared open to the sky and the toy buildings below.

"Sorry to hurry you in this way, but since we've used you, Reed, as an investigator in the past, I didn't want anyone to see you in the reception area and wonder what you're here for today."

Talk was general. Then they spoke about a time frame. Was I available for the next few days? Maybe every other day for three days, or tomorrow and the day after tomorrow and then the following Monday?

"We don't want him to say that it happened just this one time because he had a fight with someone or his grandmother died," said Brad. He kept pulling at his blue silk tie. This man in the pin-striped suit was very tense about this meeting.

"Right," said Reed. "But we have to make a case for reasonable continuity." He turned to Brad.

"It's terrible. I think it has been noticed every day." Brad turned to me. "He usually goes out for lunch at about twelve-thirty..."

"But C should be ready for him an hour before that.

There is the chance he might go earlier," said Reed. "Can you be down here in the building at eleven or eleven-thirty tomorrow?"

"Yes. Of course," I said. "But what is this all about? I haven't heard a word about the problem. What are we trying to accomplish? What are we after?"

"Sorry!" breathed Brad. "Reed and I talked on the phone, and I—" He stopped and started again. "One of our partners experiences a total personality change during the day. No one can understand it." He sighed. "We attribute this to something that he does or to something that happens to him during lunch."

THE NEXT MORNING AT eleven-fifteen, I stood in the marble lobby thinking, *I know why cooks don't want marble floors in kitchens.* Maybe I also knew why detectives are called gumshoes. The smart ones probably wear them.

There were eight elevators, appallingly large elevators holding at least twenty-five people in each. I was interested in the two farthest away labeled 40–55. The bells pinged when the doors opened, so all this pinging was going on. Heads would bob out, attached to hurrying bodies. Women with shoulder-strap bags, men and women with briefcases. There'd be a surge of humanity charging through the lobby. Two exits or entrances, both with glass doors, both at least sixty feet away.

I stood, trying not to lean against the planter, which came to midthigh. I pinched a shiny green leaf and realized the poor thing was real. I thought of it longing to be in a field somewhere instead of in the lobby of an office building in the financial district of New York City.

The field. *Out in it again*, I thought. No graham crackers, but there was a nearby newsstand for Oreos. *Ping. Ping.*

I focused on the mass of heads. I looked at my watch. More pinging, more heads, as we neared twelve, then twelve-fifteen. I told myself to watch all the elevators because what if he had gone to another floor for a document or for a meeting? Then he might be descending in the elevator marked 20–39. Or in the one marked 1–19.

Yesterday had been ridiculous. Brad Dutton had told me that he'd walk down the hall in front of me and when he was in front of the subject's open office door, he would say something about the weather. I was to glance in that doorway and get a look at the subject I was to follow today. We walked quickly down a long corridor of open doors and people at desks in front of computers, and suddenly he turned around and said, "I hope we don't have a hot summer again." Then he kept walking. I looked in the open door, and the office was empty. A chair, a desk, and two framed prints of clipper ships.

Brad stood at the end of the hall beside his office, holding the door open. I went in, sat next to Reed, Brad closed the door, and said, "Okay, did you get a good look?"

"There was no one there," I said.

I nearly laughed. This man was so nervous. He left me and Reed, and then he came back and said he had found him in the library and there were three other men at the table with him, but he was the shortest. Reed asked for his height and weight, and Brad was mystified. You'd think he'd been asked for a secret of the universe. "He's the shortest one sitting in the library," he repeated.

I said, "But if they're all sitting down, won't they all look about the same?"

Reed gave Brad a look that said, "She has a point." Brad left the room again and came back with the news that the subject was wearing a red tie.

"Terrific," I said, and stood up. Brad told me the library

was the third door on the left after the main reception area.
I began walking.

The door was half-open, and I could see four people at
the table. A glimpse of a maroon tie, a gray suit, balding
head, but the head was down. No face. I kept walking, then
I turned around and walked back. You should never make
eye contact with a subject you're surveilling. I knew it and
I risked it. This time he happened to be talking, and I could
see him in profile. Olive complexion. Sideburns perhaps a
little longer than the style, eyebrow a little more angled than
usual. No facial hair, no scars, no big nose, nothing unusual
about this man that I could see.

I walked back to Brad Dutton's office and closed the door
behind me. "Think you can pick him out tomorrow?" asked
Reed.

"Absolutely," I responded, and Reed smiled with relief. *I
have a chance*, I told myself. *There* is *a chance I could pick
him out.*

Brad was a wreck. You'd think he was ratting on his
brother and the Mob was going to whack him for doing it.

So there I was, checking every balding man under six feet
tall and trying to remember the shape of those eyebrows.

The edge of the planter was digging into my thigh, and
I realized I was sitting in the peat moss. A tall, uniformed
porter was staring at me from across the huge lobby, so I
moved away from the tree like a guilty little kid. *Ping! Ping!
Ping!* It was 12:58. *Ping! Ping!* Five elevators were arriving at
once, and more than a hundred people poured out of them.
I thought I saw him. He walked toward the back entrance of
the building with a man and a woman and carried a brown
envelope.

Oh, but was he that chunky? *Was* that his head? The ears
were flat, but I couldn't see the sideburns from this distance.
He was nearly at the door, about to go out of the building.

The elevators were pinging like mad, like xylophones. *Ping! Ping!* If I followed the wrong man and the right one arrived behind me, the subject would be swept away by the lobby crowd like a twig in a river, and I'd have wasted the whole day. I had to make a decision.

I sprang into action, walking quickly across the lobby, through the door, and outside into the spring day. He was crossing the street. I was tense, praying to the patron saint of detectives: *Please let this be the right man.*

Traffic separated me from the short, stocky man. He wasn't more than five foot four inches tall. I stepped out, played chicken with a taxi, and then stepped back. *No case is worth death*, I told myself. *I just won't charge anybody. I'll tell them I wasn't here, that I was throwing up all night, that I think it's a mix of tuberculosis and anthrax. I'll begin tomorrow.* I watched the man go into a store that sold greeting cards and candy. This was the beginning of his mysterious lunch hour. Would I follow him to a hotel and watch him meet a glamorous hooker? Would it be S&M? Would he get naked with animals?

I crossed the street. Rushed to the store. Then I took a deep breath and slowly pushed open the glass door. The stocky man was paying for something. Back of bald head. Was this the right bald head? Something changed hands. A drug deal? In a store that sold Hallmark cards? Anything was possible. But it seemed to be a receipt and change from a ten-dollar bill. I stood behind a treelike display of hanging stuffed rabbits and peeked between them.

Being a detective had raised my threshold of embarrassment. I wondered if anything could ever humiliate me again.

Please turn to the side, please turn to the side, I sent the brain waves to him as he bent over the display of candy. I felt like leaping out from behind the bunny tree and shrieking, "Show me your eyebrows!"

He abruptly straightened up and headed for the door. I felt someone standing beside me. "May I help you with something?"

"Um, no. Not today. Thanks. I'm just looking." I bumped the display, and stuffed rabbits swayed crazily in my face between me and the clerk.

I left the store and looked to the right and to the left. There he was. Going into the bank, using the automatic teller machine. I stood outside and prayed I wasn't wasting my time on the wrong man.

Eight minutes had passed since he'd descended in the elevator. How many hundreds of people had poured out of elevators in these past eight minutes? He came out and started down Beaver Street. A wave of relief hit me. The eyebrows! It was the subject!

Thrilled, euphoric, I walked about forty feet behind him, refusing to give in to the urge to click my heels in the air. I did give two happy little skips, and a banker type passed me and smiled. Oh, this was great. This was being a kid again. Subject walked quickly, with a purpose. I noted shoes, I noted cut of the suit, I noted the brown envelope and was close enough to see the brad closing. Whatever he'd gotten at the shop was in his pocket.

I was wild with curiosity. I had cab fare in my pocket. I had subway tokens. I felt poised to do anything to keep on him. Hotel room? That would be tricky. Would twenty dollars bribe a maid? I'd never bribed anybody before. Oh, except the customs official at Algeciras when all his men had raised their machine guns at me and at my knapsack. I'd just gotten off the ferry from Tangiers. "No drugs! *¡No droga!*" I had yelped, with arms raised. "Carnation Slender!" Chocolate marshmallow Carnation Slender, if one wanted to be specific. Those black patent-leather hats above those stern, unsmiling faces. "Just taste it!" I'd insisted. "*¡Con leche!*"

I implored them. Me with my fear of starving to death. Me carrying a piece of baloney in the clear photo sleeve of my little green wallet in first grade. That went on for years. It always left grease on the picture of my dog, but it made me feel safe. In Africa I'd graduated to biltong, dried elephant meat that was gray until you licked it and it turned blood red.

The subject was slowing down, so I did, too. The streets were narrow, felt worlds away from Broadway. I could suddenly sense New Amsterdam. This part of the financial district was of a human scale, with sunlight, buildings that were one and two stories high, and without crowds. I followed the stocky figure as he hurried up Beaver Street. He turned under an awning that said, "Lounge," and disappeared in the front door.

I crossed the street and looked at the squat one-story building. The two small windows were cheap stained glass on one side of a heavy dark wooden door. The place was meant to look like an old-fashioned English pub and was actually called The Cork & Bottle. Quaint it was not.

I waited four minutes, then took off my scarf and sunglasses and with my raincoat over my arm pulled open the heavy door. I was excited. This was it. I was going to solve the mystery of the personality change. For Reed. For Brad. For all the partners of that high-in-the-sky investment firm.

The room was quite dark. Within four feet of the open door, the subject turned on his bar stool and looked directly at me. I dropped my eyes like the demure detective I am, let go of the door, and walked in. The entire room, which stretched back eighty feet, went silent. Dozens of men looked me over. I stood still. The bartender, rosy-cheeked, with a white apron over a paunch, lifted an arm and said, "Sit anywhere. What can I get you?"

I sat down hurriedly at a table about twenty feet from the

subject and called out, "Diet Coke, please!" I cringed at all the attention I was getting, but conversation began again and a young Hispanic waiter appeared with my drink. I realized I was the only woman in the place.

The subject was sitting on the bar stool nearest the door beneath a large suspended television with the sound cut off. I saw him drink from a stemmed glass filled with ice and an amber liquid. He then called for another.

I wrote on the cocktail napkin that the second drink had arrived and the time was 1:20 p.m. The bartender poured a shot from a bottle behind the bar. In my report, I would carefully say that it had a black label and white printing. It was, of course, Johnnie Walker Black. I would verify this later. The subject lit a large cigar, which was probably his purchase at the card shop, and turned to his right to begin a conversation with the heavyset man on the next stool.

This man had gray hair and wore a plaid shirt, khaki trousers, and running shoes. I watched for any passing of an envelope, for any unusual thing to happen. Eyebrows finished his drink, called for another. Each drink was a shot of Scotch and a spray of water or club soda. I wrote down 1:32, then 1:45, then 1:52. Astonishing. But yes, he was really pouring them down his throat and the glass was always empty before he asked for a refill.

Subject raised his arm for another drink at 2:01. I had a second Diet Coke and pretended to study the open notebook in front of me on the table. I heard the cash register clang for the first time and saw that the subject had paid the bartender and no change was returned. *Oh, Eyebrows! What are you doing to yourself?*

This drink went right down; another was poured and put before him at 2:12. Eyebrows paid and I heard the cash register, but no change was returned. At 2:19 the bartender poured him another, and he paid. I was now writing in my notebook. How could this be happening to that man no taller than five feet four inches during his lunch hour!

I was poised to follow him somewhere, anywhere, even to the men's room if I had to, with the idea that there might be something more to these lunches. But the subject never left the bar stool and ate nothing. He smoked a cigar and consumed nine drinks.

At 2:30 p.m. the subject stood, left a five-dollar tip, then departed The Cork & Bottle, still smoking the cigar. I followed him, taking in great whiffs. He walked, swaying slightly, on Beaver Street to South William Street, crossing Broad and then walking on Stone. It was an easy tail, with few people between me and the subject and very little chance he'd turn around. At 2:35 p.m. he waved at someone in the window of the A. J. Kelly Bar. At 2:36 p.m. he was back at his office building but standing outside as he finished the cigar. At 2:42 p.m. he entered the building, proceeded to the elevators, and ascended. I watched him step in and saw the doors close behind him, and then I sighed with great relief. I'd spotted him, I'd followed him and not been burned, and I knew exactly how he spent his lunch hour.

"That's right. Nine shots of Johnnie Walker Black." I was in the phone booth in the alcove behind the newsstand. The door was closed and I'd paged Reed, who'd called me right back. "Yes, that's it. And the cigar must mask the smell of liquor on his breath."

Reed breathed, "Well, now we know. I'll give Brad Dutton a call and confirm that he'd like you to do this again."

"I think it would be fair to the subject if we did."

"Yeah." Reed paused. "Hey, good work! Thanks! I'll call you later and let you know if it's on again."

The surveillance was on again the next day. This time I

watched Eyebrows pay $2.32 for the cigar and followed him without that panicky sense of "Where the devil am I going? Will I lose you?" tension inherent in every tail.

Once in the bar, I sat farther away this time, but it was not good being recognized by the bartender and then asked by the waiter if I worked nearby. I had to invent a job in the financial district and being new in town.

I thought of my days at Citibank. It was when they'd just decided to hire women to be in training as officers. That first day was interesting since my line and Walter Wriston's were crossed and I got all the chairman's phone calls. Plunging into my new career, I read the biography of Bernie Cornfeld, skimmed *The Wall Street Journal* every day, and thought, *Oh, wow, I'm a banker.* I was an officer in training in the Capital Goods Department way up on the tenth floor, in charge of all the accounts for General Electric and nine other big, Fortune 500 corporations. I would check the balances and chirpily recite them to the treasurers who called every morning. Tedious stuff, but I had my own secretary and everyone thought it was this wonderful job. Actually, I've never had my own secretary again. People were so impressed with my position, with my title. But I wasn't. I was bored. I told one of the treasurers that I weighed 382 pounds and was very grateful to have any job at all. I described my specially reinforced chair. We laughed so much; he believed I was this fat, jolly banker. I'd happily tell him the balances, which were always in the millions.

Meanwhile, downstairs, Citibank had given me my own checking account. This was as mysterious to me as trigonometry. I didn't really trust banks, but of course I hadn't mentioned this during my interview. I had gone off to college with a year's worth of traveler's checks, which I hid in my room. Each year I had done this. Mother tried to talk me

out of it but then relented. Now I was just out of college and
had this job in the headquarters of Citibank on Park Avenue
in New York City.

One Saturday morning, I was awakened by the telephone.
The woman at the frame shop on Lexington began yelling at
me because my check had bounced. I apologized profusely and
said I'd bring over the $27.50 that very day and that I would
certainly speak to the bank about it. On Monday, I certainly
did speak to them about it!

"Didn't you open this account for me? In my name? And I
have all these checks with my name printed on them!" I was
very annoyed at the situation. "You have really embarrassed
me. I wrote a check and the woman at the frame shop called
and said it was no good!"

The man on the line was not able to interrupt me, could
not say a word.

"I do not understand why Citibank would open an account
for me, tell me it is mine, print checks with my name in the
corner, present them to me, and then let this happen!"

The "service representative" burst out that I didn't have
enough money in my account to cover the check, and as a
matter of fact, I was overdrawn by thirty-one dollars.

"Well!" I retorted, amazed at him. "Isn't it your job to
notice that and to take care of it? Isn't that why you are han-
dling my account? So something like this is *never* allowed to
happen!"

This man then told me the truth about banks.

It was my first bank account, how was I to know how
it worked? Mother never discussed sex *or* money with me.
I vaguely remembered our bank in Jackson taking care of
something like this for her and then calling her later and
telling her about it. Mother had thanked him; he'd been a
gentleman. I was nearly faint with the revelation that a bank

in New York could be so different. How could this be so
serious, so upsetting to everyone? Why, if a bank were on
its toes, this simply could not happen. Not long after this
conversation, I quit my job. No one in the Capital Goods
Department wanted me to leave; they pleaded with me to
stay, my boss even took me to lunch, but I refused to recon-
sider. I think it was a narrow escape—for me, for General
Electric, for everybody.

IT WAS JOHNNIE WALKER Red for Eyebrows the second day. I wrote 1:25, 1:41, 1:45, my God, 1:50, and 2:00
p.m. He smoked his cigar, wrote on pages he'd brought in a
brown envelope, talked to the ponytailed male to his right.
Same bar stool. The subject paid sometimes and sometimes
tipped. More drinks were ordered and drunk at 2:07, 2:14,
2:18, and 2:20. We were back up to nine drinks. At 2:23
Eyebrows finished his last drink, tipped the bartender, and
stood up.

I watched him leave the bar and stood up and tried to be
casual as I pulled on my raincoat. I looked at my watch and
then walked to the door. The bartender looked at me and
said, "Hey, I'm sorry I changed the channel on you."

I smiled. "I wasn't really watching. Don't worry about it."
Oh, *why* was he trying to make conversation with me!

We talked for a minute, a very long minute, as I pictured
the subject *not* going back to the office. I had to get outside
and find him. I said, "Why does that shot glass look funny
to me?"

"You have a good eye," he said. "It's one and a quarter
ounces, and a regular shot glass is only seven-eighths of
an ounce." This was the shot glass he used for Eyebrows'
drinks. "Not quite a double," he added.

I said good-bye and walked out, let the door swing closed,

and then looked frantically to the right and to the left. It was my being part beagle that saved the day—I thought I could smell the cigar and started to run in that direction. Sure enough, around the corner and a quarter of a block away, the chunky figure was strolling along in the spring afternoon. Luckily, he walked back to the office a lot slower than he walked to the bar. I followed him, happily inhaling, and thought, *Poor man. Marinating himself like this. I hope he hates his job because he may lose it.* I felt a certain affection for him by the time I watched him get into the elevator. And I felt pity.

I reported to Reed from the same phone booth and he was happy the surveillance had been a success. He, too, felt sorry for the subject. "Maybe we can recommend that they get him some help," said Reed, and I agreed immediately.

When I typed up my report that evening, I multiplied nine drinks times one and a quarter ounces and then divided that by seven-eighths of an ounce and determined that Eyebrows had drunk nearly thirteen drinks made with a regular shot glass. It was amazing that he could even get his arms into his raincoat, could even find his office, let alone return to it and work.

The client decided he knew enough. I wrote the report, billed Reed, Reed sent me a check. Case closed.

I never really saw his face; I had looked down when he turned on the bar stool to look at me. The arched eyebrows, the olive complexion, the balding head, the overweight short figure with the swaying gait, which after lunch became that of a captain on the deck of his rolling ship. I wondered why he drank. A monstrous wife he couldn't divorce. A demanding, invalid mother who filled him with guilt. A love affair gone wrong. A child with cancer. Blackmail. Murder. Crimes against nature. All I knew for sure were those two damning words: *He drinks.*

Poor Eyebrows. Maybe the reason he drank Scotch was simple. Maybe his banking career was proving to be as unsatisfying as mine had been. Maybe losing this job in the world of finance would be a turning point, the beginning of something better. I hoped so. I thought of him once in a while.

I'll never forget that chunky figure reeling ever so slightly through the narrow streets and me, the beagle, skibbling along behind him with my nose in the air, sucking in the scent of his cigar.

A Lot of Diamonds,
a Little Revenge

Mickey was now a one-man band and had hired me as a freelance operative. We were working several cases at a time together. He'd been my favorite investigator at Parker's—the one whose judgment I trusted the most. He was honest, the brightest, and the one with the most savvy. Most of the time, Mickey and I were enmeshed in an activity that is like running to the site of a plane crash carrying a box of Band-Aids. Again and again. Every day of the week, Mickey and I did what we did at Parker's. We went after counterfeiters.

We roamed Broadway, forayed into factories in Queens, and raced through the Holland Tunnel into Jersey—always after them, relentlessly on their tail. I still slinked around Chinatown. We wore hidden cameras and hidden tape recorders and video during car chases. I fished names out of my *What to Name the Baby* book, and once in a while I ordered a new set of cheap business cards. The counterfeiters just kept on getting more sophisticated, and the goods kept getting more like the real thing.

I remember one morning the bus took forever, but Mickey had warned me not to take the subway that week. Something about germ warfare. Inside information only he and

Chiefie had. Sometimes I thought those two characters were tapping into Pentagon intelligence sources. They wanted me to think it. They loved being mysterious, loved having me plead with them to tell me more. Chiefie smiled, Mickey smirked, they teased me, and sometimes I even stamped my foot in outrage, but to no avail. I never knew when they were having me on. So there I was on the Lexington Avenue bus as it wheezed slowly downtown in the rush-hour traffic— promising myself I would not tell either one of them.

The office that summer was a room over a drugstore— eight by ten feet with a window in case of fire, guarded by surveillance cameras inside and out. All walls from floor to ceiling were festooned with the tools of the trade: two-way radios, throwaway phones, reference books, notepads, tape recorders, monitors, videos, computer programs, parkas, hats, and flak jackets. There were also about thirty framed certificates from various law enforcement agencies giving Mickey their respective stamps of approval. Guns were either worn or kept in desk drawers. A baseball bat was propped by the door. A billy club hung from a leather strap on the door and made a big noise whenever anyone came in or out. This office was prepared for attack.

When I opened the door, Mickey handed me a sheet of notebook paper. A new case. "Maybe you could call John Sykes…" Mickey was tapping on the computer keyboard, talking to me in profile as usual.

"Sykes, Talbot, and Wells?"

"A good firm."

"I know. I've heard of them."

Mickey turned in his chair and watched me standing there reading. "Give that guy—give Sykes a call before you do anything. He said it was important he go over a few things."

Turns out they wanted to meet with me. I went uptown to the Park Avenue office, had the meeting, came back, and faced Mickey. In silhouette, of course. He hadn't moved from the computer.

"There were three lawyers sitting there, around a coffee table in Sykes's office. All very nice." I sighed. "Very civilized meeting, but the thing is . . ."

"What?"

"We're their second choice. Somebody else mucked up the case and so now—"

"Fuck."

"My sentiments exactly." I pulled out my notebook. "The case revolves around a jewelry designer whose stuff is now being sold at Bergdorf's, at Bendel's, at very high-end department stores all over the country. But it's being knocked off . . ."

"Costume jewelry?"

"No. Mostly diamonds, silver, and gold. The design is bold, easy to ID; it jumps out at you." I showed him the glossy ten-by-twelve photographs. The necklaces, bracelets, and rings lay on beds of velvet. "They put the designer's wife on the speakerphone from Palm Beach. She said it had become a huge problem in just the last six months and they'd had some success in stopping it, but the big problem is right here in New York." I sighed. "Then she got her Palm Beach lawyer on the phone from his office, and it became a conference call from there to New York. Four lawyers and the designer's wife, and sometimes all of them expressing an opinion as to how this investigation should be handled at the same time. Wild." I'd been glad to shake hands and get out of there.

Mickey reached for the phone. "Diet Coke?" He ordered and then turned back to me. "So what do they want? Evidential purchases, C and D letters, what?"

"I'm supposed to go to the firm in the diamond district and order the design for my store." I took back the photos.

"Sounds cut-and-dried, but I guess if they won't sell them to me or won't consent to make the design then it's over—a dead end. Because Sykes and Mrs. Kimble are positive this company is making them, filling orders, shipping them out. And I've got the report from the other P.I. firm right here." I handed it to Mickey, who shook his head.

"This was blown to the sky only three weeks ago!"

"I know. It's a hundred percent horrible," I said cheerfully. "Ridiculous! These diamond dealers deal with their own people, and now a parade of complete unknowns starts coming in, wanting this design, within such a short time span..."

"Two guys. I know 'em both," Mickey said, reading. "Big shots at a pricey firm charging huge hourly fees and they blew it." He put the pages down in disgust. I knew what firm he meant. I'd done work for them. They were a Kroll wannabe outfit. Kroll is probably the biggest white-shoe investigative firm in the world. "When do they want you to do this?"

I shrugged. "Yesterday."

There was a bang on the door; Mickey opened it about five inches and handed out a few bills. There was barely enough room to take in the paper bag. I heard somebody say, "*Gracias*," and the door closed. The phone rang, and Mickey talked to a client as we both snapped open our diet sodas. I went out in the hall and unlocked the door for the other room Mickey had rented, sat down, and listed all I had to do. The counterfeit locations were new.

I called Nevart Badrusian. "My name is Barbara Lee Allen and I'm a private detective. I was just at Sykes, Talbot, and Wells and I've taken on a case for John Sykes, who gave me your name. Do you have a minute to talk to me? Is this a convenient time?" I dived in. It took longer than a minute, but at last she gave me what I wanted: an invitation to her office. I put on lipstick, grabbed my notebook and all the morning's notes, and jammed them into a portfolio. I locked the door behind me, then stuck my head in Mickey's room.

"Where ya going?"

"I'm going to meet with an Armenian who was busted for making this design. She's promised Sykes, Talbot, and Wells she won't do it anymore and I'd like to talk to her, see the stuff, hear anything she can tell me. The way she sells, buys, whatever." I sighed and jammed papers into the file I clutched. "I'm going to use that Houston address. These old cards I never used for the Lippman handbag case." I sighed again. "Mickey, I don't know a thing about the jewelry business. Diamonds are a girl's best friend. That's it. That's my limit."

Mickey smirked. "Yeah, you'll go far on Forty-seventh Street. Those Jews will eat you alive, Charlie."

"Well, I'll start with an Armenian who sounds awfully fierce, then work my way up to the shark tank."

Sometimes I fight with myself. I told myself to hurry to 47th and Fifth before she changed her mind, but my feet wouldn't cooperate because I was rehearsing my approach. I was holding myself back, stalling. Sometimes I felt like an actress who hadn't seen the script. I'd been pushed onto the stage and the curtain would rise, so to speak, when I walked in the door. It was quite a feeling. The adrenaline rush was terrific. Adrenaline. My drug of choice.

Summer on Fifth Avenue. Lots of tourists wearing shorts and sandals dragging shopping bags mixed with the business types wearing ties and office attire dragging briefcases. Nevart Badrusian's office was just off Fifth on 47th Street. Another world. Dominated by Orthodox Jews wearing beards, side curls, yarmulkes, and long black coats even in this heat. Was she the wife of someone? Jewish? Weren't Armenians Orthodox something? Would I have to win her over and then work on the husband, who made the decisions?

The address was right between Fifth and Sixth avenues in a sort of arcade. The glass door was opened by a bearded man in a black suit and side curls; I was hit with a whoosh of the air-conditioning. Before me were about fifty small booths, all selling jewelry, in the two-thousand-square-foot area. The shine of electric lights and glass counters was blinding. Gold chains hung on display stands and were sold by the yard; rings reclined under glass. Men in white shirts and yarmulkes called out to me to look, to "just look," and offered to "make good price." It was chaos. It was Middle Eastern.

She had said she was in room 12 on the lower level, so I took the stairs down to a collection of six-by-eight-foot offices with locked doors and glass walls. There was usually a desk and a phone in view and one glass display case. Very few stones or pieces of jewelry were in sight, but I had the idea there was a safe under the desk or behind the photograph on the wall. A small woman with blond streaks in her brown hair and big, very made-up dark eyes buzzed me in. "Nevart Badrusian?"

A handsome, black-haired man in his twenties squeezed behind me, locked the door, and flipped the venetian blinds so that we could not be seen. We shook hands and introduced ourselves. She seemed to blink in surprise.

Nevart was angry. Angry at being caught, at being fined, at the whole system. I listened to her hiss, figured she'd get tired and let me talk after a while. Feeling sympathetic at one point, I volunteered that yes, it was possible to go to a museum and see jewelry two thousand years old that didn't look appreciably different from something in the latest Tiffany catalog. "But there's something called intellectual property. You know all about it. You're bright enough to steer clear of the gray areas," I said.

She nodded, as if suddenly tired. Maybe all she wanted was for me to agree with her. With a quick snap of a gold lighter, she lit a cigarette; her brownish lipstick left a smudge near the tip. The rust color matched her long polished nails. She was tough, bright, quick, in her forties, and I liked her. There was no wedding ring, and Vahe—the black-haired man—seemed like a pet, possibly gay, possibly a kid brother or a cousin she allowed to do her bidding.

"You don't look like an investigator." She blew smoke out of her nose and slitted her eyes. Deep blue eye shadow was on her lids, and a heavy gold chain with a gold coin circled her throat.

"No. You don't," chimed in her aide-de-camp, also lighting up. He offered me a Gauloises, and I declined. Within a minute I thought somebody, the surgeon general maybe, should coin a phrase that was somewhere between smoking and secondary smoking. The Gauloises effect.

"Oh, they've come in here before, and they're so stupid. They think we don't know in two seconds, yes, Vahe? With their bad clothes, bad hair, lousy jewelry . . . ha! We know."

I was thankful I was wearing only silver. Everything good of mine had been stolen in Cyprus by that maniac Welsh fiancé who turned out to be already married to someone in an Irish insane asylum—he'd been so carried away with passion, he'd forgotten to mention her. So now it was silver and lapis and malachite. She went on, "They don't know anything about stones, and they think . . ." She was sneering as she drew hungrily on her cigarette.

"Listen, I don't know anything either. I'm here because John Sykes said you might help me."

It was strange how the situation began to change. I told her we had our eye on somebody, a dealer, but he'd been too clever for the other investigators and now they'd made my work twice as difficult because, of course, he was on the alert. There wasn't any softness to this woman, but she seemed to stop swinging her fists at me and I guess part of

it was that I'd passed the appearance test. She said it again:
"You don't look like an investigator. You actually fooled me
when you walked in. I even expected an investigator and
you fooled me." Turning, she spoke to Vahe in another language, and he left and came back fifteen minutes later with a
pizza. I was offered a cold drink and a slice, and this eating
ceremony, this spreading of napkins on the desk, this ritual,
seemed to mean something. To all of us.

I decided to trust her. John Sykes had said I could, but he
hadn't said how far. At this point, I knew her better than
I knew John Sykes. So I was trusting him and trusting her
when I said, "The man we're after is someone you might
know. It's Jacob Weissberg." I was holding my breath. I'd
gone the limit. Mickey—everybody—would have a fit if this
blew it, and it could. She could reach for the phone, punch in
his number, and tell him right in front of me in that language
I didn't understand, or she could wait until I'd left. I watched
her face break into a delighted grin. Nevart laughed aloud.

"Okay, I'll help you."

Great good luck. Or not! Did she mean it? Amazing. I
promised myself I'd never take a chance like that again. We
began in earnest. I started taking notes in my notebook and
then just focused on her voice and on the stones before me.
Don't ask for this. Don't ask for that. Don't use that word,
he'll know right away. There were carats. That I knew.
There were points. I was given a crash course in each. All the
silver would be sterling. Easy. The gold and the weights are
not difficult. I hoped I wouldn't trip up on the diamonds.

There was a knock on the glass door, and we all three
looked at each other. A man came in, spoke Armenian to
Nevart as I kept my head down over a few of the gemstones
that were scattered over the desk. I put my arm over my notebook and was still as a mouse with head turned away while

they talked. Nevart had become a rat. I wondered what diamond dealers did to cheese eaters on 47th Street.

The man left with a tiny brown envelope, the kind I used to carry my grade school lunch money in, and the door was locked behind him. "Okay," said Nevart. "I think you're ready. I'll call him. I'll see if he can meet you this afternoon. It's three o'clock."

"No, you can't do that! He'll connect it all—me and the design and later the cops—with you." Could she be that stupid?

Nevart lit another Gauloises with a click of the lighter. Two more cubic feet of smoke took up space in the little room. "Maybe not."

"He will. And you'd risk . . ." I didn't know what she was risking. Her business, her professional reputation, her life?

"I hate him. He is the reason I got arrested for this design. He knows I'm not allowed to make it anymore." She inhaled and then blew out the smoke. "So it would seem natural that I would have a customer I can't sell to and that I would be so adorable I would send the customer to him."

Adorable was not a word to associate with her. I shook my head slightly in amazement, and we all three laughed. Nevart was going to insist until the bitter end that a private investigator had been good enough to elude her radar. I'd passed her test, had fooled her, and now I had to fool him— her enemy. Best of all, she really wanted me to. Better than that—she was betting that I could.

Nevart punched in the number. "The phone's ringing," she said, and winked at me. "Is Jacob there? This is Nevart Badrusian . . . Okay, yes. Could you please ask him to call me back? . . . Yes, he has my office number . . . A few minutes? Okay, thank you." She put down the phone, and I handed her a business card.

"Here. I had these cards made up. My name is Barbara Lee Allen and my store is called 'B' and I'm from Houston..." I filled her in, hoping I was ready to sound savvy about diamonds.

"Now, when you are ordering, don't forget to barter. He'll think you're a fool if you don't ask for a better price. It's normal. You have to do it, and you have to be firm about it."

I nodded. I now knew the number of diamonds used in the design, the number of carats they should be, and all about the points. The cost wholesale and retail and the probable range. The cost of the necklaces at Bendel's and what I should tell him I planned to charge to compete with Neiman Marcus on my own turf in Houston. I knew what sort of discount to ask for, what he might counteroffer, what I should accept, and how long I should hesitate before agreeing. I knew the phrases that would give me away and the ones that would engender his respect. Nevart barked it at me and I absorbed it, knowing I couldn't sit in front of Jacob Weissberg and read from scraps of paper. My head was packed with the new information.

We waited for the phone to ring. Other dealers came in and left. The safe in the corner was opened and closed, and tiny brown envelopes exchanged hands. I never saw money—maybe it would be delivered later. It was as if they all knew each other and as if these were familiar transactions. The phone didn't ring. I asked Vahe and Nevart how long they'd been in the business. Generations, but of course. Great-great-grandfathers and back. Their wisdom was coded in their DNA. Mickey was right: The Jews were gonna eat me alive. *After* they tore me to pieces.

At a quarter of five, she offered to call again. I'd been in the office for four hours. "Look, don't seem too eager," I advised. "Tell him I've gone back to my hotel and I'll get in touch with you tomorrow. If you get a time for me to meet then I'll go. Whenever it is, I'll make myself available, but you should tell him you have to check with me, that I've got a busy schedule while I'm in town."

Weissberg's line was busy so I stood up and shook hands with them. They said, "Good-bye, Barbara," which gave me an odd feeling, but I'd thought it was for their own good to think of me as Barbara from the beginning. I walked down 47th Street wondering if Nevart had been to bed with Jacob Weissberg. Was it possible? She was very sophisticated, well dressed, and wily. Was he one of the sausage-curl men? Could he...could she...could they...? I told myself to stop it. Leave it to me to introduce sex to a case involving diamonds and lies and revenge.

I called the office from a phone booth on Fifth, but Mickey had left for his meeting uptown so I didn't bother to go back. My head ached from all the Gauloises smoke, and all I wanted was to sink into a bubble bath and wash my hair. I was halfway down the stairs to the subway when I remembered the germ warfare situation, so I began to walk uptown, talking to myself.

A few hours later, clean and on my straw mat, I fell asleep with carats and points and numbers floating behind my closed eyes.

I BROUGHT MICKEY UP-TO-DATE on the jewelry case when I got into the office at ten, and he said I had to be wired. Fine. First I called Nevart and she said, "He's at home with a migraine. I left a message for him to call me, but I think I'll have to call him in the office tomorrow."

So it was put off. I prayed I wouldn't forget everything that had been crammed into my tiny brain. Mickey tossed me a little tape recorder and I changed the batteries and the day went on.

The next day, I called Nevart and she said, "He's in the office, he's on the phone, he's calling me back in ten minutes."

"All systems go," I said to Mickey after hanging up.

"I think you better wear a backup tape recorder just in case." He put a second one on the desk in front of me.

I recognized it. "But isn't this the one that makes a noise after thirty minutes?"

"Yeah, but you won't be in there that long. Thirty minutes is a long time for something like this."

"Okay. I guess it is." It only felt like a long time, but it usually wasn't. I looked at my watch and called Nevart, and she said, "Jacob can see you anytime from eleven to lunch, and he goes to lunch at half past one." She was gleeful. She had baited the hook. I wasn't so gleeful since I was the bait.

DAMN. I HATED THE new phone booths, which really weren't booths at all. No privacy whatsoever. Ruinous for a private detective. Or Superman. Forty-seventh Street and Madison were streaming with crowds and a man was waiting to use the phone, making a big thing about looking at his watch. I put the tape recorder I liked in my trousers waistband and then pulled it out, checked the "pause" button, pushed on "play" and "record," then jammed it in again and lowered my short silk top over it. If I sneezed or coughed, my button and my zipper would be ripped right out, but otherwise I just had to be careful when I sat down not to do serious damage to my spleen.

The second recorder I prepared, checked, and then dropped into the open bag I carried with notebooks, pens, and a paperback. The mike was pointed up and in the clear. Then I licked my lips, fluffed my hair, put on my sunglasses, and exited the absurd excuse for a phone booth. Three minutes to get there—through crowds, through the noise, through the heat.

He's expecting me. I'm from Houston. I have this boutique. Nevart wouldn't set me up, would she? No. Have a little faith. I reached the address and saw that it was an elevator building with a porter and a long, flat table right inside the front door.

"Wait a minute," called the porter. No, he wasn't a porter after all. "Need to check your bag." He rummaged through my purse and then the briefcase but missed the tape recorder entirely. I signed the book as Barbara Lee Allen. "Need a photo ID."

I swallowed and tried to smile. "I have an appointment with Jacob Weissberg," I said. "The sixth floor. He's expecting me."

Would they call up to confirm? Fine. But the guard didn't reach for the phone. He held out his hand. "Need an ID— driver's license, something with a photo..." Then I saw the metal detector facing me like the guillotine, where a second and a third guard in khaki uniforms waited for me. Would this screw up the tapes? Would the alarm sound? Would they frisk me with that baton thing, and find the one I was wearing?

I gave him my new business card with the Houston address, and he handed it back. "No, this won't cut it."

"I don't have a photo ID," I said. "I changed bags today and I don't drive in the city, so I never thought I'd need it." People were passing me, having bags checked, and being waved on toward the metal detector. *Damn*, I was thinking, *will I really have to turn around and start over another day?* I couldn't stand the idea of that. "Here," I said, smiling. "What about— Take this." Lots of lunch-hour people were moving through the lobby, many were being recognized and waved through, others were talking to each other, all to my advantage.

The guard had evidently made a decision about me. I looked harmless. He didn't even look at what I gave him but photocopied it behind the counter, handed it back. I got myself around the metal detector with a quick little sidestep in the meandering crowd and seconds later I was rising in the elevator.

The sixth floor was one long corridor with one locked door. "WEISSBERG" was printed in white on the black sign. I looked up and saw cameras beaming down at me. I rang the bell and the door opened. An elderly man with side curls and a gray beard said, "Do you have an appointment?" and I told him I did. "Follow me," he directed. I heard the door to the hall lock behind me. I was led through a locked low gate, which locked behind me, into a large open area with about eight or ten men—all dressed identically in white shirts with black suspenders and black trousers—walking back and forth between tables. They all wore side curls, and most had beards and glasses.

"This way." I was motioned into another corridor, and a door clicked behind me. Locked. "Wait here." I entered a small white room with a window overlooking 47th Street. I could see the crowds on the sidewalks below. I felt a wave of missing my new Armenian pals and wondered if they were thinking of me. There was a chair on either side of the small wooden table and the window and the videocamera aimed at me. That was it. I checked my watch several times and then began to worry about the backup tape.

"Yes, you are the friend of Nevart Badrusian."

Suddenly the room was filled with the huge persona of Jacob Weissberg. Side curls, yarmulke, wire-rimmed glasses, way over six feet, over two hundred pounds. I tried not to stare. His eyes were as big and brown as a heifer's behind the magnifying lenses. He really had wonderful brown eyes. Or did he? They were cold. The beard was distracting and

I wondered how the curls stayed curled. Did these men use curling irons every morning or sleep with a pink foam roller clipped at each ear?

Weissberg pulled the door closed and it locked loudly. The lock had a solid sound like a car door closing; there was nothing flimsy about this lock. He sat down and I presented my situation. I was a new business associate of someone he and Nevart had known in the past. We also had a second and a third friend in common. I took a deep breath and talked about them. The man had been with Saks, the other woman was from Chicago and I'd met her in Los Angeles at a trade show. "My partner, Nancy, used to work with David Gottlieb and then Silverstein bought it and then Levy bought it and everybody got thrown out." Basically, I stuck to the script. A little gossip. Some things he knew, some things he didn't know. Nevart had cooked this up. I told him about my boutique. I started seeing it. I could visualize the front window and the display cases and the mirrors and the walls, which were painted bright yellow. *Stop*, I told myself. Problems with getting the jewelry with this design. How popular it was and how annoying not having it was. I was too polite to spell it out but let him know I knew that Nevart had had problems. I insinuated that it was not an issue for me and obviously the reason I was here was that I still wanted to sell the design.

I told him what I was buying from Nevart, and he asked me what price I was paying. I told him. He nodded, apparently indicating that was okay, then asked what I wanted of the design he carried. I said I wanted a good look first, and he said he'd be back in a minute. The second the door clicked behind him, the recorder started buzzing like an angry alarm clock. I grabbed the open bag and fumbled frantically to punch it off and was barely settled again when Weissberg appeared with a tray of jewelry. It appeared that the camera

was the only witness. I supposed if someone were monitor-
ing it and me, he'd arrive any second or Weissberg would be
called out and then everything would start caving in. It was
a bit relaxing to sincerely admire the jewelry as it sat on the
islands of velvet between us.

I was there in that locked room with Jacob Weissberg for
a long time. The table was so small and we were so close and
there was so much picking up and putting down that I had
to resist staring at the hair on his knuckles and then at the
way his beard had never been shaved. I pulled myself back
to the present and told him about problems with advertising
the design, problems with Neiman Marcus. All fabricated
immediately, of course. He was cold with me and oblivious
to my southern charm. That was okay. He was from another
world and we didn't know how to handle each other. I was
telling myself I was comfortable here and wondered if he
were telling himself the same story.

Weissberg left the room another two times, and both
times I was keenly aware of the lock and the noise it made.
I thought of Whitfield. The lock-in wards. I was alone with
the cyclops high up in the corner. This time Weissberg
returned with rings, and we talked about 14-karat and 18-
karat and casting and color. "Can you use rhodium to make
it whiter?" I asked, delighted to have him say that of course
he could. Rhodium! It really *did* exist. I was silently elated.

I tried on a necklace, feeling very free now that that
blasted tape recorder was off. I prayed the other was working as he stared at me with those big bovine brown eyes and
handed me a mirror so I could admire the necklace.

I felt I was there forever. I asked for and received a 10 percent discount. We discussed COD and shipping and Jewish
holiday delays in orders. We moved on to the diamonds. I
found myself talking about points. "Are these the same?" I
asked.

Weissberg said, "No. The diamonds here are thirty-two times two and two times four...the bracelet is seventy-seven and seventy-five."

I nodded and wrote this down. *That would be normal*, I thought. So far I thought I was okay. I picked a matte finish as opposed to shiny. I chose rings, bracelets, and necklaces for my Houston boutique.

At one point, I felt sorry for the man spending all this time with me, thinking he was making a sale. He talked about developing a real business relationship for the future. Time passed. I had to get him to admit, to acknowledge on tape that he knew he was copying this design by Kimble. Sometimes the eyes looked right through me and past me. Did he suspect something? What if he suddenly stood up and said, "Who are you?" or he pushed a secret alarm under the table and the downstairs guards arrived with the photocopy of my Visa credit card from Barclays Bank and shouted, "Who is this person? And why did you sign in as Barbara Lee Allen?" What if it came down to me against all ten of these men with bobbing curls and beards? I'd been locked in again and again, and everyone outweighed me. I was wired and I was lying. About everything. Beginning with my name.

"I think you should pick one of each style," Weissberg was saying, and I pulled myself back into what was happening. I told him I'd be in London in mid-September. We discussed delivery time again and calculated the total—a bit over forty thousand dollars. I quickly added up the column in my head and was amazed that he, the little shrewdy, had made a mistake in the addition and overcharged me by nearly three thousand dollars! "Oh, excuse me," he said. I looked into those eyes and realized that he hadn't thought I'd notice. I smiled sweetly and wanted to kick him under the table. Suddenly I didn't like this man at all.

This is it, I told myself after another moment or two of

arrangements. I threw in the one carefully worded sentence and waited. He could go either way. It wasn't too late. If he distrusted me, I'd lose him. If he trusted me and told me the truth, then it was on the tape. *If* the tape was still going. He bit. He said exactly what John Sykes, Mrs. Kimble, all those lawyers, Nevart and Vahe, and Mickey wanted to hear him say. At last, negotiations were over and I could stand up from that little table. The door was opened for me. I started to shake hands and then dropped my arm to my side again. Through this door and then another locked door and then through the locked gate and then a last thank-you before I left the main room. It was too quick and I never saw what was happening at the tables, but I proceeded past them and got out into the hall. Clicking, clicking, locking closed doors behind me. I waited for the elevator as the hall videos stole my soul. I went down to the lobby, sailed past the metal detector and out into the street, which fairly screamed with normal, Technicolor activity. I felt weightless, I was starving, I'd touched earth again, back from another world. I wanted to grab strangers and shout, *"I did it!"* And I couldn't wait to call Nevart and thank her.

THAT NIGHT I WAS lying on the floor, thinking. I'd moved the straw mat under the window, and there was a sliver of moon looking down at me from between the two skyscrapers on Third Avenue. Mickey had been happy, John Sykes, Mrs. Kimble, and her designer husband very, very pleased, and Nevart euphoric. She knew that I couldn't tell her every detail, but what I'd told her had made her laugh, had made her gloat. Especially the three-thousand-dollar "mistake." She did not ever tell me why she hated him, why revenge was so delicious. I would probably never know.

I looked up at the fingernail moon and thought that so

much of the day had been luck. Yes, I'd known my lines and pulled it off, but that damn buzzing backup tape recorder! The not having a Barbara photo ID, the guard not finding the recorder in my bag, not finding the one in my waistband, the sidestepping the metal detector—it could have all been over before it began.

The thought of facing huge Jacob Weissberg's wrath in the tiny locked room made me feel weak, even now, hours after the possibility. What would I have done? Maybe I would have suddenly stretched out my arms and shouted, "Okay, hands up! Open that door but stay back! Stand clear! Unlock that door and the next one and the next one! Get out of my way!" And if those men in black had hesitated? My pocketbook held everything. I laughed aloud, imagining holding a Tampax in front of me like a weapon. "Stand back if you know what's good for you! Unclean woman making an escape!"

Little Girls Who Tell Lies

For a while, though I was still doing cases for Mickey, I took on unofficial public defender work in Brooklyn. The court-appointed lawyer would introduce me, and if I wanted the case, I'd tell the client all that needed to be done and then say, "Okay, for five hundred dollars I am yours from this minute until the trial is over." My expenses would be photocopies, film, and the subway, and that was included in my fee. I'd track all alibis, talk to every possible witness, photograph the crime scene if necessary—in short, do everything in my power to help them. Anything to follow up, to question, any interview to be reconducted, any witness to be found—all they had to do was ask. When some cases were over, I probably earned four dollars an hour, but I didn't care because I felt so sorry for them, had seen the way certain lawyers had treated them, knew how helpless they felt. And—just so you don't think I'm an entirely good person—I love criminal work. They'd call me any time of the day or night with an idea, and I would follow up, keep them informed, and they'd have reports every week of where things stood. A copy of every report would go to the lawyer.

I was hired by a Haitian woman whose eighteen-year-old son had been accused of raping a twelve-year-old girl in their apartment building on two occasions. It wasn't the first time I'd been hired by the mother of a black teenager accused of rape. I always liked the mothers. The mothers with the jobs, two or three jobs, who'd gone to school at night, who'd take the day off to show up in court every single time. A husband or father was rare. But I always loved the mothers, I would do anything for the mothers.

François was over six feet tall, very thin, very black, and very quiet. He seemed to be suffering, rarely spoke, and, in contrast to the boys his age, was wearing clean, pressed blue jeans, no do-rag, no jewelry. I spent hours with him and his mother at their kitchen table in an attempt to reconstruct events of the days of the purported rapes. It was difficult. No one in the family wrote anything down; they didn't seem to have dentist appointments or meetings or plans for lunch. François worked part-time on a construction site but was paid off the books, so there were no pay stubs. I began to tag events around holidays and birthdays, as in, "Did you talk to her about this before the Fourth of July?"

His mother, Marie, had come from Haiti, gotten her college degree at night, had a good job. Three kids, second marriage. The apartment was spotless. You could smell the urine in the halls of the building and I hated touching the button in the elevator, but once Marie opened the door of her apartment, I stepped into a clean and orderly world.

Marie's entire savings to leave the neighborhood, leave New York for Pennsylvania, had gone for bail. The first lawyer they had hired took thousands of dollars from her and did nothing.

I canvassed the building, looked for witnesses who could place François somewhere else. It seemed as if every single cell phone were no longer in service and as if every single person had moved with no forwarding address or left the construction job the week before. François's best friend since sixth grade had been with him on both mornings in question, but no amount of talking could persuade him to become involved.

I went from Manhattan to Brooklyn to see Marie, François, and the kind stepfather so many times—with dirty snow in the gutters or sweating in summer heat, walking down that avenue and realizing I was the only white face since getting off the subway. Actually the only white face for the last five subway stops. The girl was lying, but she would not change her story, and her mother, jealous of Marie, was heard to say, "I don't care if it happened or not, I won't drop the charges."

I think of myself as a truth seeker, letting the facts tell me what happened, but over that kitchen table in Brooklyn hung an eight-by-ten photograph of a tiny François wearing a blue robe and mortarboard on the day he graduated from kindergarten. The portrait was head and shoulders, life-size. Was the image so powerful that I was preconditioned to believe in his innocence? I couldn't get the wide white smile, the shining eyes, out of my mind. Now that same person, Marie's son, faced at least twenty years in prison for something I did not think he had done.

Marie and I would talk on the phone several times a week, go over details. I'd worked for months, questioned everyone possible, and I could do no more. The lawyer had every report. There would be a court date, and the night before we would confer on the phone or in the kitchen and think that in less than twenty-four hours it would be over. The next day, I'd arrive at the courthouse, go through the metal detectors, get upstairs. I'd be embraced in the corridor, Marie and I would chat a little then we'd file in, sit together, and hear the prosecution say, "Not prepared, Your Honor." This happened at least four times over a span of months.

Sometimes, to my surprise, François would call me. I believed in him. Once, outside the courthouse before going up the steps, I took him aside and, looking up at him in his freshly laundered bright white shirt, pressed a tiny sea-polished stone from Watch Hill into his big hand. "It's for luck," I told him.

The extended family began to come to court, and I'd be introduced to aunts and uncles and not be allowed to sit anywhere but with them, everyone moving down and hissing, "Here! Next to me!" It was my white face right in the middle of all the Haitians.

At last it came to trial and came to an end: The girl was proved to be lying, and François was pronounced not guilty of all the charges but one. This lesser charge made no sense, but it was probation and it was over. Marie and I talked once in a while afterward; the last I heard, she was waiting to get the bail money back.

SPIESMAN, MY MENTOR, ONCE told me that each case is like a snowflake. Even if I grouped several of my legal aid cases in Brooklyn under the heading "Girl Lying," they were never the same and never bored me.

I was hired on behalf of another African-American male, eighteen years old, accused of statutory rape. The victim was fourteen. I felt uneasy as I sat in the lawyer's office with the boy and his mother.

Davon was about six foot four, wearing a do-rag, several heavy gold necklaces, and sneakers that cost $150. Muscle-bound and sullen. I knew these "boys" and that many of them already had their weekdays structured by visits to a parole officer.

I took the case with misgivings. The lawyer left the conference room for a phone call, and I laid out my terms. I had to be paid the entire fee of five hundred dollars in the next four days, and then I would belong to them right up until the last day of trial. The mother nodded. She worked at the Gap, and I hoped she could come up with the money. I thought of lowering my fee and then told myself not to. I wasn't the Red Cross. I needed that money.

Then I told them that I expected a few changes for the

court appearance. "Lose the do-rag. Leave the jewelry at home." The boy blinked, opened his mouth to protest. I said, "You are looking at me and thinking I'm just a skinny white woman bossing you around, but the courtroom is full of people like me who see a do-rag and that jewelry as a symbol, and they don't like what they think it stands for, so that first impression of you is not good. Believe me, you want them to like you. You have a jury and a judge deciding on how you will spend years of your life. A lot of them are white just like me. Do yourself a big favor. Lose the do-rag and the jewelry."

Davon's mother gave me a look of "Good for you." "You hear her?" she said to him, and he nodded, staring straight ahead. I asked if he had a white cotton shirt with a collar and sleeves and a pair of khaki trousers that fit him at the waist. He didn't know. I looked at his mother and said maybe she got a discount where she worked and could get them. She smiled, pleased with her assignment.

I spent the day with him. We took the subway back to his neighborhood in Brooklyn and walked the streets together. I was glad to be six feet tall in my boots. I sat in a waiting room while he visited his parole officer, then introduced myself to her. Davon already had two arrests, for fighting, a disorderly conduct sort of thing. Not terrible, but not a plus. I met his friends loitering on the corner and went to his house, though I didn't feel good being alone with him. He was so tall, so massive, so glowering. Twice I said, "Hey, I'm on your side!" and after the second time, he seemed to lower his guard. He showed me what he called his crib, where he and his girlfriend had sex; she'd told him she was eighteen, and he'd believed her. He told me he and the girl had dated, that it wasn't just sex, that he took her to parties and had met her father. The father who had brought charges of statutory rape.

Davon had dropped out of high school two months before graduation and spent his days on the street talking to his pals, who seemed to have the same sort of biography. He would have sex with the girl in his house while his mother was at work. Davon had no idea she was in junior high school across town. She told him she was pregnant and he borrowed two thousand dollars for an abortion. The girl had the abortion, told her father, and Davon was arrested.

I talked to the lawyer about it. He said I could not approach the girl. "What if she calls me to talk?" I asked.

"I'm not holding my breath," he said.

"What if she does? Can I make sure she understands who I am and talk to her?"

He looked at me, disbelieving. "Absolutely. But she sure as hell isn't going to call you to have a chat." I smiled and left his office hearing Mother's voice. You never know.

I told Davon to put it around the neighborhood that I had a phone number and would talk. Little Denise called within two days; I answered the phone and pushed the "record" button, just in case. This is legal in New York State if one party is participating in the conversation. I made it clear who I was, who had hired me. She was desperate to tell her side of the story, felt so sorry for Davon, said she still loved him, had no idea her father would have him arrested. She cried when she told me about the abortion. I felt sorry for her. I let her go on and on, asking a question here and there. Then she said just what I wanted her to say: "I told him I was eighteen because I knew he wouldn't have anything to do with me if he knew how old I really was. I told everyone he introduced me to that I was eighteen. Everybody believed me."

I gave the tape to the lawyer and all charges were dropped.

This case won't go away for me. I feel so ashamed for thinking Davon was guilty because of the way he looked.

The Last Summer

How's your mother?" asked Mickey one day without looking up from the computer. He'd gone through so much with his own mother. She'd lived for two years after the priest had given her the last rites. Mickey has a highly developed sense of responsibility toward anyone smaller or weaker than him. Particularly mothers and dogs.

I rearranged the flak jacket we used as a chair cushion and sat down. "Not good. My brother said I'm not allowed to talk to her doctors, and it's true that I'm never put through, but I talk to the nurses. They say that she is very frail and should be coded." I stopped. "My special delivery letters have no effect." Mickey knew I talked to Mother every day.

"You know, Mickey, it's the only time in my life I wish I'd married somebody. To have an ally. For the first time ever, I wish that I had money." I tried to breathe normally, not to gasp. I lived on the verge of tears. "I could have rescued her from them before it was too late."

In the past year, I'd gone down to see her as often as I could, trying to change things. But the trouble had started years before. I'd wanted Mother to move to Florida, offered to pack up her house, do everything for her when we caught my brother going through her checkbooks, going into her safety deposit box. He used to come into her house when she was out shopping and, when it was still expensive, make all his long-distance calls from her kitchen. My brothers had written "anonymous" letters to the Mississippi Highway Patrol, but Lyndon stepped in and arranged for a driving test, which she'd passed effortlessly. There was the insistence that she was never to be believed, that she had Alzheimer's. "She was easy prey," Lyndon told me.

Things got worse. Much worse. I'd begged her to confide in her sisters in Vero Beach, but she'd snapped at me, "Do you think I want anyone to know I have a son like that?"

Mother had been tricked out of her house into the hospital, then been put in a nursing home, and was now in the hospital again. Three times her heart had stopped, but they had yanked her back to life. Mother wasn't ill, had never been ill. She was nearly eighty-eight and she hated the tubes, what they were doing to her, the air-conditioning. At first she'd wanted to go home but she now knew there was nothing to go back to.

"Is there anyone who can persuade them to code her?" asked Mickey, handing me a file.

That summer I'd lived with her I'd talked to her about a living will, but she'd said it was silly, couldn't imagine ever being weak or incapacitated. Just the way she could never imagine that any son or daughter of hers could behave badly. This would reflect on her and she was a good mother, above all else.

"It's up to 'the family,' according to the nurses. I've written letters, I've called and begged them to stop the tests. I've reminded them that Mother was one to let nature take its course. Always." I blinked away tears and opened the file. "But they don't care what I think."

"Maybe they feel guilty and are standing around her bed trying to get forgiven," he said.

"No. They are totally self-righteous. Don't ever forget that they are good Christians."

"But why a spinal tap? Feeding tubes? You said they were X-raying her head and doing brain scans? Why?"

I thought of Mother weeping on the phone after the spinal tap. Only once before had I ever known her to cry. "My brother said, 'We jes' wanta git her back ta where she wuz a month ago.'"

Mickey turned to look at me. "Pieces of shit. Fuckers."

I felt tears streaking down my face and swiped them away quickly. "It's three against one. They have total control over her and control over what I'm told."

Mickey and a few close friends knew pretty much all of what had happened. Stanley Rosenfeld, the maritime photographer, and his wife, Heather, were confidants from Rome. They knew Mother. Stanley was in his eighties and very wise. The year before, I'd had the idea to ask Mother if she would sell her house in Turtle Creek and come to live in New York with me. The money would go for a one-bedroom apartment with an elevator. It was never proposed because Stanley said my brothers and my sister "would cheat you and find a way to keep you in debt to them for the rest of your life."

Caro said she'd give me money for the plane ticket, but what was the point of it? Mother, who used to say, "As long as I've lived, I've never eaten apple pie as wonderful as this!"—and mean it—no longer wanted to eat, no longer wanted to live. If she had said, "Come," or, "I want to see you," I would have hitchhiked to get to her but she knew I had no power against the others.

It was a cruel circle: She couldn't protect me at the start of my life and I couldn't protect her at the end of hers. We weren't the sort to ever trade I love you's, but on the phone she once said, "Thank you for being my friend." The words still ring in my ears; I hated myself.

One afternoon in August, she suddenly began to describe a beautiful white light coming in the window and filling her hospital room and her voice became young and happy. She was speaking French. I listened to her for a minute and then she said the light was gone. So was her youthful voice. What if she had died on the phone with me? Would alarms have sounded and people rushed in? To yank her back from what she wanted?

Night and day I prayed for her to die, and then I thought about the machines so I didn't know what to pray for. I prayed for the machines to break, I prayed for them to let Mother go.

SOMETIMES DURING THIS DESPERATE summer, I'd come to the office and Mickey would take one look at me and say, "Get outta here. Go home." I would have been crying behind sunglasses from 65th to 34th Street on the Lexington Avenue bus.

"No! Give me some locations. Come on."

So he'd call out addresses, and I'd write them down as tears fell on the desk and blurred the numbers. Mickey would rig up the video for me, checking batteries, and in a few minutes I'd be out the door. Walking west on 34th Street, I would decide to be Veronica or Vanessa, who had a chain of small, elegant boutiques that sold only handbags and costume jewelry. Or I would be Lucy, who was just starting a sporting goods store in Atlanta. I would blow my nose, put on eye makeup standing in one of those poor excuses for a phone booth, click on the hidden video, and sail into the factory, the showroom, the warehouse. I would be all smiles, deal with the bad guys as whoever I wanted to be. I was somebody else for a few hours; undercover was a holiday from what was happening in Mississippi to Mother.

I hated myself for not saving her. Undercover was a holiday from being me.

Other days, I'd leave the office for twenty minutes, walk on Madison to the Morgan Library and stride right through the lobby. For some reason, no one ever asked me to pay admission. Maybe I looked crazed. I'd go down to the ladies' room in the basement, make sure it was empty, then I'd put my fist in my mouth as far as I could and scream with rage and sadness. It only took about five minutes for me to be exhausted. Then I'd wash my face, put on lipstick, brush my hair over my head upside down—which I'd read calmed women in labor, though I don't know if you want to be upside down having a baby—and go upstairs. I'd stride through the lobby and go back to the office. Now I wonder if anyone ever heard me, but then I didn't really think about it.

ONE MORNING IN AUGUST, I picked up a car at Budget and on my way to New Jersey realized that Mother was beside me in the front seat—riding shotgun. I talked to her driving to the location, then I worked for three hours with the Jersey cops ID'ing counterfeit product. All the way back to Manhattan, I talked to her, hot tears soaking the front of my T-shirt.

Mother made her escape a few hours later, that evening. She embraced me as I lay crying on the straw mat on the floor.

When I was a little girl, I'd told her why I would not go to her funeral and she understood so she came to me the next day and the next. Occasionally in the coming year, I would see her smiling behind me in the mirror; she was in my apartment sometimes and later on would leave messages. When she died it was a conversation interrupted, but as long as I can hear her laugh, her voice, she will always be with me.

PART V
The Open File

I can pretty much call my own shots now and work for the clients I like, accept the cases I want. I went through a phase of painting my nails Swiss Army knife red, though Revlon doesn't call it that, and I take a bubble bath before the rare stakeout. I'm getting away from the physical, getting paid more, too.

I realize that I have a network of P.I.'s and men with intelligence backgrounds who are generous to me. I just pick up the phone. Mickey is my first choice for certain things, Spiesman is my first choice for others. Esposito at the New York Stock Exchange is more corporate in his approach but it depends on the situation. He has a law degree, too. All of us have the same sensibilities about doing the right thing, as Mother would say. Among just the three of them, and their three very different viewpoints, I have access to over a hundred years of experience.

One summer, I flew all over the country on a class action case, and at every airport a former FBI agent was waiting to take me to the interview. It was so restful, for once, not to have to assume the entire responsibility for whatever happened. What adventures they'd had, what stories they told. We'd have hours of talking time—in the car, lunches, dinners, cold beer at the end of the day. I feel they're out there, in Utah, in Texas, all over, if I need them.

The big firms keep giving me work, and I always seem to get along with the chief investigator, especially if he has a Company background. It is unspoken, but we know.

My corporate cases often begin around an enormous oval table with six lawyers trying to tell me what they want and then, all too often, telling me how to get what they want. As Mickey says, "I don't tell them how to litigate, so they shouldn't tell me how to investigate." Most of the time, however, I like them, and they appear to appreciate how I do my job. If they are behaving badly, I can always complain to Mickey and Spiesman about it, and Spiesman will remind me that "we [detectives] are just the towel boys in the whorehouse."

I've met dazzling characters. Experts in their field.

Once I was sent to Hartford, Connecticut, to work with a forensic document expert who examines everything from autographed baseballs to parchment to canvas to ransom notes and counterfeit bills. Age, authenticity, type of ink, you name it. He's in demand at auction houses and with law enforcement. We were to go through the offices of an insurance firm, looking for the source of a letter threatening to murder the top five executives. It had been decided that our presence during the workday would further erode company morale since there had been three bomb threat evacuations that week, so we were slated to go in at night. To read typewriter ribbons. Backward. The firm was using both computers and typewriters but the letter had been composed on a typewriter. You sweat in those rubber gloves, even with the talcum powder. We were buzzed on Dr Pepper, sucking on Tootsie Pops as we bent over machine after machine, removing the spools, unwinding them, looking for a series of letters, then rewinding the spools and putting them back. We got out of there at dawn, aching with tiredness; he solved the case soon after. It was discovered that the threats were a distraction to swing attention away from a bookkeeper who was embezzling hundreds of thousands of dollars from the firm.

Another time, another case, in a courtroom, I was accused of doctoring a tape on which I'd recorded an incriminating conversation. I was outraged and so was my client, but I was wearing my blond wig and knew I looked like a Mob moll or a small-town tart. *My God*, I thought, *no wonder nobody believes me.* The disguise was essential because I'd been warned about someone throwing acid in my face, but I still worried that I looked deeply cheap. My client hired Paul Ginsberg, a forensic audio expert, to examine my tape for any breaks or interruptions. He did this digitally in his bunker, which was filled with equipment years ahead of anything on the market, and the following week testified on my behalf. I worked on other cases with Paul; he had good stories, and we ate a lot of M&M's together. The FBI calls him to examine tapes—especially in kidnappings.

Things got very slow one freelance winter, and I called Lyndon in Jackson and he said, "Yeah, well, it's slow for me, too. Everybody's gone dove huntin'." He said he was thinking of advertising. "What I really need is to go out and expose myself."

Esposito called me from the New York Stock Exchange one rainy afternoon and asked how the detective business was going. I told him not so well but that I'd just gotten back from answering this tiny ad in the *Daily News* that said, "Actors Wanted," and I now had an agent. A theatrical agent. A real one. With an office in a huge building on Broadway. I'd had to read a scene from a script, and it was easy—just like going undercover. Esposito made a lot of jokes about my acting career, but he was always on my side, always wanted

me to succeed. Within a week I'd been cast as an extra for
Law & Order.

I called the *National Enquirer* and had an interview in
a ritzy office on Madison Avenue. Now part of American
Media, the *Enquirer* wasn't what I expected. It's celebrity-
driven, almost mainstream. When I lived in Rome, I had
an international subscription that came by ship, and about
every six months, I'd get a huge packet of old issues. For
days, I'd read nothing but stories of women who claimed to
have been raped by extraterrestrials in trailer camps outside
Albuquerque. *That* is the sort of thing I yearned to write.
So now, in New York, out of hundreds of journalists, I was
shocked to be picked to be one of ten interns to vie for a
permanent position. I was given an assignment and went
after the story like a Doberman leaping for sirloin. Knock-
ing on doors, talking, talking, talking to people. I remember
hearing Mickey say to somebody at OCID, "Charlie could
have a meaningful conversation with a parking meter," and
maybe he's right. Maybe it comes from those days at Whitfield, cheerfully chatting to a catatonic farmer. Or maybe I
just get it from Mother. Great assignment, great break, and
an eyeball-popping revelation that would have been a front-
page headline in *The Wall Street Journal.* Would have been.
My source, morbidly obese and borderline agoraphobic,
after hours of talking to me, after days of taping him at his
kitchen table, agreed to tell all. My editor was salivating on
Madison Avenue as my source was rushed from Brooklyn to
Manhattan in the back of a stretch limo with me holding his
hand the whole way, feeding him éclairs to calm him. But
he couldn't pass the poly. This is another story, and why I
am not a reporter at the *National Enquirer* is another story,
too. But this doesn't mean they haven't called me since to get
information that their reporters obviously couldn't get.

In a way I was relieved, as the words *permanent position* had alarmed me. All of these moneymaking forays were just to tide me over between cases. I was a detective and only a detective.

I was thinking of baking brownies and selling them to Jimmy downstairs to be sold at the deli. But this was not a world-class idea since I'd just gotten Mr. Suarez, who acts as the building handyman, to change my kitchen into a walk-in closet. I'd already filled up the dishwasher with my pocket-books, the top rack being perfect for evening bags. I have a baby fridge in there, like a hotel minibar, but it won't open all the way because the kitchen is too narrow. It's sort of like parking your car too close to another one. I have to hold my breath and slide in sideways if I want to get to the sink or grab wineglasses. The clothes hang on two poles way up high, and my blazers just tickle the top of my head. There is an oven but I don't use it much because the dry-cleaning bags above it start melting and get in my hair. Baking brownies was a terrific idea for an entire twelve seconds.

The lull in detective work was insane, Mickey and I agreed. It was after 9/11 that so many of our clients experienced a drop-off in sales and cut back on advertising and their intellectual property budget. But Mickey and I were dealing with the very Middle Easterners who were making the money to fund bad behavior like attacking the World Trade Center. We knew the characters, so to stop going after them made no sense at all. All this talk on CNN and *The NewsHour with Jim Lehrer* about terrorist cells and could they *possibly* already be in the country? We would moan at the stupidity.

Hayko, who'd become a close friend, offered to teach me to weave and to let me work with Zoya, Inam, and the others repairing antique rugs. I imagined myself fumbling with knots, drinking tea all day, and learning to gossip in Urdu and Armenian.

I signed up to be a census taker and took preparation classes across 65th Street in a church basement. The U.S. government paid me eight hundred dollars, which was excessive as I only got to count two people.

I read an article about how to start a minigoat farm but wasn't sure my apartment was suitable for this enterprise. Every time I saw a "Waitress Wanted" sign, I'd wonder if I should walk in and ask for an apron. But I knew I'd be the worst waitress in history because of my daydreaming and would keep walking. I did copywriting for a catalog. I was hired to write the script for a cable TV show and was elated because I could still take on cases and work with Mickey, but the funding bank pulled the plug. I got my process server's license. I started *The Scribe* to write people's biographies. I took a jewelry-making class and tried to sell necklaces to Bendel's. I had twenty projects in the works. There were times when I felt I was swimming parallel to the beach in a riptide that stretched forever.

I worked in a boutique across Lexington Avenue, selling pashminas. I thought, *I can do this once a week. I can do anything once a week.* I also thought I could read all day, but it wasn't allowed. The tough little Korean woman owner believed in the buddy system to prevent stealing, but I decided the real reason was to prevent suicides. I could fold those expensive little blankets in my sleep, and the rest of the time I imagined knotting one and looping it over a pipe in the back room. I was so bored that all I could think about was killing myself. I wondered if anyone would mention the color in my obituary, and then I would try to decide if I would choose, as my last color choice ever, Tibetan Turquoise, Sunset Coral, or Spring Grass Green. The ultimate fashion statement. After the second Wednesday, I decided the job was too dangerous for me and quit.

There were several other ideas—even less terrific than selling pashminas—and then, when I really felt ratty, the phone would ring. Elation. Euphoria. For months at a time, the phone would never stop and I'd be hired for case after case. My life would get complicated and fascinating, and I would be very happy with it but working too many hours a day, teetering on the brink of mania.

Meanwhile, about this time, Spiesman disappeared on some secret mission for several months. He wrote me letters from a foreign foxhole and I wrote him back. Just when I was thinking I should be knitting socks for him, he started sending me Travis McGee paperbacks. That was Spiesman: always concerned that I be well read and introduced to the right characters.

Case Closed

Mother leaving earth freed me from having to deal with my brothers and my sister. I had always thought that it wouldn't have turned out this way if Stirling hadn't killed himself. He was more like me and Mother, and he was the oldest of us five and wouldn't have allowed those things to happen to her.

When she died, they phoned me the next morning and called me a murderer, which made no sense at all unless they meant I didn't want her to be resuscitated again. They shouted all kinds of things, they yelled that I wasn't showing respect for her, that I didn't love her enough to come to her funeral. I didn't speak at all, just held my hand over the holes in the receiver so the tears wouldn't fall in and electrocute me.

More than a year later, I was in the middle of a murder trial and couldn't leave New York. There was to be a three-day weekend of dividing Mother's possessions, which had been in storage; Lyndon would be perfect as my stand-in. Since he was from Jackson, I thought they would be charming. My Mississippi brother, however, bellowed at me on the phone, threatening to "beat him up, run him off," until he showed them the power of attorney. One of the Boys on Broadway had heard something from Jeanette and had insisted on drawing it up for me, though I had been sure it would be unnecessary. Stupidly, I perpetually underestimated them. Lyndon said that when my corporate lawyer sister saw it, "her face turned red as a possum's bottom." After that, they realized they couldn't "run him off," but they tricked him with fake appointment times, treated him despicably, and regaled him with what a terrible person I was.

They told him I was mentally ill and that I'd resisted all their efforts to help me; they said I had never lived in New York, never had an apartment, that I lived on the street, that I had no friends, that I was a pathological liar. There was a lot more, but Lyndon said it wasn't worth repeating. He did describe how they fought among themselves, how materialistic, how openly greedy they were. They'd bicker over Mother's artwork because they wanted the expensive frame. Lyndon and I were most upset at the mocking, heartless jokes about Mother, whom Lyndon had adored.

"Your sister," he said, shaking his head. "A total bitch. She joined right in with your brothers tearin' you up. They went after you all day long. Cold as ice. All uv 'em. They were saying such cruel things and laughing. I could hardly believe it." I could hardly believe that they would show their true selves to him.

Lyndon, the tough ex–homicide detective, summed it up after three days: "They are the worst people I've ever met in my life." Somehow that made me feel better. Mother saw things were wrong in those last years but even then we rarely discussed "her children." This was a turning point for I'd never had anyone who knew them to confide in. Whatever was said or done forever after—nothing would alter Lyndon's verdict for me.

Lyndon weighed his next words carefully: "They hate you deeply." Every syllable roared through my head. I had left the South and my life was not like theirs, but I'd never done anything to them, never done anything against them.

"Why?" I asked. Finally a chance to know the truth from someone I trusted. From a man who "got it." "Why do they hate me?"

Lyndon was silent for a long moment and then said, "They know that you know who they really are."

Capers

I kept on doing anticounterfeiting work with Mickey and was at his office a lot. One morning, I was there talking about Broadway. A typical intellectual property case. Me undercover, dealing with the Arab counterfeiter we call The Bodybuilder. He'd liked me so much, he'd followed me right into his factory's freight elevator and asked me to dinner. Stripped to the waist, shining with perspiration, with pecs the size of Frisbees. I'd told him I was flying back to Atlanta that evening. Didn't deter him. Wanted to come to Atlanta to take me to dinner there.

Mickey loved it. He snapped up the phone and got McCluskey on the line at OCID, and they chortled over it. "Yeah! Charlie was with him for an hour! She got everything!" He hung up and turned to me, grinning. "All those guys in OCID are scared shirless of The Bodybuilder."

"I don't think he would hurt me," I said, and Mickey looked as if he wanted to say something and then didn't. The Bodybuilder or The Bombmaker or Salah or Ali—I treated them all the same, and they were all nice to me.

One Saturday, an investigator sent me out to a spa to get a massage and to get the Russian masseuse to tell me the story of her marriage. On tape. I groaned. "First of all, I hate hate

hate massages. Plus I'll be naked or with one little towel—how'm I supposed to wear a wire?"

He laughed. "You'll think of something."

I did, and the Russian divorcée told me everything about her Brighton Beach mobbed-up thug of a husband. I lay on the massage table, naked, facedown, panicked. The little red light of the tape recorder glowed like a cigarette butt through my canvas tote bag on the floor a few feet away in the dark room. New Age music was on to soothe me but would probably override our conversation. I was about as relaxed as a clenched fist. The masseuse, so intent on her work and her story, never noticed the red light or how loudly I was talking in a successful effort to get her to talk loudly. She massaged and she cried and her tears fell on my bare back, and the little wheels of the cassette turned round and round. The weeping masseuse told me all about her husband's depravity, his cruelty, and I believed her.

Later that afternoon, I called the investigator and told him what I had on tape and said that I hoped the husband was not the client. Silence. It was very, very unprofessional of us, but he reported that the tape didn't come out and even gave the thug his money back. Scary, too. Russian Mafia stuff.

THERE ARE HUNDREDS OF cases, hundreds of stories.

Parents call me. The father in a panic who wanted me to find his missing daughter who might be a lesbian. Yes, I found her. Living in sin in Cincinnati. Yes, with a woman.

The runaway Mafia chieftain's daughter. That nine-hour stakeout in New Jersey in a driving rain when I had plenty of time to worry I was on the wrong side.

The mother of the bride in despair. Within hours, I'd discovered that her daughter's fiancé wasn't exactly who he said he was—starting with his name, then his education.

Three times I've been asked to check on lying men who've told women they graduated from Harvard. No one has lied about Yale or Princeton. The woman up in Cambridge who did the last search for me was pretty jaded about it: "Honey, just because they walked through the Quad doesn't mean they went to Harvard."

People have problems and no one to confide in. If your brother-in-law is your business partner and he's stealing you blind, maybe you can't discuss it with your wife. If you are being blackmailed, where do you turn?

I don't do domestics. I did a few for Vinny that first month, and tailing the blond adulteress in Mississippi seems a lifetime ago.

When I get a call from a woman who is frantic to hire me because she thinks her husband is unfaithful, I tell her that I don't want to take her money to tell her what she already knows. I quote Vinny Parco. We talk. Sometimes for three hours. My own marriage was less than delightful, but I had two true friends, Julie and Renwick, who listened to me when I was sad and tedious. Renwick saved me with vodka and chocolate. By listening to another woman in distress, I'm giving something back to the cosmos. I tell her to take the money she was going to give to me and to spend it on dinner with her friend with the most common sense. They will make a plan: to leave him or to stay, to confront him or to keep quiet and consider the knowledge a secret power. Then I wish her luck and tell her to call me the next afternoon if she is still upset.

Nor do I particularly like reuniting mothers who gave up babies for adoption and their grown children. This is the last decade of that with the advent of open adoptions in one state after another. One case involved a friend of mine whose mother happened to mention, just before dying, that his father wasn't really his father. I found the identity of his father and the existence of eleven half-brothers and -sisters. His mother had been in love with a married man. My client felt this discovery answered unasked questions that he'd had all his life, so it turned out pretty well.

The next thing, I guess, will be to locate the sperm donor fathers.

Sometimes I'm sent to more exotic places than the Bronx. I was hired to go to Paris to look for a man who'd been missing for months. He'd left his suitcase in a hotel room and vanished. As I flew over the Atlantic, I clutched a French grammar and murmured, "I have to find him," as my mantra for seven hours. And I did find him. He was a prince—which made perfect sense, for I'd been told as a little girl that I would find one. Usually the princes found me.

One spring, I flew to Italy while memorizing a new identity and a new past. I had three Italian bodyguards who were to keep me in sight at all times, as I would be traveling with the bad guys. Maybe it didn't matter that one of my bodyguards had a bright red car, maybe it did. Two of them wore bright red V-necked sweaters. *So Italian*, I sighed to myself. I never knew a Roman male who didn't own at least one tomato red pullover. A red car, red sweaters. It seemed like an ominous start to this caper. The bad guys lost all three of my bodyguards within ten minutes of Siena and I was on my own, speeding off into the countryside with the counterfeiters. A little tension keeps me from daydreaming, and Tuscany is splendid no matter who you're with. The food was divine, the jeans factory was all I hoped it would be, and what a kick to pretend I didn't understand a word anyone was saying.

Once I was sent to Costa Rica and had daiquiris with the glamorous Brazilian mistress of a money launderer. Her hotel was the best, the view from that terrace was spectacular, and the drinks kept coming. Poor girl, she'd had a terrible fight with him and needed someone to confide in; she needed sympathy. And there I was.

I was outrageously lucky that trip. I got very dressed up the next morning, spent extra time and mascara on my beady mud browns, and took a taxi to the bank. A certain bank. Crowds swirled around the entrance and up the marble steps, and everyone seemed agitated. I wondered, *Coup d'état or just another currency devaluation?* I never did find out. I squeezed my way through the perspiring clots of people into the lobby, then inched my way up marble stairs to the second floor. Relayed from one clerk to another, I finally faced one with some power who, amazingly, decided to give me information about the bank account of not one but two very bad guys. Pieces of the case began to fit together. I went outside, found my cab, and went to the airport. Good fishing for being on the ground only eighteen hours.

I liked my first little foray into stolen art recovery. Trying to figure out who really owned that Vermeer that had hung in Hitler's dining room during World War II was following threads all over Europe—on the telephone—and lots of interviews on Fifth Avenue.

There are so many cases I cannot ever mention. Hundreds of my cases are covered by nondisclosure agreements, so I can't talk about them, either. It was written in *The New York Times* that Kroll handled the Parmalat case, so I think it's okay to say that I was asked to work on it but didn't. At the time, I was doing another case for Kroll in the States so had to turn down Kroll in Milan. I was very disappointed and still think I could have handled everything.

I worked for the lawyer Ben Brafman on the first Internet gambling case. Jay Cohen, our client with his World Sports Exchange located in Antigua, was targeted by prosecutors using the Federal Wire Act of 1961, which makes it illegal to make or accept bets on sporting events over the telephone.

The argument was that since Internet traffic uses phone lines, the law also prohibits online gambling. Cohen was found guilty.

Catching a respected oncologist at a big metropolitan hospital on tape as he surreptitiously pushed his bogus "miracle" cure meant becoming the wife of a man dying of cancer. It wasn't difficult to get tears in my eyes and emotion in my voice, but it was a challenge to learn all the medical terms, the names for all the treatments and medications and tests that my fictional husband had endured.

Another case involved a suspicious death in Geneva, Osama bin Laden, many millions of dollars in gold, and a couple of rogue CIA agents. Or were they?

A counterfeit pharmaceutical case meant I gave myself a crash course in basic chemistry, wore a wire, and met with the head of the American branch of the drug company. I felt great satisfaction helping to get his potion off the market.

Once I had two days to transform myself into a rich divorcée from Geneva who collected Tiffany glass. A dealer who'd sold stolen Tiffany stained glass windows was out of prison, and my client in the art world wanted to know what he had to sell these days, its origin, the prices, and if he was behaving himself. I got books, I read, I studied, I called experts with questions, I rehearsed a description of my "collection" in front of the bathroom mirror. I was wired, got what we wanted, but I was winging it like mad. An expert knows so much. Sometimes the client hires me to be a lion tamer when I've been practicing at home with the neighbor's cat.

Murder can be fascinating. I was Sante and Kenny Kimes's private investigator for several years, preparing for their trial for the murder of Irene Silverman. I was the only P.I. who wasn't fired. Mrs. Silverman, a wealthy, elderly widow, disappeared on July 5, 1998, and the mother-and-son grifters from Las Vegas were accused of killing her. No body, no forensic evidence, no witness, no weapon, no DNA, and certainly no confession. Their conviction made it a landmark case in New York State.

Dealing with Sante and Kenny Kimes meant knowing them, investigating their background, their associates, their schemes. Their history had everything: money laundering, identity theft, credit card fraud, Saudi emirs, forged documents, disappearing "friends," disappearing bankers, slavery, corporations that didn't exist, accusations of incest, insurance fraud, Lee Iacocca, and the CIA. Of course, there was murder, too, and that whiff of arson that hung over every pricey bit of real estate Sante had ever owned.

In 2004, I was the consultant for the defense team when Sante was tried for the murder of David Kazdin in Los Angeles. I couldn't help but like Sante sometimes. Not what she'd done, but her energy, her sense of humor. She's very bright. I confess that I used to smuggle her bubble-gum-pink Wet 'n' Wild lipstick into prison when I went to see her. But I did wheel it up all the way and snap it off so she was just getting paraffin and not the metal container. I didn't see any harm in a little vanity behind bars, but I didn't want her cutting somebody's throat with a shank, either.

ONE MORNING, MICKEY TOOK an ax and chopped a door in between the two rooms he rents. Now we could go back and forth without having to go out in the hall, but you had to remember to turn a little bit sideways since it's not a standard-size door opening and you had to step way up since Mickey didn't chop all the way down to the floor. But we discovered that on the other side of the new room is a phone sex service, and Mickey got hysterical. "It's a security lapse! If we can hear them, then they can hear us!" I cannot imagine that anyone would listen to our talk about the newest location in Jersey if they could be talking about sex instead. Mickey plans to soundproof that wall, but so far he's just hanging more and more equipment on it.

Mickey is overworked, overtired. He has a truly impressive roster of clients. Needs a much bigger office. Needs a vacation. Desperately needs to get out of the city and away from the lawyers. We commiserate in depth. He should take a real break from all this. When he gets depressed, he buys equipment—cameras, mostly. I buy shoes. Sometimes he's just down in Greenwich Village cleaning his guns and worrying about his cholesterol.

Last Words

It's been years since first getting printed, but I'm still a beginner, still watching everything, still taking notes. It seems like yesterday that I would hang up the phone in Vinny Parco's office and resist rushing to the mirror in the ladies' room. I was sure the lying was going to show.

Working for Lyndon was not like working for Vinny—cases, personalities, the very landscape were so different. It wasn't just the humidity—I stepped off the *Panama Limited* and into my past. Pursuing counterfeiters at Parker's was unlike anything I'd ever imagined. The settings alone were the stuff of drama. Speeding over delicate, silver-cabled suspension bridges with the radios squawking, following a perp in Chinatown during a January snowstorm with chattering teeth and soaked boots, entering a warehouse, pushing open the door of a factory, shortcuts on back streets, taking the alley, taking the dark stairway—New York City opened itself like a vibrant jungle flower to me. Ugly, magnificent, tough, cruel, glorious, black and gray, full of cool shadows and hot neon.

This adventure has meant that I've gotten to try and had to do a thousand things I never thought any half-sane person would dream up as a viable possibility. There's still the same thrill when I hear, "I've got a case for you." I'm fascinated by how people think, stunned at how much they tell me. Vinny Parco told me that first week that I'd get used to it, but I haven't. I wonder what happened to the Brazilian mistress, The Bodybuilder, The Bombmaker, the fiancée in Nassau, the prince in Paris. I wonder about everybody because, for a moment, I was immersed in their lives. I worried about them before I fell asleep and when I opened the mud browns in the morning.

The book ends here, but the story doesn't. I moved to Miami in 2003 to work on a money-laundering case, and then in 2006 I bought a row house in Philadelphia. International world headquarters of Green Star Investigations is on the third floor. I am a court-appointed investigator but still do locations for Mickey in New York, still take on all kinds of cases. How can I resist?

I am intoxicated by curiosity, driven by the excitement of possibility. Undercover, I step through a mirror, into a land of lies and more mirrors, my heartbeat slows, my voice is calm. When I catch a glimpse of myself, I'm not quite the person I used to see. Did I create an alternate universe or did it create me?

The men are an exotic blend of Boy Scout meets the Internet, whereas I like to imagine myself to be more romantic, more Sherlockian. But when I slink—it's all naked instinct.

The men are lunatics and geniuses. Brilliant and harebrained. Chance takers, thrill seekers. Maybe, sometimes, I am a little bit like that. Detectives don't wear seat belts.